P9-AGP-272

WHAT IS
TO BE
UNDONE

**A MODERN
REVOLUTIONARY
DISCUSSION OF
CLASSICAL
LEFT IDEOLOGIES**

WHAT IS TO BE UNDONE

BY MICHAEL ALBERT

A MODERN
REVOLUTIONARY
DISCUSSION OF
CLASSICAL
LEFT IDEOLOGIES

WITHDRAWN

PORTLAND CENTER LIBRARY
GEORGE FOX UNIVERSITY
PORTLAND, OREGON 97223

AN EXTENDING HORIZONS BOOK
PORTER SARGENT PUBLISHER
11 Beacon Street, Boston, Mass. 02108

Copyright © 1974 by Michael Albert

Library of Congress Catalog Card Number 74-18987

ISBN 0-87558-075-0 (cloth)
ISBN 0-87558-076-9 (paper)

Copyrights are still essential to book production in the United
States. In our case, however, it is a disliked necessity. Thus, any
properly footnoted quotation from *What Is To Be Undone*, up to 250
sequential words, may be used without permission, so long as the
total number of words quoted in any article or book doesn't exceed
5,000. For longer quotations or for a greater volume of total words
quoted, authors should write for permission to Michael Albert, care
of Porter Sargent Publisher, 11 Beacon Street, Boston, Ma. 02108.

Cover design by Nancy Brigham

SP
52
A 333

ELS 4.50 (net)

1·26·76

89 84 29417

TO ALL LIBERTARIAN MARXISTS
PAST AND PRESENT

By 8th 29411

The tradition of all the dead generations weighs like a nightmare on the brain of the living, and just when they seem to be revolutionizing themselves and things, in creating something entirely new, precisely in such epochs of revolutionary crisis they anxiously conjure up the spirits of the past to their service and borrow from the names, battle slogans, and costumes in order to present the new scene of world history in this time honored disguise and borrowed language .... The social revolution of the nineteenth century cannot draw its poetry from the past but only from the future.

Karl Marx

The struggle against religion is therefore indirectly the struggle against the world whose spiritual aroma is religion .... Religion is the sigh of oppressed creatures, the heart of a heartless world, as it is the spirit of spiritless conditions. It is the opium of the people.... The criticism of religion is thus in embryo a criticism of the veil of tears whose halo is religion.

Karl Marx

...woe betide those who seek to save themselves the pain of mental building by inhabiting dead men's minds.

G.D.H. Cole

TABLE OF CONTENTS

Introduction   1-4
Chapter One:
        The New Left in the Sixties   5-41
Chapter Two:
        The Purpose of Theory, Strategy, and Practice   42-53
Chapter Three:
        Classical Marxist Theory   54-79
Chapter Four:
        Leninist Strategy   80-101
Chapter Five:
        A Critique of Bolshevik Practice   102-132
Chapter Six:
        Critique of Leninist Strategy   133-145
Chapter Seven:
        Critique of Classical Marxist Theory   146-179
Chapter Eight:
        Critique of Classical Marxist Leninist Ideology   180-188
Chapter Nine:
        The Libertarian Anarchist Alternative   189-205
Chapter Ten:
        The Chinese Experience   206-262
Chapter Eleven:
        Humanist and Neo-Marxism   263-311
Chapter Twelve:
        A New "New Left" in the Seventies   312-321
Bibliography   322-332

INTRODUCTION

In this book we critically discuss Classical Marxism Leninism, Anarchism, and Maoism from the perspective of political effectiveness here and now in present United States contexts. 1

We demystify, criticize, and uncover the roots of old-ideology weaknesses; we seek to learn from old-ideology strengths and we try to forge a set of guidelines for the task of eventually creating our own newer and better presently-relevant revolutionary ideology.

We work from *activist* evaluative criteria. Rather than discussing all the best Marx and Lenin of the *Collected Works,* we discuss only the core of Classical Marxism Leninism as it was really employed by the Bolsheviks and as it's generally employed by sects today. Rather than struggling for 'philosophical precision,' we strive for practical relevant-to-use criticisms and alternative views. After emphasizing criticism in the discussion of Classical Marxism Leninism, rather than repeating that approach with Anarchism and Maoism, we turn more toward discovering positive aspects useful for us in the United States.

Chapter one gives a very brief descriptive analysis of late-sixties political movements. Its only purpose is to give force to the assertion that social change requires political insight; it also provides a background of some present movement needs to help orient our follow-up discussions.

Chapter two discusses the general nature of political consciousness in terms of the concepts of theory, strategy, and practice. It lays out an approach for studying political ideas we then use throughout the rest of the book.

Chapter three introduces Classical Marxism as a full consistent theory of social interaction, history, and revolution. The chapter presents Classical Marxism in a positive manner but in accordance with our critical expectations.

Chapter four introduces a significant portion of Classical Leninism. The effort is to objectively set out something close to what most Classical Leninists actually use in their day-to-day efforts, but again the discussion is organized and bounded in accordance with our critical desires.

Chapter five discusses Bolshevik Classical Marxist Leninist practice in young revolutionary Russia. While not explicitly discussing theory and

1

strategy, it evaluates Bolshevik practice so as to lay a groundwork for critiquing the guiding ideology as well.

Chapter six evaluates Classical Leninism.

Chapter seven evaluates Classical Marxism, completing the examination from practice to strategy to theory.

Chapter eight summarizes the entire analysis.

Chapter nine discusses Anarchism, looking for new insights rather than deeply analyzing weaknesses.

Chapter ten discusses the Chinese experience, again looking more to find insights than to analyze recurring Classical or other weaknesses.

Chapter eleven discusses a number of Humanist Marxist and Neo-Marxist thinkers who go beyond Classical limitations.

And chapter twelve synthesizes previous results into a number of ideas about how an improved new United States political consciousness might be developed, about what it might look like, and about what it might accomplish.

What Is To Be Undone thus has rather clearly defined and delimited purposes. If it is read with desires to find new ideas rather than to defend old sectarian ones, its worth will be greatly enhanced. In his philosophic work *Marx in the Mid-Twentieth Century* Gajo Petrovic includes the following interchange under the subtitle "Objections and Replies":

> The 'strange discussions' that have lately become frequent in Yugoslavia are free philosophical discussions about the open question of Marxist philosophy. The remnants of Stalinism in us (stronger in some, weaker in others) oppose free discussions on philosophy. An internal voice in us (or in some of us) is murmuring discontentedly:"Don't we behave too freely toward our great teachers?"
> "First of all," wrote Engels to Plekhanov, "please stop calling me teacher. My name is simply Engels."
> "However should we not be a little more modest?"
> "The truth is as little modest as the light," says Marx, "and toward whom should it be? Toward itself? Verum index sui et falsi. Accordingly toward the untruth?"
> "By a free discussion of everything will we not confuse and disorient the masses? Why should we underestimate the 'masses'? Why could not an undogmatic Marxism be at

least as conceivable to them as the dogmatic one?"
"What are the opponents of Marxism going to say? Will
they not feel they have triumphed when they see we write
critically of Marx?" "They may. But let us hope that they
will soon no longer be able to say: 'Jesuits have written more
studies about Marx and Marxism than Marxists themselves.' "
"And what will our Marxist critics, for example the
Chinese, say?" "Probably the same as the Albanian."
"But will not all these discussions weaken Marxist philosophy in its struggle against non-Marxist philosophy?" "Why
should a living Marxism be weaker than a dead one?"2

We hope all this book's readers and indeed all radicals everywhere
have Petrovic's kind of immodest spirit, and we hope our own efforts have
been true to it, and to scholarly integrity as well. We must learn from "past
teachers" to transcend them, not to enshrine, worship, or exploit them.

We believe this book reflects parts of the changing consciousnesses of
a large number of activists, and we hope its presentation will help us go
forward in creating new ideas, studying them, and adapting them to our
own real situations. It seems to us that such a trend would be vastly prefer-
able to an endless repetition of the mistakes of the past.

FOOTNOTES

1. By Classical Marxism Leninism we mean only that body of ideas that constitutes the core ideology of Bolshevik-oriented parties and/or sects. We don't, for example, mean the whole and most enlightened libertarian elements of Marx's own writings or of his most competent interpreters. Still we don't want to slight the ideology we present and discuss. We feel it's a very flexible, powerful interpretation of the Classical view as good or better than any now being used by active Leninist parties. Further we think that many of our criticisms of it, though by no means all, as we'll take pains to point out, are also applicable to Marxist thought in general. The most important point, however, is not how 'Marxist' our Classical Marxism Leninism is, but how accurate a reproduction of what Marxist Leninists use, it is. Farther on in a later chapter we'll also consider some more progressive Marxist formulations.

2. Gajo Petrovic, *Marx in the Mid Twentieth Century;* Doubleday Anchor, Garden City, New York.

CHAPTER ONE

THE NEW LEFT IN THE SIXTIES

...would you tell me please which way we should go from
here? [Alice] That depends a good deal on where you want
to get to. [The Cat] 1

Lewis Carroll

To start this book we want to view the new left from a highly critical
perspective, showing a number of rarely discussed internal weaknesses,
and we want to thereby at least partially demonstrate the need for a new
new-left ideology.

There are, however, two immediate problems we must overcome.
History should be a vehicle for human liberation. The study of past events
should be a means to understand causes, to discover roots of present
'historical trajectories,' to ascertain different ends to which present
trajectories might possibly lead, and thus to learn how to affect positively
various historical possibilities. But oppressive forces often impede attempts to use history in these useful ways. On the one hand, powerful
oppressive propagandists rewrite history to show their roles as always
virtuous; and on the other, cynics among the oppressed as well as clever
oppressors call every review of leftist errors irrefutable proof of the
impossibility of effective rebellion.

Both these phenomena are now occurring.

On the one hand the United States liberal establishment is busily
seeking to rewrite the history of the sixties to show that activities of the left
were an obstacle to reform and especially to the rapid conclusion of the
Vietnam war, and to show that the liberals themselves were from the first
always opposed to this "immoral" war, and in the end responsible for
forcing its "conclusion."

And on the other hand, but with similar effects, frustrated ex-activ-
ists now trying to succeed within the system view the new-left's experience
as a chronicle of error, excess, ignorance, arrogance, and extremism,
showing irrefutably the futility of revolutionary or even radical opposition.
These folks exude cynicism and despair, and by minimizing New-Left

5

contributions, objectively aid the liberal retelling of sixties history.

These two differing efforts to rewrite history do a horrible disservice to the honest efforts of people trying to learn from past experiences. More, they return to a semblance of moral legitimacy the previously morally undermined 'Democratic' Party and the whole system it represents, while simultaneously undercutting the historical identity and staying power of the new left, the only really humane social movement this country has seen in many, many years.

The truth of the sixties is in fact exactly the opposite of these rewrite lies. The liberals and the entire United States political establishment were never against the war: they were only, to varying extents, against losing the war and against development of too great a set of domestic problems as a result of trying to win it. Thus, as Noam Chomsky methodically shows, mainstream political opposition to the war had nothing to do with moral scruples (in the entire Pentagon Papers there is not a single reference to the devastation of Vietnamese or American lives, while there are many references to economic and domestic political costs of war policies), but instead always arose only in pragmatic attempts to minimize political and economic losses that might result from the historically unparalleled Vietnamese resistance and the domestic United States resistance in the street and military barracks. 2

Further, by undermining (in parallel with Vietnamese efforts) the American myth of benevolence, wealth, dignity, and freedom for all, by causing restraints to be put on government war policies lest they arouse too much left motion here at home, and by showing the possibility of left activity even in face of extreme inexperience and repression, the new left demonstrated the vulnerability of the establishment and the potential of people's power. The whole Watergate crisis graphically reveals the extent to which even a very germinal and inexperienced movement can disrupt the powers that be. In a very few years American political complacency has been shattered. Imperialism, racism, sexism, alienation, exploitation, have become fairly well-known concepts to the United States public. The political debate has been turned around: it is no longer "Are these concepts relevant?" but rather "Just how relevant are they?" It is not "Must there be major change?" but "What kind of major change should there be?" It is no longer "The corporations and government will take care of our needs," but "How are we to 'take care' of the corporations and government?"

These major advances in political awareness plus the powerful thrust of the new left in preventing certain escalations and in eventually helping force a settlement of the war at least temporarily beneficial to the Vietnamese as well as the contribution of the new left in working for other social advances are the historical truths which must be put forward in place of the hypocritical obfuscations offered up by liberals and/or disgruntled and demoralized prior activists.

Further, lest our own highly critical views of internal left dynamics add to establishment historians' fabrications, we now give a short recounting of new-left contributions, particularly in the area of creating new revolutionary consciousness and new tools for positive revolutionary thought and action. We also try in our subsequent highly critical discussion to keep foremost our real purposes: to show the nature and magnitude of some of the difficulties that helped undermine the new left *from within*, and to show what real life as opposed to fantasy life in the new left was like, and thereby to motivate recognition of the need for new ideology.

NEW LEFT LESSONS

The new left was an international practice-oriented movement. It was not steeped in theory; its ideas emerged primarily from trial-and-error evaluations of its own experiences. Its most creative groups actually rebelled against old-ideology ideas, rather than analyzing and then moving from them as a basis. Nonetheless the new left eventually hammered out a rough prospectus very much in tune with (even advanced beyond) the finest formulations of their contemporary more theory-oriented comrades.

Thus the United States new left started as a reaction to racism and the Vietnam war, but in time came to represent a critique of the *totality* of ways modern life impinges upon human-fulfillment needs and capacities. It went from an opposition to blatant racism in the South and war in Southeast Asia to a critical revolutionary position against racism in general, imperialism in all its forms, sexism both in society and in the movement, and the whole nexus of advanced capitalist day-to-day living-working relations insofar as they breed waste, alienation, ecological decay, poverty, hierarchy, competition, and insofar as they are unable to meet almost any of peoples' collective social needs for friendship, community, identity, power, recreation, creative and spiritual fulfillment, and so on. The new left developed an awareness of the power of United States repressive mechanisms -- the state, corporation, courts, police, schools, and family -- insofar as they coerce people but also insofar as they corrupt people by imposing false and self-alienating anti-social ideas. The new left attacked the economic side of capitalism, both as it oppresses workers in factories and as it oppresses consumers in the "free" market place. But the new left also went beyond economics to additionally consider the ways modern schooling, family life, culture, and general day-to-day living inculcate oppressive modes of behavior and thereby contribute to capitalism's stunting of human potentials.

For the new left *consciousness* was a central aspect of concern. Whether trying to force the government to end the war, or trying to build forces for eventually overthrowing the government, the new left knew that the key problem was affecting people's thoughts, and thus their political allegiances, motivations, goals, and even behavioral capacities. The new left saw changed consciousness as a prerequisite for revolution, rather than an outcome of it.

Moreover, primarily due to women's-movement contributions, the new left became aware that the question of consciousness was a very complex affair: it didn't involve only "What side are you on?" but also "How do you feel about life and people?" and thus, "Are you able to participate humanely in revolution?" For the women's movement showed how oppressive ways of thinking and acting remain even after we turn against capitalism, and it showed how those *residue characteristics* could corrupt our practical effects by consigning them to self-defeat via *internal sexist or authoritarian repercussions.* Thus the women's movement was largely responsible for showing the left that *opposition to unequal interpersonal relations and to repressive sexual or authoritarian attitudes were factors on a par in importance with opposition to imperialism and exploitation.* Similarly by struggling not just for minor reforms but for the total fulfillment of Black lives -- materially, culturally, creatively, and intellectually, -- the Black movement taught leftists that *racism has to be fought not after a revolution but as part of the prerequisite process of creating revolution, that it has to be fought both institutionally and in people's minds, and that the goal of fighting it, like the goal of fighting sexism and all other oppressions, was not reform, but the total liberation of the human personality so that it might attain the greatest possible heights of growth and fulfillment.*

Because of the dual concerns of the new left with overcoming authoritarianism and with changing oppressed consciousnesses, it developed a strikingly new style of practice.

People were to struggle collectively to overcome impediments to *societal* and also to *personal* and *interpersonal* change. *Participation* and *active individual and collective initiative* were crucial as the only modes that had "Energy" as well as anti-authoritarian impact. Thus the new left was concerned to oppose all hierarchical mechanisms including traditional Leninist parties, traditional teacher/student, organizer/organizee relations, and even traditional meeting styles where heavy well known orators could always dominate events. The new left struggled for rotation of all tasks (public-speaking as well as leafletting and typing), for participatory decision-making mechanisms, for non-repressive, participatory meetings, and for a new relationship between the experienced and inexperienced that recognized that each had things to learn from the other and that each had things to teach the other, and that what was desirable was everyone moving foward together.

Further, the new left emphasized finding methods suitable to raising consciousness both inside and outside the movement. The new left thus adopted a politics of exemplary actions, teach-ins, consciousness-raising groups, criticism/self-criticism, and liberated personal lifestyles. Thus there was a preoccupation with leadership modes that would *foster rather than stifle group political participation and initiative.*

The new left also 'discovered' the importance of an *alternative vision* and tried both to outline one and to embody its values in daily practice. It took a *total* approach to revolution and liberation and functioned creatively both in analyzing social relations and in trying to alter them (even though as we'll soon see there were a great many instances in which its successes were very limited). There were obviously many grave problems, yet the fact that in a very short time the new left discovered and even began solving the key political tasks of our time -- *creation of a goal-prefiguring practice, development of an anti-authoritarian organizational form, development of effective consciousness-raising tactics, and development of a theory and practice that could simultaneously promote the autonomous development of women's, Black, worker, youth, and community movements, while also providing a total framework within which they would all fit together and function together collectively, with the whole even more than the simple allied sum of the parts* -- is a remarkable indication of modern revolutionary potentials. For the new left's promise to be fully met, activists need only synthesize its experience lessons with those of critical analyses of other historical struggle experiences, form a new collective ideology, and embark on a new new-left political activism even more informed, self-conscious, and effective than that of the sixties. A first modest step in such a direction is a critical look at the actual internal dynamics, beliefs, and contributions of the new left as a whole and then of each of its major component movements.

THE NEW LEFT

In response to Kennedy rhetoric, material changes in wealth, growths of knowledge, Black activism, and the spector of an overseas war, American youth began coming together politically in the early and mid sixties.

They looked towards old left groups for ideological guidance. They learned about classes, the state, and revolutionary organization, but they also learned, in the words of Carl Oglesby, that the old left provides only an "almost carrion bird politics" wherein "distant and above it all the revolutionary cadre circles, awaiting the hour of the predestined dinner. Capitalism weakens, layoffs and inflation converge, a rash of strikes -- the bird moves in. But not so fast, the government also moves. A different money policy, stepped up federal spending, a public works project, selective repression of the militants -- the bird resumes its higher orbit." 3

Youth wanted more dynamism and insight than the seemingly stodgy old left had to offer. We were disenchanted with conditions of war, racism, and general cultural sterility: we moved toward direct action as our new muti-purpose tactic. It promised greater successes, it was more exciting, it suited everyone's feelings of urgency, and it suited people's personal desires to "fight now."

Black movements became militant and other leftists rapidly followed suit. Even street gangs adopted political slogans: the rhetoric of revolution spread through the land. People were "rising up angry." It was initially very conscious and serious, as well as militant. At least the first wave of activists thought long and hard about making left commitments and yet even with people's careful approaches the leftward flow continually grew.

Drop out of mainstream America. Drop into either the growing youth culture or into a more active political movement. This was the message sweeping the big cities, causing much soul-searching, and a remarkable amount of active, very concerned motion.

By and large the new left had its finest hours in its earliest days. Then it was struggling in humble, honest ways, it was trying to affect the world and itself, it emphasized participation, patience, and hard work. Weaknesses were still only latent. The left wanted to communicate, and it took itself seriously enough to think carefully about everything it contemplated doing. 4

But things became more complex as time went on. Under pressures of repression, cooptation, and competition, the movement joined a kind of revolutionary rat race. It started adopting ideas instead of developing and fully understanding them. There was rush and urgency; instead of acting creatively, the movement reverted to old ways that came more easily. Internal weaknesses (e.g., authoritarianism and hierarchy) were fostered by external conditions (e.g., repression and press sensationalism); and as conditions got tougher, bad internal movement dynamics just kept getting worse.

The old class president became the new movement leader, and the old quiet sensitive person went almost totally mum. What was to be a new way of life began looking just like the old. There was a growth of ego insecurity. The left was attacked and in self-defense regrettably became defined in terms of opposition to almost everything American. It was unsure of itself but it acted cocksure. It couldn't really answer criticisms; it didn't reply when people asked how it would do things differently. It was pushed to extremism. It went from opposing McNamara's thinking to opposing almost all thought, and from a healthy distaste of bureaucracy to an abhorrence of almost all organization. It took genuinely creative intuitions about American disciplinary methods and turned them into a hatred for almost all discipline, even including self-discipline. It took a new critique of alienated work and bloated it into a new inability to do work of any kind. And perhaps most importantly, to defend itself while it was still young, it defined itself as morally superior, and turned an initially healthy critical stance into a more and more blindly arrogant one.

Of course, different people did these things to differing degrees, but the overall dynamics were such that the trends were very pronounced in the movement as a whole. In almost all cases the movement failed to break

down false polarities, and instead merely chose new sides for itself.
Instead of work, it took play; instead of mind, body; instead of discipline,
chaos; instead of allegiance, hatred; and instead of passivity, arrogance.
We didn't synthesize -- we were largely as extremist as the people we opposed. We were as subjectivist. We were motivated at least in part by the
same self-defeating habits of polarization, competition, authoritarianism,
and self-defense. We were ignorant and overly defensive about our own
weaknesses. We didn't really admit to them and so, of course, we didn't
even come close to fully overcoming them. We opposed the main
oppressions of United States life but not, at least until too late, the subtler
ones that were already at work within our own activities.

There were people who saw these many problems at the time but they
were generally outside of or peripheral to the left. When they pointed up
our weaknesses it was to demoralize and not improve us. Their intention
was to get us to be good citizens and not good revolutionaries. We were
very unsure of ourselves, very defensive, but also very headstrong. If people
told us we were authoritarian, or insensitive, or ignorant, or overly brash,
in defense we had to scream back that we were not, and that we were going
to go on being radical no matter what anyone said. We had to convince
ourselves. We couldn't sift the wheat from the chaff in their criticisms,
precisely because we were unable to admit that anything they were suggesting might be at all true. We couldn't admit to weakness and we were
certainly unable to admit to criticisms leveled by our enemies. We couldn't
admit that there was anything that they could tell us because that would
severely threaten our need to believe that it was we who were to tell them.

We screamed back at our detractors lest we be drawn back towards
them. No one was able to break through our defenses until it was largely
too late.

If a liberal newswriter said our sloppiness was disaffecting potential
allies, we said it was untrue and roughed up our jeans a little more. A
healthy rebellion against capitalist clothing requirements and especially
against clothing as a mechanism of status, slowly became an irrational
preoccupation with a new kind of uniform. If another commentator or
parent said our language or militance or attacks on certain institutions
were incomprehensible and self-detrimental, we didn't explain ourselves
clearly, or slightly alter our styles so that we might communicate better,
but instead merely intensified our assault on "bourgeois sensibilities,"
oblivious to our actual consciousness-raising effects.

No one could be a really true revolutionary and also a sharp critic of our styles, ideas, tactics, etc. etc. And even if many individuals were not guilty of this extremism, new left activism as a whole made it appear as if everyone was.

To understand the involved processes more fully we must look at the new left's separate parts in greater detail.

THE STUDENT MOVEMENT

The student movement started at Berkeley. Ex-civil righters accustomed to southern struggles took a look at their own school and at their own situations. They saw racism, war ties, and bureaucracy. They felt alienated and had the confidence to express their anger. The ensuing free-speech movement was a catalyst to students all over the country.

Soon the criticizers developed more clarity: "The schools are socializing agents. They are like computers. They are part of and program us to become part of the whole American system. They hurt us and they support the war. They make us into businessmen's slaves and they do weapons research."

Campus movements united to change schools and fight against the war. People became seriously involved in on-going deeply consuming activities. There were sanctuaries for AWOL G.I.s, teach-ins, rallies, meetings, and occasional militant confrontations over related campus based demands -- End War Research, No More War Recruiters, and so on. The process was initially driven by concern, spirit, and solidarity. People studied their schools, America, and imperialism. They moved progressively further and further left in analysis and were then, all of a sudden revolutionaries wanting to overthrow the whole system. Calm seriousness diminished as macho-seriousness enlarged. There was deep trouble on the horizon.

Students involved themselves in campus movements usually in gut response to social pressures, deep moral feelings, and movement organizing efforts. They recognized their schools' and country's inadequacies and joined with whomever seemed most committed to overcoming them. Very few recruits were *consciously strategic*. They didn't have really good reasons for the whys and hows of their actions. They were in no position to understand effects of their actions on others or for that matter on themselves either.

People either went in and then out of the movement because their understanding remained foggy, or stayed in, simply attaching themselves to a new identity related ideology, or bore their ignorances passively. In some cases they struggled to work things out for themselves. There was little collective give and take; people who had no strategic understandings were not effectively helped by their supposed 'leaders'; they were instead indoctrinated, used, or expelled. Further, the in-and-outers couldn't help the leaders overcome their particular deficiencies, including their arrogance, defensiveness, sectarianism, out-of-touchness, immaturity, and overall blindness to the effects of much of what they were doing. Skills were not *effectively* spread and elitism was not *effectively* countered. One group had sensitivity but little initiative; another the reverse. Of course the whole spectrum was much broader than this, but more often than not societal dynamics so polarized events that each individual might as well have been at one of the two extremes anyway.

Perhaps the most incongrous events occurred when Marxist Leninist student sects confused, alienated, and attacked people under the guise of "giving ideological leadership." As sectarian groups vied for position, they wasted people's time, and drained people's energies. They dominated people's capacities for initiative, encrusting all efforts in their own stodgy formulas. Worst perhaps, their bad ways played to bad latent traits in almost everyone who tried dealing with them.

Thus people trying to eliminate Leninist infantile sectarianism were often instead sidetracked into their own potentials for sectarianism. You could argue with the Progressive Labor Party only so long before developing Progressive Labor Party-like traits. The resulting internecine conflicts did more harm than good. The Leninists attacked and baited, everyone else attacked and baited back, until the behavior became rather habitual. New people were never too impressed when they saw so-called revolutionaries fighting one another to the exclusion of seriously dealing with real issues -- and when they saw in-fighting go to the level of violent confrontations they naturally began to wonder how radicals differed from the establishment they opposed. The dynamics had more to do with pathological ego-defense than with fighting for real revolutionary gains.

The left became a kind of spectacle and most students looked on with mixtures of awe, fear, disdain, skepticism, and sometimes a little naive jealousy or just plain wonderment. The movement became a kind of caricature of itself. Its members didn't understand why some people join-

ed while others didn't, and indeed the question, despite its obvious centrality, was hardly ever even raised. Movement people didn't understand
what forces worked in their favor and what forces were hindrances.
Though strategies were espoused, none could be organically related to the
but many others (problems concerning sex, psychological passivity, school
itself, needs for real community, etc.) weren't even properly understood.
That people had some difficulties adopting or even recognizing radical
ideas was not fully understood. When trying to communicate through
leaflets, there was no accepted method for deciding what should go in and
how it should be written. When trying to decide on program, there was no
real method for figuring what was important and what tactics were best
suited to student states of mind. When trying to figure how militant to be,
there was no understanding of why more or why less and of how one or the
other would affect future possibilities. If it had had these awarenesses the
student movement might have made itself more palatable to other
students and citizens at large. It wouldn't have constantly pushed beyond
what people were ready to do and it would have created on-going
mechanisms for preserving short run gains more effectively than was
actually done. When the crucial choice came between highly escalating
campus militancy, or staying less militant but constructing well-founded
unions that could at a later date take far more people more solidly to the
left, the latter approach would have won out instead of the former.5

The student movement went from interrupting the 'free speech' of the
Rostows to interrupting and fighting each other, precisely because we
never developed a full understanding of what we were doing, why we were
doing it, and what its effects on others and on us were likely to be. We were
afraid of *cooptation* but we didn't really understand it. Paul Potter
expresses the situation as it was:

> The tyranny of liberation is believing that the reality of our
> needs can overcome what this society has done to us. That
> is not only wrong it is arrogant. It is one of our most impo-
> tent conceits. Regardless of what we say about the power of
> the military and the corporations, we seem to be incapable
> of believing that the society that crushed our parents could
> crush us in the same way. We assume that we will do better
> than they. (We deny that they could ever have been like us.)
> What we cannot comprehend is that our parents too might
> have had images of liberation once. 6

In essence we did not recognize that we were fallible and so of course we did little to guard against that fallibility. By the time we began realizing that we had bad traits and that they were hurting our efforts, it was already too late. We were fragmenting. The initial hope, energy, and enthusiasm were spent. Criticism/self-criticism was introduced as a palliative. The dictum rapidly became: rule self, rule others, and by all means don't mess with any of the really threatening problems.

The first student strategy was largely reformist, that is, agitation by arguing that certain aspects (courses, ROTC, war research, Black admissions policies, etc.) of the university are irrelevant or worse; organization of demonstrations and strikes to change those aspects; agreement to help plan new ways the school could function more relevantly; and termination of demonstrations when those new ways are adopted. The essence was to make home a nicer place. The protagonists usually wanted grading reform, living reform, course alterations, or the development of Black or radical studies programs, and all these things were fought for, not because they fit into some larger scheme, but because they seemed immediately justified.

The second strategy was somewhat more revolutionary: "The universities are complicit in many of society's larger evils. They are partially responsible for society's injustices." Students were organized around university complicity in the war, imperialism, racism, etc. Demonstrations were held aimed specifically at ending complicity and escalated to whatever extents necessary. Termination of demonstrations came only when the fully desired results were accomplished. Essentially it was a "clean up your back yard" strategy which, it was hoped, would simultaneously force others (workers etc.) to police their yards too and would bring closer the day when students could join them in that effort.

Still the strategy was mostly aimed at just getting rid of obvious evils. Practitioners were not so concerned with the effects of their actions on other people as they were with the effects on the institutions they were attacking. They were not so concerned with developing organization or mass support as with achieving concrete successes spurred by large demonstrations. They didn't want commitment, they wanted immediate victories. They had very few answers for people who said they were polarizing the country to the detriment of their own goals except to say that what they were doing was right and that it therefore had to be done. People were usually motivated by the belief that they could have short-run successes and thereby eliminate a certain amount of evil from the world. The strategy began buckling when people began realizing just how much power was needed for even the smallest change. It died when a Princeton University movement got a war research building eliminated -- the campus was gerrymandered so that the institution was no longer on it. The building remained, the function was still served, everything was the same except the campus boundary. Though struggle continued the irony was felt in Princeton and elsewhere. A new strategy was needed.

Serious leftists saw these various results and became more 'political.' They foreswore the old approach entirely: they didn't try to alter it, they just got rid of it. They didn't try to improve on past ways, they just jumped on a newer, supposedly more revolutionary third-strategy bandwagon with the same relatively blind commitment they'd had for the last one. Of course not everyone was the caricature this suggests: some understood strategic possibilities more and those who rushed ahead were considerably affected by the seeming urgencies of the moment, but the overall dynamic was such that everyone might as well have been motivated by nothing but the desire to push ahead as quickly as possible lest dynamics get somehow bogged down. People's good motivations were largely submerged in their individual and collective deficiencies. The student movement constantly viewed itself as right and moral, and therein cut itself off from improvement.

The third campus strategy was in some ways more enlightened than its two predecessors. It said that campus activism could be a catalyst for changing American political realities. It reasoned that by wrecking schools, closing them, or fighting over them, we could greatly escalate the level of national political discussion. We could create motion that would push everyone further and further left. It was a politics of example and disruption, a politics of motion -- disrupt old ways and dispense new ones, and change will come simultaneously. Different people with this view of how the left could expand had different ways of actually doing things. Some used 'drama', manipulation, and people's desires to cleanse the campuses; others tried to explain their strategy and motivate people through an understanding of long run potential. The people of the first persuasion created most campus motion and in time almost all 'leaders' succumbed to using their methods, frequently without even fully understanding what it was they were doing.

Thus the Seattle Liberation Front created a whole lot of very temporary "motion/energy" in Seattle with a politics of macho/noise, confrontation, and myth; and Mayday eventually tried to follow suit on a national scale with its supposedly self-propelling dramatic predictions of "hundreds of thousands" "converging" on Washington and "shutting it down." The more modest but politically better-conceived programs of countless local community and student groups got lost in the shuffle. That the dramatic approach could create only a lot of baseless motion but no real on-going solid organization, commitment, solidarity, or conscious-ness was overlooked in the "rush of joy" caused by the large numbers it could indeed sometimes call forth (or at least not scare away).

Further most of the third group's leaders were competitive men with plenty of charisma but extremely arrogant, oppressive, and macho styles. Though the idea of catalyzing responses in new sectors was rather good, the new left never really took the trouble to seriously consider what kinds of activities had good effects and what kinds had bad. The implicit rapidly adopted supposition was that anything directed against the establish-ment would have provocative and thus good effects on the masses who viewed it. The feeling was that though working people might not like all the specific tactics chosen they would still be inevitably pushed to the left by the tactics' net effects. Of course this proposition was partially true, but to a greater extent it was a rationalization for the inability to even consider doing things that would be simultaneously radical, liked by the workers, and constructive of the movement's infrastructure and size. There were countless arguments in which claims were made that though of course the workers hated us, they were also moving leftward, and that removing the barriers between the two groups would become easier and easier as that motion progressed. The barriers nevertheless are still quite real and of course the motion never became a stampede. In fact some of what the student left did actually pushed the workers to the right and much of it (crazy lifestyles, peculiar appearances, and opposition to free speech, etc.) gave false impressions of what being radical is all about and thereby laid seeds of cynicism that are still impeding constructive possibilities. Finally student left-politics never successfully took into account the need for tactics and organizing efforts to create *on-going institutional strengths* which act as the basis and give the necessary continuity for later continuation of efforts aimed at creating a united United States left.

Further and as a kind of extension of inadequately addressing other sectors of the population, and insufficiently organizing even the student sector, the student movement actually created the conditions necessary for its own repression. It escalated militancy while cutting itself off from main supporting elements. It was too busy, too revolutionary, and too near to winning to really notice the actual phenomena around it, to actually notice what was good and what was bad about even its own activities. The overall strategy for students to exert an exemplary influence upon the rest of the country was actually quite sound. What was lacking was the ability to apply that awareness. Students' attitudes were not always the most progressive, and even when they were progressive their abilities to transmit them were largely lacking. The tactics, styles, and overall insensitive attitudes towards other people's values were especially detrimental. The student movement never developed adequate criteria for its own activities. It hardly ever had good, carefully though-out reasons for its efforts. In a real sense it was ignorant and cut off from realizing that fact by identity problems. The best arguments were never best because they were sound or because they fit widely accepted well tested criteria of value but because they were elegant, or super radical, or fashionable, or in some other way self-serving.

The grounds for anyone now judging the student movement are roughly:

> To what extent did the student movement realign society's forces to benefit the oppressed?
> To what extent did it alter non-students consciousnesses in ways favorable to future revolutionary efforts?
> To what extent did it forge students into on-going movements that could continue struggling for change?

The student movement and indeed the entire new left put to shame all other political parties, organizations, and ideologies in the United States by showing their complicity in the war, racism, and other forms of oppression and their incompetence in dealing with these problems. Indeed the new left is the only real left that the United States of the past few years offers up for critical evaluation. Nonetheless once its great importance for breaking the hegemony of the Democratic Party and other "liberal" organizations over left politics and for contributing new methods to on-going struggles against imperialism and other injustices is admitted, there is simply no way to deny that the student movement also in many ways failed.

It fulfilled our above outlined judgement criteria only partially and in some cases even partially negatively. It did affect social consciousness, often positively, but sometimes negatively; but it did not create on-going movement organizations. There is no way to tell if it could have done better if it had had a more encompassing perspective and a more maturely self-critical style -- but it is certainly not heretical, excessively defeatist, or unjustifiably self-effacing to think that it might have. Indeed, such speculation is rather liberating, precisely because it allows us to be properly self-critical and to hope for a better student and new left movement in the future. The conditions fostering the student movement were not transitory, the internal deficiencies (and repression) that drove it to destruction and that temporarily soured students on any further efforts were and are largely transitory and therefore subject to future positive alterations.

But the student movement was only one of many parts of recent United States activism. To understand the whole more fully we must also investigate its other aspects.

THE ANTI-WAR MOVEMENT

The anti-war movement developed in parallel with the campus movement. Each affected, enlarged, and defined the other. In the beginning people became involved mostly because they saw that the war was a heinous crime adversely affecting millions of people. Draft-card movements and turn-ins, teach-ins, and marches were all deeply moving, involving affairs. During its earliest days becoming a member of the movement was a really difficult existential event involving much serious thinking and risk. Joining generally reflected deep changes of political consciousness. There was a continual push toward expressing beliefs in action, but the steps were difficult. At its birth the movement had both solidarity and patience but its immediate popularity and growth, which should have been a great boon, proved otherwise.

With time, joining demonstrations, handing out leaflets, and calling oneself an anti-war activist became less and less difficult, and regrettably their effects upon peoples' beliefs and commitments also diminished. The movement's size grew but the solidarity, understanding, and commitment of each member declined.

This, however, wasn't the whole story; there were really two bad trends at work, usually in opposition to one another, and to what would have been the good trend of a simultaneously growing and strengthening movement.

On the one hand movement activists made it as easy as possible for people to oppose the war by appealing to the most universal sentiments and avoiding many political issues; but on the other, they made it very difficult for people to be actively against the war because they made significant participation depend upon espousal of a variety of usually out of reach beliefs.

The dynamics had a schizoid property that hurt the movement in a two-edged way. Many, many people were driven away by the movement center's tendency to ideologically and morally isolate itself; the rest, those who were brought in, were made rather peripheral by the movement's tendency to be somewhat a-political about its beliefs even though continually espousing the need for politics and correct lines over and over and making them prerequisites for active membership.

People marched, trying to influence the powers that be and in the process learned more and more about the war, its roots, and the forces maintaining it. Before long a reasonable number of people knew something about imperialism and consequently something about the entire American system. In parallel to the enlightenment there also developed the "isolationist" part of the double edged trend described above.

Either one was against imperialism or one's so-called anti-warism was hypocrisy ; either one was against the whole American system or not really against the war at all. One supported the NLF or was not really against the war at all; one was against monogamy, and for the Panthers and hated liberals or not really against the war in the first place. This is what one might in retrospect call the credentials or professionalization trend of the core left, the people who planned actions, wrote articles, gave speeches, and generally made the decisions. Needless to say fewer and fewer people could keep pace with the list of necessary againsts and thereby stay in the more organized parts of the anti-war movement. They thus had to stay only on the edge of movement activity and were, between major demonstrations, rather inactive and demoralized. Who knows how many others didn't do anything active because though the demand on commitment was actually lower than they'd have been willing to welcome, the demand on political, verbal adherence was higher than they could possibly handle. And, perhaps most ironic, for those who were in the organized movement the list of "againsts" was usually as much a ticket to legitimacy as it was a clearly thought out or deeply felt set of operative values. For if it had been the latter, members would have succeeded in making the list a real part of their daily calculations, and further, would have understood the necessity for not over-demanding other people's allegiances. Anti-war politics would still have been multi-issued but in styles speaking to people in ways they could relate to rather than in ways isolating the left.

The reasons for these two-edged harmful dynamics were actually quite clear to many spectators if not to the participants themselves. Anti-war radicals had vested interests in growth as well as in a unique position in society -- we were the action and, most importantly, we had the new morality and got our sense of importance largely from that distinction between ourselves and others. Whenever the American people responded to movement efforts and went a bit to the left, ironically already active movement people got nervous about their identities and made their positions more extreme and at the same time usually more unpalatable. On the one hand, we honestly tried to reach folks and "teach" them to oppose the war, but on the other we struggled to remain pure, aloof, and better. This again was the complicated two-edged trend.

Of course much of the movement's leftward motion also reflected honestly growing awarenesses, but such growth was regrettably hardly ever adapted to the demands of building an ever stronger larger movement. More often activists took their new knowledge and used it to isolate and enshrine themselves even while also trying to draw people to big demonstrations. We adopted new attitudes and styles (trashings, etc.) that often didn't reflect insight and commitment so much as an abiding desire to gain self esteem by keeping a monopoly on "real dissent" and on the dissenting identity. The movement's core was largely unreachable because at a certain level of consciousness it wanted to be unique and small. The movement was on the one hand really massive demonstrations and a tremendous number of people sharing a variety of radical beliefs, and on the other, a very small subset of isolated masters, planners, and shitworkers, precisely because the movement's every dynamic had the schizoid property of simultaneously attracting people while also keeping them only peripheral. And the fact that no one in the movement acted quite so bad as the caricature here described and that many acted diametrically opposite to it, is basically irrelevant -- for the movement had mass dynamics that averaged away the good we did and exacerbated much of the bad. The general effect of the whole anti-war movement was thus much as it would have been if all its members, instead of just some, were trying largely to set themselves apart as more moral than all other people. So despite immense forces propelling people to oppose the war including the educational efforts of the movement itself, the core of the truly everyday active anti-war movement did succeed in setting itself quite apart, much to everyone's ultimate detriment.

The major anti-war strategy (the movement's leaders who planned activities had it, though most of the people who attended them did not) was to end the war by raising its social costs at home. The strategy was to constantly increase the number of people opposing the war while simultaneously moving already actively opposed people toward ever greater and more militant activites. It recognized that rising disenchant-ment, the threat of increased worker politicization, and the growing radicalization of students, were all war policy costs which wise politicians would have to include in their cost-benefit calculations. The strategy was actually quite sound as far as it went. Most political hawks who turned dove indeed did so precisely because they felt that the war's domestic costs were growing too great to bear. In the end, despite its overall weaknesses and its tendency to isolate itself, the anti-war movement did thus help to turn the country against the war, to keep Johnson from seeking reelection, to set back the bombing for sometimes prolonged periods, to reverse attempted escalations, to prevent really massive escalations like nuclear bombing, to narrow government, military, and propaganda options, and to finally create conditions requiring a settlement at least temporarily favorable to the Vietnamese liberation forces.

The movement's weakest link was not so much the strategy that guided its leaders as their incapacities to act on it wisely and the resulting inadequacies that plagued all activities. The movement couldn't deal with people in ways that would keep them going leftward. It couldn't turn growing dissent into effective organization and it could only reach wide constituencies in the most minimal ways. It didn't create commitment so much as temporary allegiance. There was greater concern shown for quantity of effect than for quality of effect. Movement leaders frequently

urged organizers to create drama and overplay the possible numbers of
people attending demonstrations so as to bring everyone out. They didn't
talk too much about the development of real consciousness so that people
would continue to be committed between demonstrations and work
toward reaching ever broader audiences. Nor did they talk enough about
how to make movement work quality work, how to give people new
insights into the nature of the war and the nature of America.

At its heart the anti-war movement was manipulative. It did not
transmit strategic understanding to all its levels. It did not raise consciousness in irreversible ways. Most people never got to really participate
in planning. What planning there was, was not deeply enough conceived,
and was too hampered by tendencies emphasizing drama, being more
moral, and winning now, while ignoring questions of how the American
people actually felt about the war and about the movement. Most demon-
strators perceived each event as just another failure, perhaps not during
the immediate excitement of the event itself, but almost inexorably in the
period immediately following. Most people had no really deep feeling for
process -- they saw no great changes in the state of the war, they saw no new
constituencies creating strikes or other such actions, and so they
gravitated toward the belief that nothing was being accomplished, and
movement rhetoric did more to foster these frustrations than to overcome
them. ("If the government doesn't stop the war; we're going to stop the
government.") Finally most people had no real understanding of the
immensity of the enemy and so they had a ridiculously disproportionate
set of criteria for judging themselves and their movement. Did we win,
rather than did we gain a little?

Some people fooled themselves into believing that they were always
'winning now' and others, in some ways correctly, always felt they weren't,
and eventually became demoralized and split. Only a few constantly kept a
modest strategic sense of making gains a bit at a time in an inexorable but
very slow process. And, perhaps most striking, this last group did little or
nothing to help the others achieve a new perspective, and in fact often gave
dramatic speeches that fostered wrong approaches.

For example, at a national People's Coalition for Peace and Justice
criticism self-criticism session after the Mayday actions, the criteria for
analysis of the effects of the demonstration should have been did the
action realign government powers a bit in our favor; did it move
immediate and distant spectators toward anti-war awarenesses; did it

affect participants positively; and did it strengthen the movement? The answers should have been: perhaps a bit; a little yes, a little no; maybe; and no. The mood should have been self-critical and rather 'depressed' but determined. The actual mood was different. No one set out concrete criteria for judgement. Everyone implicitly used variations of the extreme 'did we win' brand, even while many bemoaned the fact that that was the way the media were playing the whole thing: did we shut down the city or not? There was a lot of euphoria and backpatting. Some people convinced themselves the whole thing was great (a victory) and other people who thought it was not so good (a defeat) didn't bother saying so for fear of being considered defeatist. PCPJ was like most other parts of the anti-war movement in that its criticism/self-criticism hardly ever led to real improvements.

The culmination of all these various dynamics seems to have come with the Cambodia invasion. Students did everything they felt they could and very few other people seemed to them to do much of anything. Anti-war people fell into the belief that the situation was quite hopeless -- they alone didn't have the power to win and no one else was making time to join them. And besides, now there were risks. You could be jailed or even killed. In the absence of solidarity and an understanding of real accomplishments, the chief emotion became fear. Anger and determination diminished and passivity increased. The movement was neither a fruitful nor fun place to be -- at least for the great bulk of its people who weren't central, didn't travel, and didn't contribute many ideas for strategy. The movement was debilitating because it made people act in competitive, arrogant, sneaky, and aloof ways, and besides it just didn't seem to pay off. Repression was becoming a real factor too. It was more and more difficult for people to keep active faith as they began to feel their daily behavior was becoming more and more oppressive. Life became alienated, success seemed impossible, and most of the movement's attempts at good dynamics were replaced by extreme versions of the bad ways people had been taught to act in the society at large.

In essence the same dynamics hit the anti-war movement that hit the student movement. People's identities became tied up in their own righteousness and in subjective myths about the Vietnamese, themselves, and the enemy. People began fighting with each other because the enemy was too powerful, and at the same time people lost their abilities to be humble, sensitive, participatory, and patient. People went to the farm, gravitated back to the school, became sectarian hangers-on, or in a few cases, usually because of advantages, knowledge, many friendships, experience, and some kind of steady income allowing full time participation, hung in. The latter are now struggling with the sectarians for leadership of the remnants of the organized anti-war movement. If they can succeed and overcome past inadequacies perhaps they will yet be able to help develop a movement that could force discontinuation of American support for Thieu, really develop an anti-imperialist awareness and presence, and insure that when the history of the sixties is told, it gives a correct perspective to the roles of both the left and the liberal United States establishment.

The anti-war movement succeeded because it had a patently clear cause and because it had energy, good will, and at least at the beginning, much solidarity and attractiveness. It was thus able to create an effective counter-force to United States imperialist designs, materially aid the Vietnamese cause, lift the level of United States political awareness, and demonstrate the possibility of effective United States leftist action. It failed, however, because it was authoritarian, because it refused to educate itself clearly about what it was doing and why it was doing it, because it refused to study the feelings and beliefs of the American people, because its members had weaknesses which were fostered and not countered, and because its members also had immense ego-problems. It failed because, having not asked the right questions about itself or about the American people, it was unable to formulate good programs. Thus the present absence of effective, relatively large on-going anti-imperialist organizations. The anti-war movement had essentially the same leaders, the same structures, the same constituencies and the same faults as the student movement. While students and middle-class people suffered considerably for ensuing imperfect dynamics, the Vietnamese, all third-world people, and America's Blacks and poor bore the greatest long-run burdens of all temporary inadequacies of the left.

THE WEATHER MACHINE

The Weatherman movement was a kind of aberration that developed in the days when third-world heroes seemed actually godlike. If something is wrong, fight it; since "the country sucks, kick ass." Weatherman was an aberration and yet it was also a logical extension of the sixties. If the Weathermachine was moved by pathology, it was also moved by the most impressive commitment to fight injustice, to whatever extent conditions demanded, that the sixties produced. In many ways its practice embodied the logical extension of the whole new left. 7

Weatherman had an ideology and its members functioned consistently within it. They recognized some of their middle-class upbringing weaknesses and tried to correct them. The main problem was that they were one-sidedly extremist about all they did.

Their strategy was based on the premise that most Americans are too tied up in their relative advantages to be willing to take revolutionary risks. In light of the way Weatherman approached people these expectations were rather self-fulfilling. To gain Weather-praise one essentially had to admit to being a white honky pig who was repentant and willing to give all for the welfare of the third world, and then act like a guerilla facsimile of John Wayne. Weatherpeople saw themselves as a kind of Vietcong front functioning within the United States. They were the NLF, except of course that they had little of the NLF's integrity, experience, discipline, patience, or preparedness, and certainly little of their dignity or empathy for other people's perspectives.

Weatherpeople believed in the raise-the-cost approach, but felt effective mass militancy was quite impossible. They wanted a small Red Army, and though they damned just about everyone, they felt they and a few others could work 'alongside' the third-world masses. They opted for terrorism, figuring it would attract those few with guts, and at the same time raise domestic costs and put everyone on notice as to what was coming. Their vision of revolution was a blazing tank. Their early attacks on working class kids, high schools, other movement groups, street gangs, and occasionally police stations, ROTC centers, or university fraternities showed just how far astray from rationality they would eventually deviate. One had only to hear the upper-middle-class-authoritarian leather-jacketed leaders singing praises to the therapeutic values of violence to learn the Weathermachine's chief lesson: certain kinds of 'uncritical' even if rebellious thinking can pervert one to such extents that the resulting actions can be more a 'people's problem' than even the actions of official authorities. Regrettably, to teach us this commonsense but important piece of wisdom, the Weatherpeople took many very severe beatings and scared away a great many potential leftists as well.

When general activism levels slowed, Weatherpeople got somewhat more sophisticated and revolved their strategies around the idea of exemplary action - though still with a heavy emphasis on the inability of most people to respond positively. Essentially this was a useful rationale for doing whatever one wanted, coupled with an excuse for why it didn't work, all worked out before the fact -- the exemplary action idea always gains sway among the more persevering parts of any epoch's leftist movements. The idea was that bombings or 'events' of a militant kind could detonate favorable feelings in many who saw them. People could learn how possible it was to fight the behemoth. They would see that there were some people who had good values and guts and who intimated a better way of life.

The thought was a step foward but only a small one. Weatherpeople were just too out of touch to know what would push people to the left and what to the right. Certainly bombing bathrooms didn't impress too many people with Weather abilities to smash the state, and emulating a toughed up James Dean didn't impress many others with Weather potentials for living well or creating a better world. Indeed most people took away the impression that Weatherpeople were a collection of maniacs who had lost all track of their own relations to reality, and who were tripping on a fantasy about their own importance.

That image, though slightly unfair, was by no means completely off base. For the Weathermachine at its worst was the guy who got up in the middle of a meeting and gave a long dramatic rap worshipping the therapeutic effects of unrestrained violence, or the women who got up and attacked all men for their pig natures, in attempts not to educate but to score points, or the militant who hurled a petty rock at a demonstration and then beat a hasty retreat while others who didn't really know what was going on got trampled or caught by the police. It was a 'heavy dude' on the run from imaginary police pursuit, hiding out at one's house, creeping around, not talking to anyone except to say that he was the Vietcong slipping out in the morning and eventually getting busted for ripping off underwear. At its worst the Weathermachine was a band of toughs who on one day were a-cultural, anti-hippie, tight asses, and on the next, after some central committee decided on a new path, became the Kazoo Marching Band carrying chains instead of batons.

When the Weatherpeople were at their best and succeeding beyond

even their own expectations with a bombing, or a fight, or a school distur-
bance, their main effect was to make people hate them and the left. The
Weatherpeople, at the cost of a few bathrooms, gave the government
ample reason to extend its oppresive apparatuses in almost all its major
cities. This was unquestionably a dubious achievement even if it had been
accompanied by a significant growth on the left, which of course it wasn't.

The Weatherpeople had the same identity problems and the same
tendencies toward extremism as everyone else but as they made quite
clear, they also had more 'guts' for carrying their errors all the way
through to their logical ends. They saw revolution and repression around
every door. They bounced from one side of each false dichotomy to the
other, never once finding the solid revolutionary ground in the middle.

Many Weatherpeople were society's best trained, most confident,
most educated, and (initially) most sensitive youth, but the dynamics they
encountered and created were overwhelming. They rebelled against
society's discipline but made that rebellion a fetish even in their own
organizations. They rightfully discovered that a fear of violence could be
debilitating but they pushed on to worship violence as virtuous behavior
which should be 'pushed out' in almost all circumstances. They screamed
about America's gross machismo and then became crudely macho-violent
themselves. They decided that monogamy had weaknesses, moved on to
decide that it was totally wrong, and then created a kind of tribal dynamic
that forced people into a self-destructive brand of sexist polygamy. The
Weather living tactics convinced many that even justifiable attempts at
altering life styles were recklessly worthless. And finally, Weather
militance and Weather hostility pushed the machine further and further
away from the rest of the left until they lived in a kind of self-created
paranoic guerilla dream world that had little relation to the on-going
realities of American life -- except for the fact that as Weather behavior
became more extreme, they were indeed isolated and repression did grow
until their dreams became self-fulfilling nightmares. The waste of talent,
emotion, and life that was Weatherman's result is a crime for which everyone in the new left is partially responsible.

THE YIPPIES

The human   race in its poverty, has unquestionably one

really effective weapon -- laughter. Power, money, persuasion, supplication, persecution -- these can lift at a colossal
humbug - push it a little, weaken it a little, century by
century; but only laughter can blow it to rags and atoms at a
blast. Against the assault of laughter nothing can stand. 8

The Weatherpeople were not totally alone in a willingness to take
things to an extreme and camp on the fringes of reality. Youth culture, San
Francisco, rock, drugs, and new colorful lifestyles with loose mores were
all part of a supra-political attempt at revolution. The initial strategy was
quite ingenious. American lifestyles have pain, alienation, and obvious
inconsistency. American institutions are inhuman and the culture is plas-
tic. People want love, self-esteem, and involvement but are forced to settle
for debilitating substitutes. The youth culture would carve out an
existence for itself based on humane, loving values and thus be irresistible.
It would spoof and confront all that was bad and do it entertainingly. It
would reach people through their hearts and their funny bones. Rather
than trying to out compute the American computer or out fight the army,
the youth culture would pull out the plug of the first and flower-power the
second to death. Yippieism initially had a good understanding of American consciousness, a good feel for some ways to reach it, and tremen-
dously invigorating energy to sustain the whole effort. The Yippies
contributed humor and creativity to the new left. They awakened a
national awareness of the ills of alienation, commercialism, authoritarianism, and competition.

The Yippies were products of the land they hated and their own bad
traits were overlooked and were thus eventually able to subvert the good
they were doing. The Yippie lifestyle offered many new ways but it also
only refurbished a few of the old ones. Competitiveness and liberalism
were both diminished, freedom was emphasized, honesty was a high virtue, and believing in things that help people rather than in things that hurt
was the primary admission ticket. Life became more colorful, light, and
fun, and especially for men Yippie styles overcame a number of
competitive habits that had previously forced alienation upon people. But
women were still largely supposed to serve men, if anything in more
grotesque caricatures than ever before. For now there had to be colorful
clothes and liberated smiles and free sex along with an adoring deference
for the still male god. Women were allowed only in a lower echelon of

participation as "our women." The continuation and even elaboration of sexism in Yippiedom was one of its chief weaknesses -- as the going got tough that one bad trait helped resurrect a great many others until Yippie originality was finally inundated by the Americanisms inside the Yippies.

As with all other strategic attempts, when repression and cooptation became tough, approaches were polarized more and more toward old ways of doing things. As soon as the Yippie identity was threatened, a jocularly critical approach was replaced by a haughty put-on superiority and the trend continued in every area. Yippies began joining with Weatherpeople, violence was wholeheartedly adopted, the more sensitive hippies dropped out of the drop-out; outlaw styles of anti-rationality, toughness, and dirtiness began flourishing. Disease and drugs took a heavy toll. The whole affair ended in a rather dismal mess. Haight Ashbury moved from being the result of an effort to create a place that could teach people new ways, to being a youth slum that could only attract the most hopelessly disaffected. A group of people originally into sharing everything became so destructively critical that they could hardly share anything with anybody. The only tastes that mattered were their own and they too became more and more irrational. A group that was going to ride people's funnybones to their consciousness was in the end considered arrogant, elitist, sexist, self-centered, divorced from reality, and often just totally obnoxious.

Here again, it was partly because people were much too headstrong. Yippies were unable to develop flexible identities and methods. They couldn't simultaneously balance criticisms from outside, accepting the wise and ignoring the badly motivated, and they couldn't aim their communication to where people actually were. The Yippies were therefore not confident or wise enough to pursue their intuitions in the face of establishment repression and cooptation, or in the face of leftist baits urging them on toward heavier positions. The Yippies didn't have and couldn't give each other enough humble self-confidence. For all their insight they didn't know enough about themselves or America, they underestimated their enemies, and they didn't have any real methods for improving their own deficiencies. Although the make-them-laugh approach could never really have eliminated all the "colossal humbugs" and all the colossal powers behind those, as a partial element in an overall process it could have been much more effective than it finally was.

Perhaps most contributory to their decline, the initial Yippie disposition toward 'happy tactics' didn't stem from conscious respect for traditional American lifestyles or for traditional Americans. In the beginning most Yippies had intuitively humanistic aspirations but very little understanding of why American people act as they generally do. In the beginning Yippies had enthusiastic faith in people generally, and when there was no pressure to defend their new styles, they evinced no hostility toward the 'jumbled' ways in which normal people were trying to deal with their own problems. But as time went on the Yippies were forced to distance themselves more and more from the mainstream so as to have clear, strong, identities. They inevitably became disdainful of everyone else -- they never developed a solid understanding of other people's motivations and so under pressure became intolerant of them. They grew to like themselves and no one else. And they really had few other options, they didn't have enough awareness to retain self-respect while at the same time also respecting the contradictory attitudes of other Americans. As a result Yippie efforts to talk to others became constrained and patronizing. They were no longer trusting guides. They became arrogant, sloppy critics who had less and less to offer. Yippie ideology and behavior threatened mainstream America's identity while having few redeeming traits and so the Yippies gradually became a favorite target for abuse and even violence. 9

The Yippies rejected patriotism, the police, puritan sexuality, the work and success ethic, consumerism, education, and the assumed goodness of the American social order continually more and more strenuously and with less and less sensitivity, as well as with diminishing abilities to offer any attractive alternatives. They pulled the rug out from under people's self-images without offering any ways for people to otherwise stand erect. What solutions they offered were totally unworkable for most Americans, and in the end even for themselves. They were critical in sectarian rather than in loving ways and it worsened with time. They did not speak in ways people could understand and then act upon. The Yippies started by trying to build a new way of living based upon communal love. They ended by telling kids that the only way they could become revolutionaries was to kill their parents. Recruitment lagged. 10

The Yippie experience teaches mostly the same lessons as the Weather one. The dynamics of rebellion are risky. The sole criterion of value can't be only the idea of winning or losing now. Without humble self-confidence and patience leftists are often likely to become their own

worst enemies, hated as well by the people they are trying to reach. Without methods for understanding what one is doing and why, and what its
effects are on all concerned, one's activities are probably going to do as
much harm as good. Without real understanding and empathy,
communication is impossible; creativity and love of self is simply not
enough. The enemy is too big to be brought down by a group of clever
comedians. But the Yippie experience also taught many people much
about social interaction and about the importance of dealing with interpersonal dynamics effectively. It taught the importance of confronting the
totality of American life, including its cultural, sexual, artistic, and
spiritual sterility. But it especially taught that even as youth we were not as
incorruptable as we would have liked to think. 11

THE BLACK PANTHERS

The new left Black movement was in many ways the core element of
sixties activism. Beginning with the participatory Student Non-Violent
Coordinating Committee (SNCC) and extending through various nationalist groups to the avowedly revolutionary Black Panthers, the Black left
was the most militant, most politically experienced, and most forcefully
opposed. Its contributions in helping reawaken Black political awarenesses, advancing consciousnesses of racism, forging new Black goals and
identities, and aiding the Vietnamese through anti-war activity especially
within the Army itself, were immense. Its chief teachings are again the
viability of radical activism, the centrality of racism to all United States
political possibilities, and the need for revolution if United States Blacks
are ever to fully achieve liberated existences. To have accomplished so
much in so few years, despite the "legal" police murders of over a hundred
activists, and despite imprisonment of hundreds more, armed invasions of
offices, and immense police infiltration programs is remarkable testimony
to the power of an organized opposition force. Nonetheless, as with all
other new left groups, frequent successes were accompanied by many
failures, and at least sometimes the reasons for failure were internal rather
than police-imposed. In this section we discuss only the Black Panthers as
they were the best-organized and most avowedly revolutionary of all the
various Black organizations.

The Panthers started with an empathy for their people and for their own plight that was much deeper than any comparable views held by white groups. They understood why oppressed Blacks frequently act in self-defeating ways and even had some grudging respect for all kinds of survival tactics. They dealt with the problems of being baited by racists and therein developed strong racial self-images. The Panthers were aware enough so that no pressure would make them become racist, either against whites or against their own people. They understood the nature of racist tendencies and where they came from and were able to control them. The Panthers knew that racism against whites was a dead end and were able to incorporate the awareness into their own behaviors. They also had significant roots in the Black ghetto and thus a real feeling for the day to day needs of their people. Their ten-point program was one of the few concrete political programs espoused by any part of the United States new left and itself makes clear many of the injustices the Black movement opposed and brought into public awareness:

> 1. We want freedom. We want power to determine the destiny of our Black Community.
> 2. We want full employment for our people.
> 3. We want an end to the robbery by the white man of our Black Community.
> 4. We want decent housing fit for shelter for human beings.
> 5. We want education for our people that exposes the true nature of this decadent American society. We want education that teaches us our true history and our role in the present-day society.
> 6. We want all Black men to be exempt from the military service.
> 7. We want an immediate end to *police brutality* and *murder* of Black people.
> 8. We want freedom for all Black men held in federal, state, county and city prisons and jails.
> 9. We want all Black people when brought to trial to be tried in court by a jury of their peer group or people from their Black communities, as defined by the Constitution of the United States.
> 10. We want land, bread, housing, education, clothing, justice and peace. And as our major political objective, a

> United Nations supervised plebiscite to be held throughout
> the black colony in which only black colonial subjects will
> be allowed to participate, for the purpose of determining
> the will of black people as to their national destiny.

But the Panthers didn't have so powerful a grasp of insights concerning --
nor the capacities to deal with -- the ills of sexism and authoritarianism,
and therein, as we'll see, lay the roots of much of their weakness.

The Panthers chose a series of tactics that were in some sense schizoid
-- "we'll increase our support with serve the people programs and newspapers, but also by showing how tough we are and how well we can deal
with the man." During their early days when they chose to go to the
California State House armed, they sealed their ultimate fate. For though
they had the self-awareness around race necessary to ward off bad racist
tendencies, they could not do the same with their macho and sexist
tendencies.

The line was a direct one from the glorious state house 'show' to
eventual isolation in small armed camps daily attacked by the police. The
Panthers formed authoritarian organizations and these fostered all the
bad tendencies that hierarchical societies inevitably give to their citizens.

The organizations became more and more authoritarian and the leaders
lost touch with reality, tripping out on their own inflated visions of their
self-importance. As latent aggressive, hostile attitudes poured forth
unchecked, they had to be rationalized and incorporated into the whole
Panther ideology. The Panther image grew inextricably entwined with
militance, toughness, and courage. They grew more and more isolated.
Their worship of revolutionary suicide was only slightly less ridiculous
than the Yippie plan for parenticide. With isolation and militance came
inevitable repression. There was no great defensive upsurge because there
was no great empathy for a group that seemed bent only on violence. The
image of Eldridge Cleaver strutting through Congress with John Stennis'
head on a platter did not overly entrance this country's Black population.

The Panther understanding of the need to build a base in the ghetto
was offset by members' inabilities to effectively organize, and to stave
off their own tendencies toward machismo. The Panthers went the same
way every other group of the sixties had gone, good beginnings, through
bad times, to polarizing defensive tactics and self-images, to severe inner
strife, arrogance, and external obscurity. They were stronger and had

better intuitions than white groups, but their enemies were also better armed and more eager to repress. The final responsibility for the deaths of many Black Panthers and the incarceration of countless others rests first with the state and society. The immediate responsibility rests with a strategy that lost track of itself and got caught up in self-indulgent rationalization.

NEW LEFT WOMEN'S MOVEMENT

The New Left Women's movement went essentially the same routes as the male led elements. Myths had it that women would be able to avoid competitive strife because of the types of oppression to which they'd been subject, their long-standing low position in society, and their gut understanding of machismo's harmfulness. Ostensibly since women were arising in a defiance of competitive machismo, their movements wouldn't have to worry about succumbing to its particular dynamics. In fact this belief was a great error. Every group in the United States has potential for every kind of oppressor/oppressed behavior. Everyone raised here has to one degree or another been affected by surrounding environments and thereby picked up countless bad traits, some of which dominate behaviors, some of which are only subtly active, and many of which most often only lie dormant awaiting opportunities to emerge. The difference between one United States group's identity and any other's is that for each, good and bad traits occur in different combinations, and in connection with different sets of emotional feelings and needs. Women are thus generally oppressed and reticent in company of men until they understand their oppression and start opposing it. Once that occurs, however, the situation alters drastically and so do behaviors.

When women began rebelling in the mid-sixties, they developed fine intuitions about the nature of American male-female relations, about what a woman's movement could include, and about what it could do. The first activists had tremendous empathy with their sisters' needs and emotions, and tremendous enthusiasm due to their new self-images and imminent liberation. They had participatory, non-competitive, anti-authoritarian aims. But at the same time their respect for other non-movement women's efforts to survive through capitulation was none too great, and their defensiveness concerning things male-related was still quite strong.

Initially women formed consciousness-raising groups for understanding their own oppressions and the circumstances of the society in which they lived. They used very effective militant ways to confront movement men about machismo, sexism, and competitiveness. They successfully 'rediscovered' the heritage of United States feminist activism and began hammering out a new type of aware, strong, female personality. But at the same time there were growing problems of male attacks and difficulties of movement growth. The early activists reached middle class women effectively enough but had neither the time nor the experience to think effectively enough about reaching working-class women. Women's group discussions became highly self-centered. In time there were external attacks from movement men ridiculing feminism, even assaulting women, and always calling on them to spend their time more effectively: instead of challenging our leadership, follow it. Under these attacks left women strengthened their identities regrettably by tying them ever more completely into the most 'radical' conceptions they could formulate. Movement women lost touch with non-movement women who didn't think as they did, and had no patience for any men, even for those who were really trying to understand, but had not quite made it yet. Movement women simply refused to recognize their own tendencies towards the kinds of behavior they hated in their male counterparts. They didn't admit they would often manipulate meetings, degrade opponents, compete amongst themselves, and generally create the same bad kinds of dynamics that men create when they hold themselves to be superior.

Inside the movement, dominant women began developing oppressor roles and reticent women began gravitating toward more passive ones. By and large the new oppressors determined the movement's public images precisely because they were its most energetic members. Hierarchy began to rule.

Movement women were unable to develop firm enough understandings of their own backgrounds and their own weaknesses and strengths. They were unable to create flexible identities. They couldn't be careful and patient about developing new modes of actions in the urgency to rush their efforts. They worried about being oppressive and spent countless hours discussing it but didn't fully understand all its potentials for occurring and had, like the rest of the new left, no tools for effectively warding it off. They didn't formulate programs in an unhurried, objective way and in time that omission cost them severely. They espoused heavy-handed criticisms of monogamy and then had to act on those criticisms to their own detriments. They glorified lesbianism and found themselves pushed hard by lesbians who had views different from those of many other women in the movement. The developing dissensions caused many problems and disaffected many potential adherents.

The movement had no tools for adequately understanding the tremendous rush of new situations which pressed upon it. It developed hierarchies of womanliness which gave some people distinct powers over other people. There were the ins, the partials, and the outs. Like the members of all other new left groups, women were unable to perceive their identities independent from immediate actions; they were unable to act in accord with their ideology's own dictates.

Under assault by society and the male part of the movement women activists took the same road as all their male compatriots. They began getting their self-images from believing in their own worths as compared to other people's weaknesses. Who is the purest liberationist? Who is the best? Leaders and followers emerged. The leaders were implicitly regarded as better than the followers and ipso-facto had more privileges, and the followers in the movement were similarly better than everyone else outside it. Everyone could see, feel, but do almost nothing about these dynamics because they were too deeply rooted. Women's groups began planning demonstrations, meetings, and newspapers that lacked sensitivity and organization and almost always contained competitive dynamics.

And yet even with its various weaknesses the new left women's movement unleashed a tremendous force in the United States. It helped many people develop understandings of the dynamics of sexism and authority and of what men and women could and someday would be like. It gave countless women new understandings of their histories and present lives, and new goals for their future efforts. It brought people into motion, but regrettably it was a motion that didn't yet incorporate enough of the critical anti-authoritarian, anti-sexist lessons on which it was premissed. The New Left Women's Movement "ended" in a kind of disorganized frustration with only the non-revolutionary elements maintaining significant organizational strength. Nevertheless overall women's political awareness was still on the rise, and the potential for a truly effective, anti-sexist, revolutionary organized feminist left seemed great.

A FEW LESSONS

The new left was internally without a strategy. It had ego problems, it wasn't adequately self-conscious, and it was immature. It judged practice by asking very narrowly either how much motion was accomplished or how much was created. There was little understanding of sustained process or of patient struggle towards growth. Hierarchies fostered people's worst traits, competition thrived; people's politics got tied to their identities in ways leading to extreme sectarianism. There was no powerful guiding ideology. Practice was intuitive and generally very problematic. It made many gains but often incurred even greater costs.

The results were predictable: morale and effectiveness declined together. Either people left depressed, or stayed but usually became caricatures of what they had hoped to be. And yet even with all this the American left of the sixties had many important successes. It was struggling against the strongest enemy any left has ever encountered, both in the state apparatus and in its cultural socialization processes. Despite the great odds, it created an effective counter-force to the Vietnam war, a growing American awareness of America's weaknesses and of the viability of protest, and an understanding within the left itself of the multiplicity of oppression that is America, and of the complexity of the problems confronting modern revolutionaries. In this last category, perhaps most important of all, it put sexism, racism, authoritarianism, and general interpersonal dynamics on the revolutionary agenda on equal footing with class struggle.

Though at times indulgent, irresponsible, and even 'pathological,' the new left of the sixties did make honest courageous attempts to confront the totality of America's injustices. If it failed to create a viable revolutionary movement, it did at least create some new awareness and a bedrock of experience upon which such a movement can likely soon be constructed. It certainly did much more than anyone could have predicted at the time of John F. Kennedy's election. Despite the sacrifice, the errors, and the losses, the efforts, because of the future left activity they prefigure and provide a base for, were well worth it.

But even our very brief presentation shows that to grow anew the left needs a new and enlarged political consciousness which can among other things:

Understand our society's institutional, cultural, and ideological relationships, identify those that are truly oppressive, those that are largely neutral, and those that are
potentially useful to liberation, and then understand all
their various interrelations.

Understand revolutionaries and all social groups with
respect to how they are oppressed by, how they rebel
against, acquiesce to, and even in part support their
oppressions, and thus how they might be affected by
changes in their environments -- and most specifically by
changes caused by revolutionary activities.

Understand future goals and means of transition well
enough to posit short term programs and strategies suitable
to all local contexts and incorporative of the knowledge of
the two points above.

Our analysis also shows that to accomplish such ends any new politics
will have to take account of and explain racism; sexism; hierarchy;
authority; and consciousness in general and at concrete local interpersonal levels; and to explain effectively all the more traditionally addressed
material politico-economic relationships.

The new left needs a better consciousness than it had in the sixties.
What it then knew intuitively it must crystallize now; what it then didn't
know it must learn now. One route to such creative ends is to build upon
critical analyses of past revolutionary ideologies. As a first step we next
clarify our usage of the concepts 'theory,' 'strategy,' 'practice,' and
'political consciousness.' We provide definitions and also evaluative
criteria which we go on to use throughout the rest of *What Is To Be
Undone* in our critical studies of Classical Marxism Leninism, Anarchism,
and Maoism.

FOOTNOTES

1. Lewis Carrol, *Alice in Wonderland,* McMillan and Co. London.
2. See Noam Chomsky, *For Reasons of State,* and *American Power and the New Manderins,* Vintage Books, New York.
3. Carl Oglesby, *The New Left Reader,* Grove Press, New York.
4. See the "Port Huron Statement," in *The New Left: A Documentary History,* edited by Massimo Teodori, Bobbs Merrill, New York.
5. In Boston the choice was perhaps somewhat more conscious than many other places. The 'leadership' was in effect confronted with a choice: We could proceed with a city wide anti-war struggle focused on MIT's war complicity, very militant and very anti-capitalist, or we could do the more patient job of continuing to build left support throughout the city so as to move later on a larger more together scale. We choose the former way mostly because we felt it was necessary to make a ruckus about the war that could provoke others elsewhere into doing the same. Our reasoning was understandable but quite wrong. In general we should also now point out that this whole chapter is primarily about Boston-Cambridge experiences, though the lessons, we expect, are more widely applicable.
6. Paul Potter, *A Name For Ourselves,* Little Brown, Boston.
7. The quoted phrase had its origin on a Boston subway on the way to a demonstration to confront a Boston University mixer -- it arose spontaneously during a rap to the "transfixed" subway riders.
8. Mark Twain in Phillip Foner, *Mark Twain Social Critic,* International Publishers, New York.
9. See George Harrison, "Blue Jay Way" and the whole of the album "Magical Mystery Tour" for a cultural description of roughly the same phenomena.
10. See Jerry Rubin's and Abbie Hoffman's books for the quickest rundown of the Yippie "ideology."
11. Ibid.

CHAPTER TWO

REVOLUTIONARY THEORY, STRATEGY, AND PRACTICE
METHODOLOGY FOR OUR CRITICAL INVESTIGATION

What a man sees depends upon both what he looks at and
also what his previous visual-conceptual experience has
taught him to see. In the absence of such training there can
only be in William James's phrase, "a bloomin' buzzin'
confusion." 1

Thomas Kuhn

We wish to present and critique Classical Marxism Leninism to
develop insights for improving it to fit our own modern contexts. What
should we study most? What aspects of the whole should we emphasize?
In what order should we discuss various aspects? Can we give our study a
guiding thrust that will help organize the whole effort? And in a prior
sense can we even motivate our study with a clear precedent understanding about how theories are generally developed and judged?

People answer these questions many different ways. We base ours on
a general store of scientific training and on an extension of Thomas
Kuhn's analyses of similar issues, precisely because those analyses seem
the most accepted, the most suited to our ends, and the most correct of any
available.

Kuhn says the natural sciences move foward by way of alternating
evolutionary and then revolutionary periods. During evolutionary
development a widely held collection of thoughts, methods, beliefs, and so
on, are advanced in accord with their own internally determined dictates.
During revolutionary development the same consciousness collection, or,
as Kuhn calls it, the same *paradigm*, is overthrown, which is to say,
advanced by negation and replacement due to developments lying outside
its own previous visions and criteria.

In the evolutionary period there is what Kuhn calls *normal science*. The generally accepted paradigm is applied to ever greater numbers of phenomena. Scientists improve, verify, enlarge, and adapt it by constant reapplications. Essentially, in Kuhn's words, they engage in "puzzle solving." They try to fit the world to their paradigm's category/dynamic expectations. They guide their efforts according to their paradigm's dictates. They approach problems because their paradigm orients them so, and because it says they can succeed in finding solutions.

> Closely examined, whether historically or in the contemporary laboratory, that enterprise seems an attempt to force nature into the preformed and relatively inflexible box that the paradigm supplies. 2

But during the *evolutionary period*, as the many new problems to which any paradigm gives rise are being sorted out and solved, some prove quite intractable. Others, also intractable, are discovered accidentally, outside the realms toward which the paradigm actually pushes practitioners. Eventually there is an accumulation of "anomolous" problems which practitioners find important and troubling, but which are seen as unimportant within the context of their paradigm and in any case unsolvable by it.

Many practitioners, then, simply put the problems aside (and often don't even recognize them in the first place) due to their normal-science faith in their well-tested beliefs. Others however can't help but see the importance of the new problems and begin trying to alter their paradigms in accord. Then normal science reaches what Kuhn calls a state of *crisis activity*.

Resolution comes by way of supercession of old paradigms by new ones. The scientist who saw reality in terms of one set of beliefs, concepts, and methods before such resolution sees it by a different set after. In a sense, practitioners' world views alter. The debate between old and new during transition is generally extremely impassioned and confused. Each side initially approaches issues differently. What one says is important evidence in favor of its paradigm is irrelevant to the other and vice versa. Nonetheless, by dynamics Kuhn describes, in revolutions there is a gradual transition to a new paradigm and then to a new normal science. 3

> Probably the single most prevalent claim advanced by pro-
> ponents of a new paradigm is that they can solve the
> problems that have led the old one to crisis. When it can
> legitimately be made, this claim is often the most effective
> one possible. 4

In moving the analysis from the hard to the social sciences the
contours change but nonetheless Kuhn's model remains at least roughly
applicable. Thus in revolutionary science, *paradigm equals ideology*,
equals *theory, strategy, and practice;* equals Marxism Leninism, or Anarchism, or Maoism.

There are three questions that must be answered in the application of
Kuhn's model to our subject. First, what is the purpose of a revolutionary
paradigm and of each of its parts? Second what are the parts in more detail,
including potential roots of strengths and weaknesses? And third, how do
the parts interrelate to form a whole and what are its specific dynamics?

A physics paradigm of the kind Kuhn centers his studies on informs
its holders about the real physical world and gives them ways of understanding and affecting it. It guides their endeavors by giving methods and
directions of concern.

Similarly a revolutionary paradigm informs its holders about the
socio-political-economic world, gives them ways of understanding and affecting it, and guides their efforts by providing methods and directions of
concern.

Yet even though each seems to do pretty much the same things for its
practitioners) the ultimate purposes of the two types of paradigms are
somewhat skewed from one another. Thus with the physics paradigm the
ultimate emphasis is on knowledge; whereas with the revolutionary
paradigm the ultimate emphasis is on change.

For both the physicist and the revolutionary, knowledge and activity
are to serve each other. Each must provide guidelines and ways of improving
the other. And yet in the last analysis, the physicist experiments to further
knowledge; while the revolutionary uses knowledge to further experiment,
which is to say struggle.

There is a critical inversion of theory/practice priorities and it is this
that complicates a Kuhnian analysis of socio-political paradigm development, and that must be recognized, to answer the question, "What is the
purpose of revolutionary paradigm?" and to get at the more detailed

analysis of the purposes of revolutionary theory, strategy, and practice.

Normal science is in the revolutionary context the process by which Marxist Leninists, Anarchists or Maoists pursue studies of the world and engage in practice in accord with their own ideology's dictates. Thus each group sees things somewhat differently from the others, employs different priorities, and so on, but at least when functioning normally, each moves steadily and calmly forward in what are generally self-consistent ways. Like for the hard scientist functioning normally, day-to-day revolutionary practice encounters few surprises and is essentially a puzzle solving (and doing) dynamic that occurs very much in expected and preordained ways.

Crisis science is, on the other hand, the process by which the paradigms struggle with one another and with non-revolutionary alternatives for social dominance. They generate debate about each others' suppositions, and even more than with the hard sciences (because of the extra involved interests) the debate is a tortuous one in which no side gives much credence to the formulations of any other.

Resolution in the area would be the success of any one revolutionary paradigm in gaining full domination over all the others.

For the purposes of this book, however, we begin by asserting such a resolution, with Clasical Marxism Leninism as a core around which normal activities now proceed. Later, after dealing with Classical Marxism Leninism as if it were the only ideological possibility, we admit the existence of Anarchism, Maoism, and some contemporary neo-Marxist views and consider them too.

Thus for the moment our available revolutionary paradigm is Classical Marxism Leninism. We feel a definite crisis. The anomalous problems to which it denies importance, and, in any case does not help solve, revolve around useability, racism, sexism, authority, socialization dynamics, the relationships between consciousness and general day-to-day activity, the dynamics between social and movement relations and people's consciousnesses, the nature of bureaucracy, the ability of people to understand local situations and analyze local tactics, and so on.

According to Kuhnian logic our task is to therefore define our Classical paradigm precisely and then examine it with reference to its various problems. We try to discover how the paradigm might yet eventually solve them, or how, if it can't, some other altered one might. In the latter event we could then try as our first tentative alternatives the Anarchist and Maoist paradigms, to either adopt one or reject both, while learning still more about what a finally successful paradigm would have to be like.

Our critical study is thus justified by the state of *crisis* we perceive in Classical Marxism Leninism's abilities to handle today's crucial revolutionary problems. A good result of our study would be either a recognition of how the Classical paradigm can finally solve its problems or of why it can't and how an altered new paradigm might be able to. And how then should we proceed with our critical study? In what order should we approach the body of Classical Marxist Leninist thought? What should we emphasize and what should we only gloss over? To answer requires a better understanding of the internal relations of any revolutionary paradigm's three component parts: theory, strategy, and practice; an understanding will tell us how to study each part with an eye toward most readily discovering from where the whole's 'anomalous' weaknesses are derived.

THEORIES

What are theories, how are they constructed and used, what are the loci of their strengths and weaknesses, and how might they be studied most effectively, especially when one is looking to 'overthrow' them and their whole parent paradigm?

Theories are collections of ideas people use to understand the realities they encounter. Theories have one part which describes the elements of reality and another part which talks about how those elements interact, thereby allowing predictions concerning what they will do in varying situations.

Social theories refer to realities of people and institutions, but are necessarily *abstract*: they do not explain everything in their reference systems but only those parts considered important. Thus 'what is important' and included in discussion, and 'what is unimportant' and abstracted out, become crucial questions in social theorizing. As Paul Sweezy writes:

> The legitimate purpose of abstraction in social science is never to get away from the real world but rather to isolate certain aspects of the real world for intensive investigation. When, therefore, we say that we are operating at a high level of abstraction we mean that we are dealing with a relatively

small number of aspects of reality; we emphatically do not mean that those aspects with which we are dealing are not capable of historical investigation and factual illustration. 5

Thus there is a first guideline for theory construction: for clarity, conciseness, and useability one must abstract out all that is unimportant; for correctness and wholeness one must include all that is important. *One must abstract away the unessential while making sure not to eliminate from consideration anything essential.*

But this suggests a problem. How does one determine what is essential before having a theory which explains the whole? The best way around the enigma is caution and a flexible willingness to reformulate one's views over and over as one's insights grow more and more complete. The usual subjective and obviously flawed way around the enigma is to determine what is important on the basis of self-interested speculations, and to then bend everything to suit that first determination rather than vice versa.

For example: a factory owner runs his enterprise according to a certain social economic theory of business. It produces well, profits continually rise, his life goes according to plan, and he is reasonably content with the whole situation. He doesn't notice his factory's effects on his employees' lives, or on their families, or on the ecology, or on the consumers. Others bear the costs of his profit-taking and he goes unaware of all that occurs outside the abstractions of his business-school theories of life. Then his workers strike and he alters his views somewhat by including references to salaries in his calculations. Then consumers protest and ecologists clamor and again he adapts his theories precisely to the extent to which he is forced.

The lesson of our capitalist's behavior is relatively clear. Social theories are often rooted in self-interested desires. They are often narrow but nonetheless the users usually convince themselves the theories are not narrow but complete. They get away with this self-interested self-deception prescisely because their theory's narrowness obligingly hides from view, in a sense behind its own absent elements.

Narrow theories often seem complete because they are logically sound and force their practitioners to overlook such narrowness by steering their attentions away from the ensuing flawed results. *Narrow theories appear good to their believers because they are looked at through self-created blinders especially adapted to block out all that is flawed.*

All of this applies to leftists as well as to capitalists. When revolutionists use a narrow theory they too can be expected to create partially counter-productive programs that ignore certain relevant aspects of the total spectrum of effects of their implementation. Narrow-minded revolutionists function very similarly to narrow-minded capitalists. They too blunder on in their mistakes, blind to the realities around them, precisely because their theories so constrain their perceptions.

Theories can therefore be weak in at least three different ways. They can have inaccurate or *incomplete* descriptions of important realities; they can have *incorrect* understandings of the ways important realities interact; or they can be too *narrow*, they can exclude from consideration details actually intimately connected to the results a practitioner's actions might have. Thus social theory must correspond to social reality as closely as possible; all its lacks of correspondence must be well understood by practitioners. Its positive assertions and its abstractions must be equally justified.

To construct a social theory we should try to organize our efforts in light of these insights. In criticizing a theory we can profitably do the same. We will set out descriptions of Classical Marxism Leninism's views of world reality and of world interactions, we will examine the relations between its theory and its practitioners, and we will take into account the accuracy and justification for abstractions of all types.

But just *understanding*, even in rather deep complexity, is never quite enough; one wants also to *affect*. Marxist Leninists with goals and general theoretic understandings form more or less detailed plans of action or strategy. To have a full program for analyzing the Marxist Leninist paradigm we must also know how we should approach its strategic aspects.

STRATEGY

Strategies guide us toward desired goals. How well do they derive from theory, do they get us where we wish to go, and do they minimize 'expenses' and side complications? These are our criteria for judging strategies and they are certainly easy enough to apply, at least if one is an objective and well informed evaluator rather than participant in a specific set of events.

The communist, for example, feels that the capitalist's approach to transportation problems is idiotic precisely because it creates even larger problems than those it was aiming to solve. The communist thinks that capitalist strategy is poor and would at least in some cases explain it by saying that capitalist theory is self-interestedly narrow. On the other side of the coin, the capitalist feels that communist strategy is ridiculous because even if it does solve a few social inadequacies it does so at too great a cost in never-to-be-regained human freedoms. Here too the smart capitalist would probably find the roots of the problem in self-interestedly narrow authoritarian theory rather than in the incompetence of the theory's practitioners.

Strategies move from vagueness to preciseness as their practitioners learn more and more about the systems on which they are working, the goals they are seeking, and the tools they are using. Strategy emerges from theory. The more comprehensive the theory, the more potentially precise the strategy. The more incomplete the theory, the more vague the strategy greater the need for constant enhancement.

So analyzing strategies is essentially a problem of seeing whether they really do fit the environs they are applied to and aim at the goals they are supposedly seeking. *The problem exists in translating an understanding of a theory's strengths and weaknesses to the level of its compatible and thus similarly powerful or afflicted strategy.*

PRACTICE

Practice is a favorite word of leftists, usually used in reference to the activities of people trying to change their environments and in turn being changed by those environments.

Tactics, another often used word, are well defined ways of practicing that occur over and over whenever roughly the same conditions arise. So there are military tactics, race car driving tactics, medical tactics, business tactics, house painting tactics, production line tactics, literary tactics, and revolutionary tactics; most practice is simply the application of variations of such tactics in concrete active situations.

Tactics are chosen because of the ways they fulfill strategic dictates. When there is no strategy, practice often becomes problematic and thus ineffectual. Strategy affects tactics and vice versa. Strategy allows a rational choice of tactics, and knowledge of all available tactics allows formulation of the most economical strategies. Consider two military strategists. Confronted with obstacles and a goal, effective strategist has a knowledge of available tactics and a theory for understanding the whole situation and the varying effects that differing chosen acts would have upon it. The ineffective one does not. The effective one forms a strategy based on a complete understanding and begins implementing it and thus moving toward inexorable success. The ineffective one perhaps forms a plan that depends on tactics that aren't even available options, or whose effects are misunderstood, or perhaps forms no plan at all, merely blundering ahead in redundancy and error.

POLITICAL CONSCIOUSNESS

Good strategy uses whatever is available to accomplish as much as possible. Knowledge of tactical options and their likely outcomes provides a *foundation* for creating powerful strategy and good strategy then in turn provides general criteria for deciding what tactics to actually use in what sequences.

But even when a practitioner has a highly accurate theory, a good knowledge of tactics, and a good strategic sense, things are never likely to occur exactly as planned, if not because of error, then certainly because real practice often leads to *unforeseen developments* which then demand changes in theory or strategy.

The militarist comes up against an unforeseen situation in the field and alters strategy, or someone discovers new forms of weaponry and that leads to an enrichment of military theory. Or similarly for the painter, or doctor, or revolutionist, or whatever...

In general, social theories are incomplete and depend upon descriptions of very complicated 'objects'. They must constantly be adapted in accordance with new experiences and insights discovered through on-going normal practice. Only then can they approach correctness and provide a basis for ever enriching strategy.

In summary, strategy provides *criteria* for choosing tactics. Practice is the means for implementing and correcting theory and strategy. Theory provides the framework within which strategy and tactics function, a means for anticipating their various possible effects, and a means for *understanding* what goals are realistic for any whole situation.

Revolutionaries are usually concerned with changing the whole natures of their societies. In their work they want the smallest possible margin of error, and especially of the repetition of error. They thus require that the flow from theory to strategy to practice and back include effective corrective mechanisms.

Ideally the revolutionist functions with a good social theory and a broad flexible strategy for change. He or she develops a full understanding of as many tactics as possible, (strikes, boycotts, parliamentary electoral tactics, ways of organizing and communicating, civil disobedience, marches, sabotage, styles of behavior and living, etc.) and of the ways their use affects various relevant situations, and then engages in self-conscious practice. Again ideally the revolutionist learns more and more about tactics while constantly refining strategy and theory to make them more accurate and richer in content.

So, good revolutionary theory, strategy, and practice, or good revolutionary politics and practice is a *totality* which is always incomplete but constantly going forward, each aspect providing the criteria for the worth and growth of the others. Theory provides world view. Long term strategy provides guidelines for activity. In conjunction with goal, theory, and strategy together compose a *revolutionary paradigm* which guides revolutionary thought, analysis, planning, and action.

To minimize errors and dogmatism such a consciousness must be self-correcting and *growth-oriented*. It must not stagnate. It must alter to fit changing realities rather than to merely rationalize changing realities in order to preserve itself. It must be rational verifiable rather than irrational 'religious'.

Though a revolutionary ideology may have weaknesses, it should eliminate them over time. *Indeed, good revolutionary consciousness should have a tendency toward continual re-alteration built right into methods and especially into strategy and associated practice.*

CLASSICAL MARXISM LENINISM

Classical Marxism is a revolutionary social theory and Classical Marxism Leninism is a revolutionary ideology or paradigm. Virtually all Marxist Leninist organizations I have had contact with consider their social theory and strategy *immutable*, and indeed seem to get their identities and authority from that avowed permanence. This constitutes a dismal state of affairs, not only because of the stagnation involved, but also because the theory and strategy are actually flawed. Our purpose is to formulate one version of Classical Marxism Leninism in as clear a manner as we can so that we might discover what parts of it are useful, what parts are not, and in what ways it might be enriched or altered. To the same ends we shall also talk about Maoism and Anarchism.

Since we already know that present consciousness needs and correlated immediate revolutionary crises revolve in, part around our getting new methodologies as well as new, very organic, useable understandings of racism, sexism, authority, consciousness, and motivation in general, our expositions of Classical Marxism Leninism, Anarchism, and Maoism, are organized in accord. We go step by step examining those aspects reflecting most on our particular needs, eventually building edifices in which the origin of the strengths and weaknesses with regard to those needs is clearly evident.

Thus as an answer to our definite need for a 'plan of approach' we first present Classical Marxist Leninist theory and strategy, and then criticize practice, strategy, and theory in sequence, with a final summary for clarification. The middle three chapters presenting Classical Leninism, criticizing Bolshevism, and criticizing Classical Leninism have considerable overlap, but it is to be hoped that that aggravation will be offset by the gain in logic of exposition, and by the fact that the material discussed is not very well known.

In the end we hope we will have some agreement about the weaknesses of the Classical Marxist Leninist paradigm. Then after discussion of the Anarchist and Maoist alternatives we hope we'll also have some agreement about where to jump off in forming a new revolutionary paradigm that could more effectively guide future revolutionary practice than any other past ones -- it is necessary for us to move energetically but also competently. As Fidel Castro put it:

> The duty of every revolutionary is to make the revolution. It is known that the revolution will triumph in America and throughout the world, but it is not for revolutionaries to sit in the doorways of their houses waiting for the corpses of

imperialism to pass by. The role of Job doesn't suit a revolutionary. Each year that the liberation of America is speeded up will mean the lives of millions of children saved, millions of intelligences saved for culture, an infinite quantity of pain spared the people. 6

FOOTNOTES

1. Thomas S. Kuhn in *The Structure of Scientific Revolutions*, Chicago Press, Chicago Ill 113.
2. ibid. 24.
3. Perhaps one of the most important criticisms to be made of Kuhn's study is that it implies that the kind of science and scientific study that has gone on so far is the only kind that can ever go on. It seems quite palatable to me that in future contexts scientists can be rather more flexible, rather more able to use a paradigm and simultaneously be quite open to and even anticipate its demise than they ever have been in the past. Concomitantly the dynamic of upholding one's immediate paradigm that Kuhn attributes to some kind of logical necessity of the whole scientific process actually has at least as much to do with weak identities, and strong material and vested ego interests of all previous scientists, Kuhn probably, and most others now engaged certainly, included.
4. Kuhn, op. cit. 153
5. Paul Sweezy in *The Theory of Capitalist Development,* Monthly Review Press, New York.
6. Fidel Castro in *Fidel Castro Speaks,* Grove Press, New York.

CHAPTER THREE

CLASSICAL MARXIST THEORY

The suggestion has been made, and its irreverence does not make it irrelevant, that Marxism as a religious system, has its bible, its orthodoxies and heresies, and its exegeses, sacred and profane.... Marxian Socialism was never rigorously or even systematically formulated as a canon or dogma... various social groups in their attempts to dominate the scene, claimed the authority of the founder for their expositions and interpretations of his teachings.... It seemed necessary not only to wage bitter battles against those who ignored or challenged 'Marxism' but also to engage in fratricidal struggles over its correct meanings. Marx, weary of the epigones who took his name, was moved to exclaim that he was not a Marxist, but the debates and disputes continued. 1

Arthur Rosenberg

Even the briefest readings of Karl Marx show him an awesome revolutionary thinker. Regrettably, however, most people's readings never get past that first brief cursory stage. The real Marx is reflected through what the reader wants or takes Marx to be -- often based on what he or she has heard him to be, on what use he or she has of him, or on what assault he or she wishes to make upon him, and so on.

Marx's writings are so extensive that with enough rummaging about one can discover most anything desired, most particularly to the exclusion of understanding the great flexibility of Marx's entire work.

This has historically occurred to such a point that people calling themselves Marxists have continually been at one another's throats, disagreeing on scores of critical issues. Some have even drifted so far from revolutionary commitment as to support even the most heinous of 'mother country' or 'mother party' crimes.

Our task, though certainly aimed somewhat towards critiquing actually-held Marxist views, and, most particularly, held views that have drifted from the original fullness of Marx's own efforts, is really directed in the first place toward another end. We aren't evaluating a powerful vulgarism so much to get it and variations on it out of some people's heads, (though that is a to be hoped for result) as to move beyond it to newer, more useful formulations.

Thus in this chapter we specifically present *one version* of Classical Marxism including a discussion of its historical context, and of its theories of dialectics, human nature, human consciousness, materialism, history, classes, capitalism, socialism, and revolution. The result is only a sketchy approximation, but one that nonetheless scrutinizes some of Classical Marxism's great strengths as well as many of its fundamental weaknesses.

HISTORICAL CONTEXT

Classical Marxism evolved when scarcity was the primary material fact of life. Metaphysics rationalized oppression by claiming its perpetual inevitability. Radicals saw through the mystification and wanted revolution to eliminate serfdom and create democracy, or in more advanced settings, to eliminate capitalism and create socialism.

Classical Marxism set out to counter the two great metaphysical sins
   that of working in a practical vacuum and that of basing most conclusions on self-interested speculations. According to Classical Marxism metaphysics ignored reality, and viewed things as lifeless and isolated rather than as parts of an interactive whole. As Engels put it, metaphysics was a world view which exhibited "natural objects and natural processes in their isolation, detached from the whole vast interconnection of things; and therefore not in their motion, but in their repose: not as essentially changing but as fixed constants, not in their life, but in their death." 2

The day's doctrine, *idealism*, was that reality arose out of men's conceptions, and Classical Marxism countered that fiction by moving toward the opposite position: that man's conceptions arose out of concrete conditions of reality.

Classical Marxism evolved amidst scarcity, in reaction to metaphysics, and in pursuit of revolutions to eliminate feudalism in favor of democracy. Europe between 1840 and 1880 was a place where knowledge of technology was minimal, the nature of government was primarily dictatorial, scarcity was a predominant force in thought and in action, and human material need was the only obvious motive force behind going out to work each day.

It was in this context that Marx worked toward understanding history and society in order to alter their courses for the better. His theory of dialectics was aimed at determining the bases and causes of historical changes, so that people would be better prepared to understand them, and to profitably *affect* them.

The theory is never actually made explicit and can only be gleaned from a study of Classical Marxism's more analytic descriptions of actual historical occurrences. Nonetheless, as Marx himself said, "Dialectics is the science of the general laws of motion, both of the external world and of human thought." 3

CLASSICAL MARXIST THEORY OF DIALECTICS

The science of dialectics is essentially the assertion that significant historical changes are not matters of straight-line, progressive alteration but of rupture, not matters of evolution but of revolution, not matters of continuations of flows but of resolutions of spiraling contradictions.

It is the assertion that real changes are due not to factors outside reality and imposed upon it, but to factors within reality from the start and only slightly affected by conditions imposing from without. It is the assertion that history does not change by the effects of some absolute, or in pursuit of some absolute, but rather in accord with its own internal contradictions and their continuously evolving resolutions. 4

At least in its Classical pre-Maoist formulations, the science of dialectics is a very general, loose *methodological* assertion. That is, to understand historical situations one must understand the contradictions they embody internally and most specifically one must understand those contradictions whose eventual resolutions entail overthrow of the original situation's defining characteristics. That is, one must understand situations insofar as they, by their very natures, toss up against themselves the forces of their own *dissolutions*.

For Classical Marxists, systems necessarily undergo fundamental changes whenever they embody the contradiction of trying to *perpetuate* themselves, while at the same time *undermining* themselves. Thus Classical Marxists interested in understanding and affecting historical situations have a clear methodological imperative: they must constantly uncover how systems simultaneously foster their own continuations and their own demises; *they must study motions of conflicting tendencies and forces precisely in regard to those critical contradictions and precisely so as to find ways to most beneficially help along the factors favoring their revolutionary resolutions.*

But such efforts obviously require prior understanding of many important and prevalent real-world systems, like productive mechanisms, social groupings and institutions, and laws, and perhaps most importantly, human beings as they are in actual settings.

CLASSICAL MARXIST VIEW OF HUMAN NATURE

In the Classical Marxist view human nature is something that constantly changes and steadily develops -- it is neither mechanistic, nor idealistic, but dialectical. It is a "variable in an interactive context." [5]

People can think, need safety, food, shelter, and sex, and strive to get each. But people exist in a time and in a context. And so, "the human essence is no abstraction inherent in each individual, in its reality it is the ensemble of social relations." [6]

For Classical Marxists people are what they do -- if at different times in history people act in different ways it is because their very natures have changed. Most importantly, people interact with their environments, change them, and are in turn changed by them. Central to the whole process is the formation and development of consciousness.

And yet before discussing the formation and effects of consciousness we should point out that Marx's actual understanding of people, and Marxist theory's understanding, contain a kind of tension between two pictures, the Classical one expounding the above, and the more humanist one found throughout many of Marx's own earliest writings and many of the most recent formulations of his whole thought. [7]

In that second view people are still dialectical processes but they are understood in more depth. They are viewed as having emotional, spiritual, cognitive, aesthetic, and creative as well as sexual and physical potentials. They are understood in their tensions with society -- society can either thwart or foster their potentials. With an increasing domination of nature comes an increasing play of human capacities. People create their own environments and the ones first encountered are not always the best possible. There is a societal progression and a parallel development of human potentials. History is *alienated* from people precisely because the environments it presents them are not as well suited to human capacities as they might be.

Out of this second orientation toward human nature and being, there naturally flows the Marxist theory of alienation and a number of other results usually encompassed by the title Marxist Humanism. Although historically important and critical to study as a basis for going beyond Classical views, Marxist Humanism is not immediately relevant to this book's tasks. 8 *Historically Marxists engaging in practice have had no very effective ways to make links between their broader views of human interaction and their actual day to day efforts to affect reality. There has been no theory of motivation or personality linking subtle views of human potential with concrete strategic needs in the field.* Thus, though Marx himself had a broader understanding than that drawn from his work by the Classical Marxists, even he, in strategic practice, tended to leave behind the broader views, working with only those Classical ones that could be adequately understood to be pragmatically employed.

Thus Marx's own thoughts and writings are often above our criticisms and can still very likely serve as good starting points for efforts to go beyond Classical formulations. At the same time, however, we are not in any way short changing Classical Marxism Leninism by attributing to it a weaker understanding than Marx's; for we attribute to it exactly the conceptions it actually used in its concrete practical efforts. 9

THE DIALECTICAL THEORY OF KNOWLEDGE

As we understand it, the dialectical theory of knowledge puts *practice* in the highest position. Practice leads to knowledge and then determines its worth. Theory is based upon practice and serves it. Consciousness emerges from practice and creates the conditions for its future improvement. It is real-world events that are in the first place the roots of insight and not vice versa. Knowledge is thus a reflection of reality.

Does it require deep intuition to comprehend that man's

ideas, views, and conceptions, in one word, man's consciousness, changes with every change in the conditions of his material existence, in his social relations, and in his social life?

What else does the history of ideas prove, than that intellectual production changes in character in proportion as material production is changed?...

When people speak of ideas that revolutionize society, they do but express the fact that, within the old society, the elements of a new one have been created, and that the dissolution of the old ideas keeps even pace with the dissolution of the old conditions of existence. 10

The Classical view says that all consciousness is reflection but that it need not always correspond precisely to what it reflects. To the extent it does, it is good; to the extent it does not, it is bad. Evaluation comes by means of practice. The Classical view says human knowledge depends mainly upon *productive work* since it considers such work to be the basis of all practice. True, men learn of others and of relations between people by way of culture, art, study, and politics, but as we'll see more fully shortly, Classical Marxists believe that the most important extra-work way of people learning things is *class struggle*, which is, in its turn, also totally and irrevocably intertwined with the nature of productive work. And so Classical Marxism decrees, again as we'll understand better later, that if production is backward it will hinder all human knowledge and development.

In general then, people's conceptions evolve in parallel to their work and work-associated situations. Consciousness of all kinds has roots in practice, expands through testing by practice, and has value really only insofar as it can guide practice to effective ends. Consciousness is simply a reflection and has value to the extent it reflects accurately.

The essence of Classical Marxist understandings of people and of people's consciousnesses entwines with the dialectical method at root of the historical materialist view of historical change. People must survive. They must *produce and reproduce* the conditions of their own existences. To that end they band together and form societies. Their consciousnesses exist and develop in accord with their necessary and fundamentally historically determined life activities. The world of ideas thus derives from the world of productive interrelations rather than vice versa -- it changes in accord with changes at the material level, and those changes, by our dialectical understanding, result not from steady evolutionary flows, but from the fact that the methods of production and reproduction of life's conditions of existence always toss up the forces of their own furtherance as well as of their own dissolution. Thus there is a dialectical flow at productive levels and a reflection at ideological levels -- this is the basic historical materialist awareness before refinement into a more completely defined and fuller theoretic structure.

CLASSICAL MARXIST HISTORICAL MATERIALISM

Classical Marxism's theory of history rests on foundations we've already unearthed: the Classsical theory of dialectics, of human nature, and of human knowledge. The derivative theory of history emerges the way any theory must -- Marxists observe the phenomena of their times, develop perceptions about those realities, then form concepts, engage in practice and further those concepts, and finally logically put all their learnings together into a theory to explain the whole historical reality around them. Over a longer or shorter time that is how various Marxists have developed the theory that people now interpret as Classical historical materialism.

In the Classical view, historical development corresponds to the increase of human powers to satisfy human needs. It is constructive in the sense of being a product of human activities, though not necessarily of intentional human activities.

All historical theories accept the premise that people make science and also material goods. Social idealism says, roughly, the concrete world of events is the realization of our ideas, reason grows autonomously, and the rest follows. Social materialism says, to the contrary, causal primacy is at the material-development level, with ideas following from that.

Classical Marxist historical materialism turns Hegel's dialectic upside down, putting the primary motion at the level of *material aspects* (forces and relations of production as we'll soon see) with ideas following along in the wake of class struggles based on those changing primary aspects.

Classical historical materialism revolves first around a belief in the primacy of material production. It asserts that production determines the ways men live and the nature of their consciousnesses. It says that social and economic organization flows through four *possible* stages until it finally reaches the last stage of advanced communist society. It says that:

> Just as our opinion of an individual is not based on what he thinks of himself, so we cannot judge of such a period of transformation by its own consciousness; on the contrary, this consciousness must be explained rather from the contradictions of material life, from the existing conflict between the social productive forces and the relations of production.... In broad outlines Asiatic, ancient, feudal, and modern bourgeois modes of production can be designated as progressive epochs in the economic formation of society. 11

Classical historical materialism says that changes occur dialectically and that specifically changes from one mode of production and social organization to another occur through revolutionary ruptures. Further, the theory develops the category class, and explains how classes evolve naturally from the dialectical interactions of men with their environments, and how *classes become the motive actors of all history*. Finally, the theory explains how a society has a structural *base* that is fundamentally economic, and a *superstructure* that is political and cultural; how these two levels interact, how the base is almost always primary, and how the class struggle is the major factor contributing to the nature of the super- structure. The theory has value precisely to the extent it explains history's flows, including an understanding of why history has been beyond men's control, an understanding of how it will change in the future, and an understanding of how individuals and groups can affect the ways it will look. 12

To begin, then, Classical historical materialism says that since people always strive for survival and material reward, production and reproduction of the necessities of life determine labor, and labor is necessary and conditions men's interactions with their environments and with one another. It says that labor conditions human character: that "to live men must labor" and that it is a "process in which man, through his own activity, initiates, regulates, and controls the material relations between himself and nature," thus essentially creating and defining himself collectively alongside and inevitably in interaction with his fellow producers. 13

To exist any society must produce goods enough for its own survival needs. To maintain its defining characteristics, and especially its characteristic divisions of wealth and power and thus the interests of its ruling classes, any society must also reproduce its relations of production; it must never sacrifice those relations to desires for more goods or greater technical efficiencies -- those can both be sought and indeed must be, but only within the bounds of never disrupting the social relations that give the ruling groups their dominance and make the search worthwhile in the first place. *Thus we say that to survive any society must have a productive core and that to maintain its overall power relations any society must simultaneously produce enough to ensure survival of the producers, enrichment of the rulers, and continuation of the divisions between the two, in ways non-disruptive of those same divisions.*

Classical Marxism sees labor and human nature inevitably determined by four factors: humanness, social organization, technique, and nature.

> The way in which men produce their means of subsistence depends first of all on the actual means they find in existence and have to reproduce. 14

So production depends upon and is determined by the tools and the nature that man encounters and must act upon.

> ...in production men not only act upon nature but also on one another... They enter into definite social relations. 15

Social relations between producers as well as the human characteristics of laborers are thus also determinants of production, and in consequence, of any society's historical human nature.

The Classical Marxist view thus says that societies must *inevitably produce and reproduce* by way of a mode of production determined by human, social, material, and natural givens. It says changes in human consciousness and behavior come about because of changes in the overall nature of man's interrelationship with his environment and with his fellow men, and that these in turn can arise only due to changes at the productive level of society, which is to say in any society's core mode of production.

When societies historically emerge, this view says that first an economic base or mode of production inevitably appears, and then a more or less elaborate socio-cultural superstructure follows:

> Political, juridical, philosophical religious, literary, artistic, etc. development is based on economic development. But all of these react upon one another and also upon the economic base. It is not that the economic position is the cause and alone active, while everything else has a passive effect. There is rather interaction on the basis of economic necessity, which ultimately always asserts itself. 16

Men enter into labor to survive and primitive communism evolves as the first societal form. There is a simple mode of production and a simple cultural and political superstructure. This is the Classical view. Why then do such simple relations disappear with time? Why do new social forms emerge? If a given society has a certain historically determined mode of production and a certain superstructure that has arisen from it, why should it evolve into some new societal form? These are the next key questions the Classical view raises and must answer.

Dialectics says that change occurs only when there is contradiction. Classical Marxism says that the two aspects of the contradiction that 'move' history are the old and the new modes of production embodied in any society at any time. The new manifests itself in what are called the forces of production, and the old in what are called the relations of production. The two aspects conflict almost continually though they may look different at different times in their histories. Their resolution through conflict, the new finally winning out over the old, is revolution.

Further, forces of production must not be understood mechanically in repose but as *dynamic* entities. They are not one or more of the four conditions of production but varying combinations of those four conditions; they too have internal contradictions and alter with time.

> In the youthful period of a system all the elements of a mode of production -- the human, the social, the natural, and the technical -- are also forces of production. In its old age some of these same elements cease to be forces of production. 17

In every case of revolutionary upheaval Classical Marxism shows that certain relations of production *cease to be productive* and set themselves up in *opposition* to the growth of society. They then come to represent the old mode of production while the growing forces represent the new one.

> We see then: the means of production and exchange on whose foundation the bourgeoisie built itself up were generated in feudal society. At a certain stage in the development of these means of production and of exchange, the conditions under which feudal society produced and exchanged, the feudal organization of agriculture and manufacturing industry, in one word, the feudal relations of property became no longer compatible with the already developed productive forces, they became so many fetters. They had to burst asunder; they were burst asunder. 18

And so, according to Classical Marxism, productive forces grow and eventually come into conflict with their *fettering productive relations*. And in every non-communist society the ensuing struggle is the motive force that creates revolutionary change in the mode of production. In times of revolutionary ferment new property relations support the growth of new forces of production and a change in the whole mode. With age, however, these new forces grow so strong that they grow beyond the means of their parent property relations and eventually *burst* them asunder. And similarly the superstructure which is created by a change in mode first fosters the development of the new mode, and then eventually hinders its continued growth. In a society's late stage therefore, the superstructure represents the old mode and the growing base represents the new. 19

> Modern bourgeois society with its relations of production, of exchange, and of property, a society that has conjured up such gigantic means of production and of exchange, is like the sorcerer, who is no longer able to control the powers of the netherworld whom he has called up by his spells. For many a decade past the history of industry and commerce is but the history of the revolt of modern productive forces against modern conditions of production, against the property relations that are the conditions of existence of the

bourgeoisie and of its rule. It is enough to mention the com-
mercial crises that by their periodical return put on its trial,
each time more threateningly, the existence of the entire
bourgeois society. In these crises a great part not only of the
existing products but also of the previously created productive forces are periodically destroyed. In these crises there
breaks out an epidemic that, in all earlier epochs, would
have seemed an absurdity, the epidemic of overproduction.
Society finds itself put back into the state of momentary barbarism; it appears as if a famine, a universal
war of devastation had cut off the supply of every means of
subsistence; industry and commerce seem to be destroyed;
and why? Because there is too much civilization, too much
means of subsistence, too much industry, too much commerce. The productive forces at the disposal of society no
longer tend to further the development of the conditions of
bourgeois property; on the contrary they have become too
powerful for these conditions, by which they are fettered,
and so soon as they overcome these fetters, they bring
disorder into the whole of bourgeois society, endanger the
existence of bourgeois property. The conditions of bourgeois society are too narrow to contain the wealth created by
them. 20

Classical Marxists understand social history as a series of revolutions in
the "modes of production and exchange," brought about by unfolding
contradictions between forces and relations of production. They believe
that "political relations indubitably influence the economic movement,"
but also that "before they influence that movement they are created by it."
And they believe that the dialectical nature of the process and of all its
involved parts insures that "no social order ever disappears before all the
productive forces for which there is room in it have developed; and new
higher relations of production never appear before the material conditions
of their existence have matured in the womb of the old society." 21 Which
is simply to say that for as long as new forces can develop, the contradiction
between forces and relations is not fully manifest, and that until the basis
of new property relations has been developed by the old processes of
production and reproduction, such new relations must remain beyond

human possibility.

> According to the materialist conception of history the
> determining element is ultimately production and repro-
> duction in real life. More than this neither Marx nor I have
> ever asserted. If therefore somebody twists it into a
> statement that the economic element is the only determin-
> ing one, he transforms it into a meaningless, abstract, and
> absurd phrase. The economic situation is the basis, but the
> various elements of the superstructure -- political forms of
> the class struggles and its consequences... also exercise
> their influence upon the historical struggles and in many
> cases preponderate in determining their form. There is an
> intersection of all these elements in which, amidst all the
> endless hosts of accidents... the economic movement finally
> asserts itself as necessary.... There are innumerable inter-
> secting forces, an infinite series of parallelograms of forces
> which give rise to one resultant, the historical event. 22

If the contradiction that moves Classical Marxist history is between
forces and relations of production, the question naturally arises, how does
this contradiction manifest itself as struggles between people? How does it
take form in real day to day relations of life, and more concretely how does
it lead to revolutions?

THE THEORY OF CLASSES

The search to answer these questions brings the Classical Marxist to a
need for understanding social groups, and especially to a need for understanding social groups of workers; for obviously if production is societally
paramount, one would expect worker activities to be similarly critical.

*Classical Marxism defines a class as a group of people all of whom
have the same relations to the means of production of a given society.* 23 It
says that an individual's consciousness is formed directly and indirectly by
his class ties, and that people of any one class all have roughly the same
world view because they all produce and reproduce in roughly the same
environments and because they have approximately the same powers,

duties, privileges, and educations with respect to their fellow citizens. And Classical Marxism says that the critical factor of any group's relationship to the means of production is the kind of ownership it has: workers own their own labor, capitalists own capital, farmers own farms, slaves own nothing, and petit bourgeoisie people own small businesses.

Classical Marxism says that classes emerged as important factors in history's flow when primitive communism disappeared and ownership rights were established. From then on there were various classes in all societies and these classes were always in conflict. Further class affiliations determined where and how people worked, relaxed, went to school, etc. According to Classical Marxism *classes are primary* in determining the *human natures* of all historical epochs since the first. Thus there is working class consciousness, slave consciousness, peasant consciousness, petit bourgeois consciousness, and bourgeois consciousness, and for Classical Marxists each of these constitutes the nexus of essentially different human natures. 24

And so societies always divide themselves into classes including the privileged and the dispossessed, the exploiters and the exploited, the rulers and the ruled. The owning classes are always in positions to rule and to keep much of their society's wealth for themselves.

> The history of all hitherto existing society is the history of class struggles.
> Freeman and slave, patrician and plebeian, lord and serf, the guildmaster and journeyman, in a word, oppressor and oppressed, stood in constant opposition to one another, carried on an uninterrupted now hidden, now open fight, a fight that each time ended either in a revolutionary reconstruction of society at large, or in the common ruin of the contending classes. 25

Classical Marxism says that scarcity and fairly minimal possibilities for production caused inequalities to grow in history and it says that those were then institutionalized by the development of classes with relatively consistent though very narrow world views. The ruling classes of any time owned the various existing means of production. They had a world view which included a rationale that gave them the right and even the duty to push 'their' system to the *limits* of its productive capabilities. Under every system up through advanced communism this could only mean that the ruling class would exploit all other classes to their detriments and its own advantage. To accomplish this Classical Marxism says that ruling classes inevitably control the intellectual as well as the material resources of the societies they run. To stay in power they try to make their ideas the ideas of the whole society:

> Each new class which puts itself in the place of the one ruling before it, is compelled, simply in order to achieve its aims, to represent its interests as the common interests of all members of society. 26

Further,

> The ideas of the ruling classes are in every age the ruling ideas; material control gives control of the intellectual forces as well. 27

The ruling classes of any time are then *dominant* even at the superstructural level -- and even further, as we shall soon see, it is class struggle that fills out the content of most day-to-day living in class-stratified societies.

So far the Classical Marxist has a society with some classes and with an underlying contradiction between forces and relations of production. The question we must ask is how Classical Marxists see all this leading to struggle and thus to the revolutionary evolution of the one society to a new form with a new mode of production.

The ruling classes push all other classes to accept their ideas and their leadership. The other classes try to maintain their own conceptions and further their own material security. As conflicts between productive forces and productive relations in any society become intense, the ruling class lines up with the old ways; the oppressed classes, because they have ever-growing needs, line up with the potential new ways and with the increased productivity they promise.

> At a certain stage of their development the material forces of production in a society come in conflict with the existing relations of production, or what is but a legal expression for

the same thing, with the property relations within which they have been at work before. From forms of development of the forces of production these relations turn into their fetters. Then begins an epoch of social revolution. With the change of the economic foundation, the entire immense superstructure is more or less rapidly transformed. 28

Since established ruling classes desire the complete development of all existing productive possibilities, they inevitably set the stage for revolution -- they exacerbate the contradictions of the society they lead, and they create the preconditions for a new society. The whole process and the whole historical flow is to Classical Marxists more or less inevitable. The only real question is what effects do interruptions and accidents have, and how can conscious people take advantage of them and of the momentary possibilities they create.

In summary: in any society, at any time, classes determine the division of labor and the forms of men's consciousnesses. The ruling class determines the dominant ideas of the period, but each class also has its own particular world views which it seeks to strengthen. Society is class stratified: the education, advantage, work, power, and consciousness of all people are largely determined by their class affiliations. Even interpersonal relations are largely mediated by class conflict and bias and further, each class, because of its inevitable needs and views, seeks to enhance its position and struggles for its own material and political advantage. As the society's primary contradiction becomes more and more intense the struggle heightens. The hypocrisy of ruling class claims becomes more and more evident, the potential for development under new property relations becomes clearer, and eventually the struggle leads to the defeat of the old ruling class and the establishment of a new one. But if all this describes in outline Marxism's view of history, what is its rough view of the particularity of capitalist society?

When the forces of production in feudal society grow, a new class begins forming. The bourgeoisie develops under feudalism, forms a new consciousness and a new set of institutions, and with the help of the laboring masses, lines up with the growing forces and carries out a 'democratic' capitalist revolution. In most instances the bourgeoisie becomes the new ruling class.

THE CLASSICAL THEORY OF CAPITALISM

The bourgeois revolution, though made in the name of liberty, ushers in *wage slavery, private ownership of the means of production, and the manufacturing division of labor.* With revolution at the base a new super-structure emerges to dominate the old; a new political edifice arises and fosters dynamics favorable to the bourgeoisie. The capitalist state becomes a tool for the maintenance of bourgeois rule and private property. And the same type of process unfolds at the intellectual and emotional level: The bourgeoisie uses its advantages to determine which ideas are good and which bad. It 'distributes' knowledge in accord with class backgrounds and through class-stratified educational systems.

Classical Marxism sees two key capitalist institutions, *the corporation and the state.* They work in unison to serve the interests of the ruling classes -- workers who own nothing save their bodies must sell labor to the corporate rulers and pay fealty to the capitalist state. They earn wages lower than the value of what they produce and the surplus goes to the capitalist. This process is called *exploitation* and is upheld by the laws of the state.

The capitalist worker has the right to sell his labor for exploitative wages but he has few rights concerning the ways that labor will be accomplished or the ways its product will be used. His labor is *alienated* from his needs and desires and in essence *he works only to survive and to enrich others.*

The capitalist takes the workers' excess products as profit. In addition, the capitalist uses the surplus to further his profit, and to maintain the conditions that allow his class to dominate all others. He changes it into new capital to create ever growing profits -- he expands the base and increases the forces of production. Classical Marxists claim capitalists *must* so act or the economic inequities upon which their powers are based would diminish or even disappear. Because of his competitive position and the power of his whole class the capitalist always expands existing forces of production to their utmost power and creates new ones where possible, thus furthering the conditions of his own historical demise. His very human nature as a capitalist, as well as the dictates of his competitive environment, demand it.

To change surplus labor into capital and thereby prosper, the capitalist must first use labor to enlarge his enterprises or to start new ones. But to accomplish either of these ends he requires materials, wealthy buyers, and people who are so poor that they are willing to sell their labor relatively cheaply. *According to Classical Marxism, then, the whole system recreates itself at every turn, but always by creating conditions that are eventually conducive to its own overthrow.*Since buyers, materials, and workers are necessary, they are created by any effective means, and since force and deception are time-tested, they are often employed first. Capitalism inevitably spreads, eating new markets, oppressing new workers, and gouging new materials the world over. It becomes an international system Classical Marxism calls *imperialism*. As Woodrow Wilson put it:

> Since trade ignores national boundaries and the manufac-
> turers insist on having the world as a market the flag of his
> nation must follow him, and the doors of the nation which are
> closed must be battered down. 29

Classical Marxism says that societies change due to internal contradictions between existing and potential modes of production, the former reflected in relations, the latter in forces of production. In capitalism specifically, the conflict between forces and relations is manifested in the fact that "production is accomplished socially while appropriation is private and individualized." The conflict is translated into struggle by the working class which is inevitably forged into a revolutionary force.

> Modern industry has converted the little workshop of the
> patriarchal master into the great factory of the industrial
> capitalist. Masses of laborers, crowded into the factory, are
> organized like soldiers. As privates of the industrial army
> they are placed under the command of a perfect hierarchy
> of officers and sergeants. Not only are they slaves of the
> bourgeois class and of the bourgeois state, they are daily
> and hourly enslaved by the machine, by the overlooker, and,
> above all, by the individual bourgeois manufacturer
> himself. The more openly this despotism proclaims gain to
> be its end and aim, the more petty, the more hateful, and
> the more embittering it is. 30

The proletariat goes through various stages of develop-

ment. With its birth begins the struggle with the bourgeoisie. At first the struggle is carried on by individual laborers, ... But with the development of industry the
proletariat not only increases in number, it becomes
concentrated in greater masses, its strength grows, and it
feels that strength more. The various interests and conditions of life within the ranks of the proletariat are more and
more equalized.... The modern laborer, on the contrary,
instead of rising with the progress of industry, sinks deeper
and deeper below the conditions of existence of his own
class. He becomes a pauper and pauperism develops more
rapidly than population and wealth. And here it becomes
evident that the bourgeoisie is unfit any longer to be the
ruling class in society, and to impose its conditions of
existence on society as an overriding law.... The essential
condition for the existence and for the sway of the bourgeois
class, is the formation and augmentation of capital; the
condition of capital is wage labor. Wage labor rests exclusively on competition between the laborers. The advance of
industry, whose involuntary promoter is the bourgeoisie,
replaces the isolation of the laborers, due to competition, by
their involuntary combination, due to association. The
development of modern industry therefore cuts from
under its feet the very foundation on which the bourgeoisie
produces and appropriates products. What the bourgeoisie
therefore produces, above all, are its own grave diggers. Its
fall and the victory of the proletariat are equally inevitable.
31

As the contradictions between classes become more aggravated the
role of the state becomes more and more important. It acts precisely as a
military force to guard and further the interests of the bourgeoisie and at
times it does even more. When the conditions so demand, the state tries to
hold back the contradictions of capitalism for as long as it possibly can.
The state creates ideological myths that support the capitalists; it buys
from capital with workers' taxes at rates that could never be established
otherwise; and it finds and defends overseas markets for capital. The state
helps create and recreate the conditions of capitalism by defending its
relations and at the same time creating new buyers, sellers, and workers.

In fact the state becomes "but a committee for managing the common affairs of the whole bourgeoisie." 32

SOCIALIST REVOLUTION

"Masses of laborers crowded into factories are organized like soldiers." *The working class eventually opposes the capitalist system because they naturally seek to further their own interests and because the system just as naturally perpetually denies those interests.* As capitalist contradictions increase, Classical Marxists claim that capitalists are forced to exploit their workers to greater and greater extents. Workers spontaneously progress from natural hostility toward their situation to organized opposition in trade unions. As matters get continually worse, workers' conditions are made more generally equal and dismal. They are simultaneously immiserated and brought together with one another. They are literally forced outside the system in the desire for alternatives. They become open to revolutionary ideas. Their struggle with the bourgeoisie for daily betterment becomes constant and daily inflamed.

Capitalism, of course, goes to great lengths in self-defense. First it tries to forestall struggle, and then it tries to employ all powers that it can command so as to win. Classical Marxism claims that the bourgeoisie's gestures, no matter how destructive to life, are finally quite futile:

> The conditions of bourgeois society are too narrow to comprise the wealth created by them. And how does the bourgeoisie get over this crisis? By destroying or shackling productive forces, conquering new markets, or thoroughly exploiting old ones. That is, by paving the way for more extensive and more destructive crises and by diminishing the means whereby such crises are diminished. 33

The crisis which Marxism says is inevitable is *overproduction* -- the conditions wherein there is too much surplus to be used effectively and where economic calamities then ensue. The struggle between labor and capital continues unabated until finally, in the context of severe crisis, conditions become so unbearable and the rationalizations of the capitalists so unconvincing that the working class throws off the old system and ushers in the new. According to Classical Marxism, a *dictatorship of the proletariat* stage exists as a *transition* to a classless society. The working class becomes the new ruling class and then oversees transition to a truly communist situation.

So Classical Marxism sees that the material contradictions inherent in capitalist systems cannot be circumvented in any way. There are no permanent solutions to be found within the confines of the old definitions and styles:

> Neither planning nor education, even if either was possible, would be any kind of solution -- they would not end the conflict in capitalism that prevents what might be from being. The solution lies in changing the basis of society by changing ownership relations. 34

Classical Marxism says that planning under capitalism could only affect hows, never whats or whys, the major problems can never really be addressed, and thus it could never eliminate dislocations or the parallel class struggle.

Socialist revolution is abstractly like all others -- it is to be carried out by oppressed classes, who, upon achieving power, install themselves as the new ruling classes. The one fundamental difference from other mode-of-production revolutions is that in the view of Classical Marxists the anti-capitalist revolution augers the final end of class struggle. The new state of the proletariat is to *wither away* in the sense that it will eventually *administer only things and not people.* Communism will then ensure that "each produces according to his ability and each receives according to his need." All people become volitional, freedom prevails, and thus alienation is finally eliminated. History as a process coordinated by conscious people begins, precisely as the previously unavoidable class struggle ends.

And so Classical Marxists see that it is the class struggle of any country that provides the context within which people can exercise an influence upon history.

> Men make their own history, but they do not make it just as they please; they do not make it under circumstances chosen by themselves but under circumstances directly en- countered, given and transmitted from the past. 35

Classical Marxism says that under the conditions of capitalism, a person is free who seeks to exacerbate the class struggle, and to take advantage of it as much as possible until there is successful revolution. It goes on to say that the revolutionary process is not totally spontaneous; it requires organization and cannot be carried off by the working class alone. They need guidance. Classical Marxism feels essentially the same about the bourgeois and the proletariat revolutions in this one respect. The former could not be carried out entirely by the bourgeoisie -- they need the help and even the leadership of the workers. Similarly, the latter could not be carried out solely by the workers -- they need guidance from intellectuals and in some countries help from other strata. But in both cases the internal dynamics of the involved societies would always inevitably make all the conditions required available, revolutions would ensue, history would continue to unfold along its more or less inevitable course.

> Politely history is a by-product, in truth, it is a mere precipitate of the clash and jangle of conflicting human interests which constitute the running chronicle of class struggle. 36

But for Classical Marxists the fact that history has been a rather ugly display of man's inhumanity toward man, has little or no implication for its future possibilities.

> The most important historical activity of men, the one that has raised them from bestiality to humanity and which forms the material foundation for all their other activities, namely the production of the requirements of life, that is today's social production, is above all subject to the unintended effects from uncontrolled forces and achieves its desired ends only by way of exception and much more the exact opposite. 37

And so man has dealt successfully with technology but poorly with social history, "because he has never been in a position to prevent the means of production from entering into destructive conflict with the relations of production." "Preoccupied with competing for his own living, man has been unable to anticipate and control the long term historical and human consequences of his productive activities...if human history, as distinct from cosmic and biologic history, is defined as the development of consciously intended relations that are appropriate to human life, human potentialities, human consciousness, and the already achieved degree of human control over nature, then there has not yet been any human history at all." 38

According to Classical Marxism, what there has been is "the history of class struggle" and of the resolution of economic contradictions at the base of heretofore existing societies.

Classical Marxist social theory explains the nature of historical change in terms of contradictions and class struggle. It is not a complete theory. It makes few predictions about day-to-day events. It does, however, talk clearly about the overall contours of change, and about the nature of the more important social forces and how they interact. It also provides a perspective and tools for understanding more about any specific situations at the societal level than any non-Marxist theory.

> What I did that was new [says Marx] was to prove 1-That the existence of classes is only bound up with particular, historic phases in the development of production, 2-That the class struggle necessarily leads to the dictatorship of the proletariat, and 3-That this dictatorship itself only constitutes the transition to the abolition of all classes and to a classless society. 39

> Just as Darwin discovered the law of evolution in organic nature, so Marx discovered the law of evolution in human history. He discovered the simple fact, hitherto concealed by an overgrowth of ideology, that mankind must first of all eat and drink, have shelter and clothing, before it can pursue politics, religion, science, art, etc. And that therefore the production of the immediate material means of subsistence and consequently the degree of economic development attained by a given people or during a given epoch, form the foundation upon which the state institutions, the legal conceptions, the art, and even the religious ideas of the people concerned have evolved, and in the light of which those things must be explained, instead of vice versa as had hitherto been the case. 40

If it has been true about all past history "that what each individual wills is obstructed by everyone else, and what emerges is something that nobody willed," Classical Marxists say that it must not also be true of future history. For "the philosophers have only interpreted the world in various ways; the point however is to change it." 41

For Classical Marxists an individual becomes free when he or she realizes three things: that classes are the motor of history; that people will only gain ascendency over history after they eliminate class struggle; and that the road to ending class struggle lies in winning it on the side of the proletariat, pitted against the bourgeoisie. Free Marxists are precisely those people who do not just theorize, but instead also formulate strategy, and engage in practice, trying to take advantage of all the potentialities of their times. They have an understanding of social reality, of its future possibilities, of the ways change comes about, and of their own possible roles, and they take advantage of that knowledge in their concrete activity.

FOOTNOTES

1. Samuel Hurvitz in the introduction to Arthur Rosenberg, *A History of Bolshevism,* Doubleday and Company, Garden City, New York. xv.
2. Engels quoted by Vernon Venable, *Human Nature: The Marxian View,* Meridian Books, Cleveland, Ohio. 35-36.
3. Marx quoted by Lenin, *Karl Marx,* Foreign Languagues Press, Peking China.
4. Though in some sense this and the coming thoughts have to be gleaned from Classical formulations rather than directly quoted, there is to my knowledge little debate about their general descriptive accuracy, though much, as we shall see later, about their more concrete actual worths.
5. Marx quoted in Venable, op. cit. 5.
6. Marx, "Sixth Thesis of Fuerbach," *Selected Works: Volume One,* International Publishers, New York. 472-473.
7. See for example Gajo Petrovic, *Marx in the Mid Twentieth Century,* Doubleday Anchor Books, Garden City, New York.
8. There are many references to Marxist Humanist studies in our bibliography.
9. Obviously this is a debatable assertion -- our later analysis of Bolshevik practice in Russia will, we hope, give it convincing strength.
10. Marx, *The Communist Manifesto,* Monthly Review edition, New York, N.Y. 37.
11. Marx, *Contribution to the Critique of Political Economy,* International Publishers, New York, N.Y.
12. Perhaps the single most compact presentation of the theory is in Maurice Cornforth's *Historical Materialism,* International Publishers, New York.
13. Marx in Venable, op. cit. 49-50.
14. Marx, *Contribution to the Critique of Political Economy,* op. cit.
15. Marx, *Wage Labor and Capital,* International Publishers, New York.
16. Engels quoted in Venable, op. cit.   30.
17. Venable, op. cit.   106.
18. Marx, *The Communist Manifesto,* op. cit.   10-11.
19. See Cornforth, op. cit.
20. Marx, *The Communist Manifesto,* op. cit.   11-13.

21. Marx quoted in Venable, op. cit.
22. Engels in a letter to Bloch, *Marx and Engels: Selected Correspondence,* International Publishers, New York. 475-477.
23. See, for example, Shlomo Avineri, *The Social and Political Thought of Karl Marx,* Cambridge University Press, for a flexible formulation of Marxist class views.
24. Avineri, op. cit. or especially Venable, op. cit.
25. Marx, *The Communist Manifesto,* op. cit. 2.
26. Marx, *The German Ideology,* International Publishers, New York. 36-37.
27. ibid. 39.
28. Marx, *Contribution to a Critique of Political Economy,* op. cit.
29. Wilson quoted in Michael Tanzer, *The Sick Society*, Holt Rhinehart and Winston, New York.
30. Marx, *The Communist Manifesto,* op. cit. 14-15.
31. ibid. 16-18.
32. ibid. 5.
33. ibid. 12-13.
34. Venable, op. cit.
35. Engels quoted in Venable, op. cit. 149.
36. Venable, op. cit. 149.
37. Engels, *Dialectics of Nature,* International Publishers, New York. 148.
38. Venable, op. cit. 78.
39. Marx quoted in Venable, op. cit.
40. Engels in *Selected Works: Volume One,* op. cit. 16.
41. Marx quoted in Venable, op. cit. 573-575.

CHAPTER FOUR

LENINIST STRATEGY

What is to be done? 1

V.I. Lenin

...we must pretend to ourselves and to everyone that fair is foul and foul is fair; for foul is useful and fair is not. Avarice and usury and precaution must be our gods for a little longer still. For only they can lead us out of the tunnel of economic necessity into daylight. 2

J.M.Keynes

Classical Marxism provides a social, political, economic world view. It is neither complete, nor determinist. It allows some predictions, but does not help with certain others. It facilitates our understanding of some situations but says little or nothing about the others. Lenin the revolution-ist took on the responsibility of formulating sound strategy based on the dictates of his own theory, the experiences of his own interactions with his own peculiar environment, and his understanding of the interrelation of each of these with the others.

Leninist strategy covers multitudes of situations and comprises countless volumes of writings. Here we are concerned not with the whole of it, but solely with its longer-term more generally accepted strategic and tactical dispositions -- for in coordination with a grounding in Classical Marxist theory Leninist theories provide Classical Marxist Leninists with the main tools of their arsenal of revolutionary weapons. Thus we must try now to understand and later critique them in order to follow rationally in the Leninist tradition, or decide that it is deficient and should be updated or even considerably overhauled.

Lenin was a strategic pragmatist par excellence -- he recognized the absolute necessity of working with material at hand to accomplish as much as possible:

> We can and must begin to build socialism not with imaginary human material, not with human material invented by us, but with the human material bequeathed to us by the capitalists. 3

He always attempted to work scientifically and although of course he was not the first to take up the socialist struggle, he was, at least according to Georg Lukacs "alone in thinking through every question radically to its very end: in radically transforming his theoretical insight into practice." 4 Lenin even wrote:

> Of course without a revolutionary mood among the masses and without conditions favoring the growth of this mood, revolutionary tactics would never be converted into action; but we in Russia have been convinced by long, painful, and bloody experiences of the truth that revolutionary tactics cannot be built up upon revolutionary moods alone. Tactics must be based upon a sober and strictly objective estimation of all the class forces in a given state as well as of the experiences of the revolutionary movements. 5

Lenin believed and Classical Leninists now believe that revolutions are created by only those people functioning in certain specific contexts, and functioning effectively in those contexts. And so a revolution's "creation is facilitated by correct revolutionary theory, which in its turn, is not a dogma but assumes final shape only in close connection with the practical activity of a truly mass and truly revolutionary movement." 6

Many of Classical Leninism's initial strategic biases come directly from the Classical Marxist legacy. Classical Marxism says workers become a class because their similar position with relation to production gives them 'one' world view. It says workers have power because of their numbers; they are organized by their factory milieu to respond easily to discipline and to function easily in parties which can lead revolutions; and they eventually join such parties and revolt precisely because their situations become steadily worse to the point of unbearability.

The Marxism of the *Manifesto* drew a very clear distinction between immediate and future tasks. Immediately and most specifically in Germany, communists were to aid in carrying out the middle-class revolution against feudal monarchy, and at the same time lay a groundwork for future conflict between the proletariat and the middle class. Marxism's analysis of the conditions in Germany at the time of the *Manifesto* made it clear that the proletariat must carry through and perhaps even lead the bourgeois revolution and that it must do that by means of a powerful *party*.

Marx and Engels the strategists, as classically interpreted, actually considered the party a vehicle for better leading the working classes. If a party was deficient or caused them personal difficulties the solution was to eliminate it. Marx and Engels saw themselves as the world's most effectual communists and believed their relation to revolution and to a party of revolution had to be different from that of other people.

> What have we to do with a party that is nothing more than a herd of asses, and that swears by us because their members look upon us as their equals? 7

The answer: we lead such a party for as long as it suits us. Marx and Engels had a fetish for the need for other people's discipline, they felt it central to successful operations, but their own behavior was to be different precisely because they were the brightest of the intellectuals. They would never submit themselves to any outside authority but others would certainly have to. Shlomo Avineri describes this aspect of their attitudes very clearly:

> Marx's and Engel's theoretical awareness of the limitations of proletarian revolutions and their need for intellectual guidance was coupled with disdain, if not outright contempt, for those leaders of the movement who were themselves of working class origin: especially so far as Marx was concerned, a certain intellectual hauteur is clearly visible in his comments. This attitude is exemplified by Marx's behavior toward Wilhelm Weitling, to whom he occasionally used to refer as "a tailor's king"; even one of his

own most loyal followers, George Eccarius, also a tailor by trade, came in for a generous measure of unearned contempt from his teacher and master. The Marx-Engels correspondence abounds in numerous allusions to the worker's intellectual limitations, stupidity, and narrow-mindedness. Sometimes they are dismissed in such derogatory terms as "asses," "Knoten," "Straubinger." In a letter written in 1870 Engels voices some anxiety at the decrease, since 1848, of the supply of intellectuals in the socialist movement, being apprehensive lest a situation come about in which the workers will have to do everything by themselves. 8

And in another place Avineri says:

Marx's position may consequently be stated as follows: in Western, industrialized societies, socialist intellectuals are bound to hold leading positions in the proletarian movement; this is indispensable for the very success of the revolutionary effort; it gives it direction, historical insight, leadership, moderation, and endurance. 9

Classical Marxism's strategic gift to Lenin came out of Marx's analysis of Germany's need for a democratic revolution led by the German proletariat. Marx and Engels were both concerned that the German middle class couldn't engineer such a revolution alone.

Thus the Marxist program called for the workers to lead the middle class revolution, to give it a proletarian orientation, and to lead it toward future class struggles and a future proletarian revolution. But the workers had no experience in such matters, and since they could not spontaneously get such experience, Marx, at least in the Classical interpretation, saw the need for a revolutionary party of iron discipline led by class-conscious intellectuals and followed by all proletarians.

Lenin was the foremost intellectual of that type in Russia. According to Classical Marxism *if he was to succeed as a leader he would have to be guided by the dictates of Classical Marxist theory, by the content of his own Classical Marxist analysis of his surroundings, and perhaps most importantly by his own practical understanding of the interrelations between theory, strategy, and tactics.*

Lenin often created tactical guidelines: victory is impossible unless attack is as well known as retreat; unless legal and illegal activities are combined into functional programs; unless fighting is never initiated at a time advantageous to the enemy; and unless the strictest discipline and centralization of organization is employed in all practice. But at the same time Lenin never allowed himself to get blindly caught up in such formulations -- he understood that the lessons of one situation could never be randomly applied to another, and that there were no iron clad rules except perhaps those in the body of theoretical Marxism itself. In this context and in reference to the needs for a multitude of tactical alignments for his forces, Lenin favorably quotes another as having said that, "political activity is not the pavement of the (straight) Nevsky Prospect;" one must change to fit changing situations. 10

This meant the problem'what to do and how to do it' wasn't one with a timeless principled answer, but was instead one with reference only to *specific situations and specific times,* and with answers which would therefore vary, and tactics which would also vary as contexts and times changed too. Lenin understood that a theorist was only consequential insofar as he could refer the general to the specific and insofar as he could be flexible enough to change as the specific itself changed. Perhaps it was for this reason that Lukacs said:

> Lenin's greatness as a dialectician consisted in his ability to see the basic principles of the dialectic, the development of the productive forces and the class struggle in their innermost essence, concretely, without abstract prejudices, but also without being fetishistically confused by super-ficialities. He always related all phenomena to their ultimate basis -- to the concrete actions of concrete (in other words class-conditioned) men in accordance with their real class interests. 11

Lenin's emphasis on the mutable nature of tactics was evident in his attack upon what he called leftist tendencies toward arbitrary irredeemable tactical rules:

> ...to refuse beforehand to maneuver, to utilize the conflict of

interests (even though temporarily) among one's enemies, to refuse to temporize and compromise with possible (even though transitory, unstable, vacillating, and conditional) allies -- is not this ridiculous in the extreme? Is it not as though, when making an ascent of an unexplored and hitherto inaccessible mountain, we were to refuse before-hand ever to move in zigzags, ever to retrace our steps, ever to abandon the course once selected to try others? 12

The leftists seemingly feared zigzags while Lenin in some sense adored them as additions to his tactical arsenal -- and up to this point he was quite right. *The real question, though, was how well he could assess the values and costs of potential zigzags given his theoretical armature.* How well could he perceive which was a straight path and which a crooked one, and more importantly how well could he recognize which held pitfalls and which were relatively safe for travel?

The relation one takes to the question of *compromise* often illuminates one's understanding of the nature of tactics and strategy precisely because the question of compromise is often fraught with debate surrounding the need for principles and steadfastness. Before proceeding with Lenin's general strategic views, and by way of an introduction to his tactical style, it makes some sense to consider his ways of relating to the idea of compromise with existing authorities.

Lenin felt that one should or should not compromise, not on the basis of some timeless principles, but rather on the basis of specific analyses of specific situations. He felt that compromise was a tactic and that like all other tactics it had use at some times but should be ignored at others. He wasn't arbitrary and he was never inconsistent. He related well to compromise when it was made necessary by objective conditions or when it seemed likely to lead to large gains. He related poorly to compromise when he felt it ill-suited to the demands of a specific situation, when it seemed unnecessary, or of course when it seemed likely to lead to unnecessary losses.

So, for example, when the so-called infantile leftists argued that working in parliament was a backward step, Lenin was taken aback. And when they went on to say that parliaments were obsolete and that leftists should accept the principle that compromises with parliaments were universally detrimental, he was totally shocked. He felt that the position amounted to sheer lunacy. He argued that it was quite necessary to use parliaments to reach workers and that no such principled stances about tactics made any sense anyway. He analysed the specific tactics with reference to the specific conditions of their times and in this case determined that working with parliaments was useful because it could create allies inside; because it could be an educational tool; because it could demonstrate parliamentary inadequacies; and because in crises people in parliament could be very useful. He also determined that compromise in this situation could also have potentially detrimental effects because people might believe that the left had sold out, but on balance he thought the tactic should be used, though carefully, and he lashed out at the 'leftists' with little mercy:

> You want to create a new society, yet you fear the difficulties
> involved in forming a good parliamentary faction, consist-
> ing of convinced, devoted, heroic, communists in a
> reactionary parliament. Is this not childishness? 13

In almost everyone's eyes Lenin had reduced his opponents' arguments to rubble while at the same time challenging their revolutionary competence and sincerity. He well understood the relations of tactics to strategy and theory. He was as competent, consistent, and logical as any leader of Classical Marxist persuasion. Weaknesses if they crept in at all could come only from his ideas and not from any inabilities to act upon them effectively. He was well endowed; he could think, he could express himself quite clearly, he had courage, and most of all he had a firm grounding in Classical Marxist ideas and methods. What, then, did he actually do in Russia, what were his strategic beliefs, and how did they emerge?

In 1905, Lenin confronted a Russian situation rather similar to Marx's Germany. He saw that to overthrow czarism the peasant army had to be won over -- he couldn't abolish private property but he had to attack the church, and all other czarist authority forms. He had to establish a *democratic republic* through the instrument of a broad *coalition* including socialist, working-class, peasant, and middle-class parties. But above all else the Bolsheviks had to persevere and rise above the rest; they had to gain the strength necessary to rule the new democratic republic in the name of the proletariat. And Lenin thought the Bolsheviks could do this

precisely because they had the discipline, the theory, and the most competent leaders. 14

In 1905, Lenin said that he "would postpone the revolution to the
spring if he could" but that he would not be asked. He viewed even the
upheaval itself as a tactic which like others should be employed carefully
in accord with conditions, possibilities, and goals. He was undisturbed by
the failure of 1905; he felt there had been a crisis that did not totally rupture
society, that much had been learned, and that there would be more opportunities later. 15

Even the young Lenin had a clear conception of party organization
and discipline -- 1905 further substantiated all his convictions. He thought
workers were the only ones who could successfully carry through a revolution, but he didn't think they could do it alone. He felt they needed *allies,
leadership, and discipline.*

He was convinced that the proletariat had to assist in the middle-class
revolution even if only as a first necessary step towards its own greater
interests. But he also saw that such activity was beyond then existent
proletarian consciousness. He concluded simply enough that it was
ridiculous to wait for communists to give all workers higher consciousnesses. He decided that his task was to gauge when a *vanguard* could seize
power, and when it would receive enough support to consolidate that
power -- his ideas made it quite clear, when the time came, he and his party
would have to be quick, their actions would have to be decisive.

He knew as did all others that:

> ...classes are led by political parties; that political parties,
> as a general rule, are directed by more or less stable groups
> composed of the most authoritative, influential, and exper-
> ienced members, who are elected to the most responsible
> positions and are called leaders. All this is simple and
> clear. 16

But what was to be the specific nature of the revolutionary party, who
was to lead it, and how ?

The answer had already come with the birth of Bolshevism. Lenin felt
that its party was the epitome of revolution. He believed in the idea of a
relatively small coterie of *professional revolutionaries*. He believed that
breaches of discipline should be considered tantamount to treason. He

believed that the problem was not so much the political self-determination of the masses or even of the many political workers carrying out the tasks of the party, as it was the question of accuracy and efficiency and flexibility. *He felt that success depended upon a tactical alignment of forces that included absolute discipline and put intellectuals in command -- for in this way efficiency and the ability to effectively change positions in the face of a changed situation would all be most enhanced.*

He felt that professional revolutionaries should convince the proletariat it was their business to seize control of the imminent bourgeois revolution, and he felt no other approach could work.

Nowadays many people suggest that Lenin foreswore a democratic party in favor of hierarchy because of the constraints imposed by the repressive power of the czarists, but this was not really the case. For as Rosenberg noted, "the real reason was of another and deeper nature: such a (democratic) party would not be able to carry out its revolutionary tasks," not just because of repression but because of the need for strict leadership from the most enlightened, far-sighted cadre. 17

Lukacs also attributes the same perspective to Lenin, though admiringly rather than disparagingly:

> ...the Leninist form of organization is inseparably connected with the ability to foresee the coming revolution. For only in this context is every deviation from the right path fateful and disastrous for the proletariat; only in this context can a decision on an apparently trivial everyday issue be of profound significance to it; only in this context is it a life and death question for the proletariat to have the thoughts and actions which truly correspond to its class situation clearly in front of it. 18

And in another place:

> This degree of adjustment of the life of the masses is impossible without the strictest party discipline. If the party is not capable of immediately adjusting its interpretation to the ever-changing situation, it lags behind, follows instead of leads, loses contact with the masses and disintegrates. 19

Lenin felt that the working class had to successfully lead a middle class revolution and parlay it into a proletarian struggle, and that the workers could only do that if they were led by a "tribune of the people." He felt that a person or persons of simple trade union consciousness could not get the job done, and that *socialism was only understood by "educated elements of the propertied classes,"and that its concepts were beyond the spontaneous learnings of the workers:*

> The history of all countries shows that the working class, exclusively by its own efforts, is able to develop only trade union consciousness, ie, the conviction that it is necessary to combine in unions, fight the employers, and strive to compel the government to pass necessary labor legislation etc. The theory of socialism, however, grew out of the philosophic, historical, and economic theories elaborated by educated representatives of the propertied classes, by intellectuals...
> 20

Classical Marxism says the proletariat is never spontaneously revolutionary and Lenin agrees and draws what seem like sensible conclusions: The party has to lead the proletariat toward the proletariat's best interests, whether the proletariat immediately perceives those interests or not. Marx, Engels, and Lenin, and for that matter most of the rest too, were all intellectuals. Without reservation they adopted the task not of representing or aiding the proletariat but of leading it. These men's entire discussion about discipline, organization, and consciousness occured in context of the need to take power away from one class and give it to another; their solutions were always in accordance with the logic of Classical Marxism and with what they perceived to be the conditions of their times.

And so Classical Leninist strategy wherever it has ever been employed has involved a disciplined, relatively small, hierarchical party, whose central will is to be eventually followed by the workers.

As Rosa Luxemburg, who was not so favorable to Lenin's views, characterized it:

> ...the two principles upon which Lenin's centralism rests are precisely these: 1-The blind subordination, in the

smallest detail, of all party organs to the party center, which alone thinks, guides, and decides for all. 2-The rigorous separation of the organized nucleus of revolutionaries from its social revolutionary surroundings. 21

Whether Leninist organizational forms are the only ones that a Classical Marxist can uphold is certainly unclear but it is quite obvious that they are at least consistent with Classical Marxism's understandings and are in fact the form that most Classical Marxists, for one reason or another, gravitate towards. With regard to questions of organization as with regard to questions of tactical decision-making, Lenin was consistent with his Classical Marxist heritage and as good in employing it as anyone else.

Shortly after its inception Lenin became convinced that the First World War would lead to revolution in Russia. He felt it, but he needed to be sure, and he needed to know how. Following the imperatives of a scientific approach to social change, he commenced a study of the war, and of its effects on various forms of social organization. The study was completed in a relatively short time and was released under the title *Imperialism: The Final Stage of Capitalism.* The book was a new addition to Marxist theory (though others had also contributed similarly). It added analysis based upon descriptions of systems that Marx hadn't fully foreseen. Lenin enriched Marx's ideas in accordance with the changing dictates of his surroundings.

Lenin's book showed that when Capitalism became *monopolistic* it lost all its progressive content -- the drive to increase productive capacity diminished while the drive to increase profits by any and all means increased. Lenin saw that peacetime capitalism could create conditions not totally unfavorable to the proletariat but he also saw that imperialist wars were inevitable and that miserable conditions would result in all involved countries. The only alternative for such a country's proletariat, peasantry, and lower middle classes was revolution. Lenin felt that if the wartime Russian proletariat moved, everyone else would follow -- the coalition approach to a proletariat led middle-class revolution could now work, precisely because the war was almost universally abhorrent. But there was one proviso for success that obviously followed: the leading elements of the coalition had to avoid involvement in the imperialist war.

Lenin had a careful analysis of the whole war situation: 1-He didn't want to see a German victory; 2-He felt that the cause of the Russian revolution and therefore the world revolution necessitated the overthrow of the Czar; 3-He felt that prospects for successful revolution depended upon internal Russian opposition to the war's continuation. Anyone who supported the war effort had to become inevitably and inextricably caught up in the dynamics of imperialism, and such a person or party would be totally incapable of waging an effective opposition to the Czar.

Lenin then reversed one of his earlier positions. He decided that the Bolsheviks had to have complete sole control of the middle class revolution; everyone else and most specifically the democratic socialists had adopted the wrong war position. The other parties were bankrupt as revolutionary agents and there could be no coalitions with any of them.

To Lenin the Menshevik cry, "Revolt for Victory," was total insanity. In 1905 he would have welcomed a coalition victory as progressive but in 1915 he opposed any coalition government attempts. The popular parties had the wrong war positions and so a new government with them in it would have a wrong war position and would not be deserving of support. It would be unable to do anything differently from the Czars. The dynamics of imperialist war would prohibit social change.

Because Lenin decided it would be fatal to coalesce with any of the social-chauvinist or middle-class labor parties who would try to defend war gains, and because he also felt that a coalition of forces was necessary, he was left with only one strategic alternative. The Bolsheviks had to go it *essentially alone* but yet had to develop at the *base* throughout the country. They had to adopt policies which would take people from pro-imperialist organizations into the Bolsheviks or at least into support of the party.

Thus, Lenin supported pursuing a 'democratic dictatorship' aimed at the interests of the workers and peasants and administered by the Bolshevik Party in a totally *centralized disciplined* way. He moved from a theoretical analysis of the conditions of imperialism to an understanding of the position of the various sectors of the Russian population, to a strategy for victory.

Trotsky thought Lenin's plan was naive on one point. He was convinced that in a revolutionary unheaval the workers would go further than Lenin outlined and so he supported a drive toward the establishment of a proletariat state dictatorship. "Trotsky favored democracy among the workers at the same time that he advocated the suppression of all other classes by the proletariat." 22 Lenin on the other hand favored a broad national Russian Democracy within the limits considered desirable by the leaders of the governing Bolshevik Party. The two were able to work together; though they disagreed about the goal they agreed on the main steps toward it.

By 1917 the peasants were war-weary and their desperation was spreading through the whole army. The cities were without fuel and people were starving. By March discontent was almost universal: from below, the workers, peasants, and army were demanding peace and bread; and from above, the middle class was demanding victory in the war. The Petrograd workers' revolt spread through the whole country -- the workers and peasants overran the Czar's authorities, and the liberal middle classes took over the committee that had been established to replace the Duma.

The Social Revolutionaries were strong enough to do what they liked, but were content to be an opposition and didn't push hard for separate peace. The middle classes were slowly joined by reactionary land owners and each kept a concern for winning the war and of course defending property rights. The upheavals' social institutions, the soviets, were led by Mensheviks and Social Revolutionaries, and they chose to help the other parties establish a provisional government.

Lenin returned from exile in 1917 and from the first fought against the 'old' idea that a coalition form of government was sensible since war views were relatively secondary. In March he developed a full strategy. He saw a liberal government using the tools of the old police forces, and a parallel soviet government supported by armed workers. The way seemed clear. The soviets were a new-found means to victory. Lenin planned to overthrow the provisional government by establishing the soviets as the sole organs of power. He adopted as his demand, and as the Bolshevik demand, the already mass cry for peace, bread, land, and liberty. He was quite convinced that the liberal government could in no way meet those demands so long as it was preoccupied with war and property. It would crumble of its own weaknesses.

His goal was to use the soviets to destroy Russian imperialism. His problem was to figure what tactics to use in order for the Bolsheviks to take control of those same soviets.

By May things were critical. The liberals had proven themselves totally bankrupt. The soviets, still under the control of the Menshevik and Socialist Revolutionary parties, had to take over the government. But the new rulers were not to fare much better. They too became victims of the dynamics of imperialism. They too were unable to deal with land and bread demands, and they even launched a failing offensive on the war front. Very quickly old forms began reasserting themselves, most especially in the army where the czarist commanders were again taking control and eliminating opposition. The soldiers and peasants were losing faith in the government; the workers in the cities had been dubious about the new government right from the start.

> The revolution was not the work of the Bolsheviks. Their service lies in the recognition by Lenin and Trotsky that at midnight a great anarchical revolt would occur. Five minutes before midnight Lenin and Trotsky gave the order for a Bolshevik uprising and in so doing created the impression that the tremendous occurrence at midnight was their work. It was in this manner that they won for themselves the authority necessary to enable them to govern Russia. 23

The Bolsheviks fought against Kerensky's July war offensive, but then they also fought against Kornilov's putsch attempt aimed at upseating Kerensky from the right. When the time for them to lead came, their record was impeccable: they favored peace but also supported revolution.

At Lenin's own admission their economic goal upon taking power was the establishment of state capitalism. They didn't want to alter the city's basic property relations. They wanted the workers to have power but not ownership. This was Lenin's plan, but as Trotsky had accurately predicted the workers were out in front. There was upheaval and revolution, all the old ways were dying; the workers took over the factories and the entire economy for themselves.

Arthur Rosenberg characterizes Lenin's strategy on taking power and then implementing it:

> In their capacity as organs of the spontaneous will of the masses the soviets were from the very beginning an unwelcome and extraneous element of Bolshevik doctrines. In 1917 Lenin used the soviets to destroy czarism. Once that had been accomplished he created his own state machinery

after the true Bolshevik pattern, ie, the rule of the small
disciplined minority of professional revolutionaries over the
great and undisciplined masses. 24

But we needn't rely on Rosenberg's description, for Lenin made his
own dispositions quite clear:

The Bolsheviks could not have maintained themselves in
power for two and a half months, let alone for two and a half
years, unless the strictest, truly iron discipline prevailed in
our party. 25

...the dictatorship of the proletariat is a most determined
and most ruthless war against a more powerful enemy, the
bourgeoisie, whose resistance is increased tenfold by its
overthrow. 26

...absolute centralization and strictest discipline of the
proletariat constitute one of the fundamental conditions for
victory over the bourgeoisie. 27

Though Trotsky had similar inclinations, however, at first he
still leaned toward a more open and democratic party organization, in the
context of the party's standing dictatorially above everyone else. He felt that
the Red Army, for example, should be disciplined and hierarchically
organized for two reasons: first and most obviously, it would be the most
efficient way to fight the Civil War; and second, it was a good way to gain
control over the peasants, otherwise not easily accomplished inside a
democratic system that included peasant soviets.

To foreshadow some of our later critique, we might well ask, as many
then did, if it wasn't perhaps possible for a party with another more
democratic disposition than Lenin's to have succeeded -- Was a better
approach outside the realm of Lenin's thoughts and desires or were his
thoughts well suited to the potentialities of his times? Are they well suited
to the potentialities of our time?

Leninist strategy, however, is concerned not only with taking power,
but also derivatively with using it in building a new society. Moreover the
Leninist role in this in Russia was certainly much more than it had been in

the upheaval itself. Perhaps most characteristically Lenin and Trotsky felt that *capitalist tools of development were tactics. They could be put at the disposal of socialism as easily as capitalism.* And so at the beginning of 1918 Lenin said that:

> ...In the present circumstances, state capitalism would mean a step foward for the Soviet Republic. If, for example, state capitalism firmly established itself here after six months, that would be a mighty achievment, and the surest guarantee that, after a year, socialism would be finally and irrevocably established here. 28

And that the task of the Bolsheviks was:

> To study the state capitalism of the Germans, to spare no effort in copying it, (to not) shrink from adopting dictatorial methods to hasten the copying of it. 29

At the eleventh Party Congress, in attacking the opponents of state capitalist strategy, Lenin said:

> State capitalism is capitalism which we shall be able to restrain, and the limits of which we shall be able to fix. This state capitalism is connected with the state, and the state is the workers, the advanced section of the workers, the vanguard. We are the state.... And it rests with us to determine what this state capitalism is to be. 30

Lenin and Trotsky were Classical Marxists, they were always concerned with *who* was in *power* and with what their *goals* were, rather than with how precisely those in power operated. With the Bolsheviks, the so-called Party of the Proletariat, in power, there was only one rational criterion for judging tactics: were they effective in achieving Bolshevik goals or weren't they? There was no worry about side effects or about the validity of goals, and how could there be? The goals and the methods of the Bolsheviks were by definition those of the proletariat as a whole, and thus inherently quite above suspicion.

Lenin and Trotsky were both concerned with the need to increase production but they thought about the problem in bourgeois managerial terms. They thought that managerial techniques could be put at the disposal of socialism. Trotsky said he felt it was an a political affair who ran the factories and how they were run, just as long as the dictatorship was in the hands of the proletariat represented by the Bolshevik Party.

> It (one man management) may be correct or incorrect from the point of view of the technique of administration. It would consequently be a most crying error to confuse the question as to the supremacy of the proletariat with the question of boards of workers at the heads of factories. The Dictatorship of the Proletariat is expressed in the abolition of private property, in the supremacy over the whole soviet mechanism of the collective will of the workers, and not at all in the form in which individual economic enterprises are administered. 31

In 1919, Trotsky submitted a set of theses on the need for the militarization of the work force -- it was distributed to the public by a left faction and Trotsky was forced to defend his ideas to the people.

> The workers must not be allowed to roam all over Russia. They must be sent where they are needed, called up and directed like soldiers. Labor must be directed most intensely during the transition from capitalism to socialism. 32

And in another context:

> ... it is essential to form punitive contingents and to put all those who shirk work into concentration camps.... coercion, regimentation, and militarization of labor were no mere emergency measures and the worker's state normally had the right to coerce any citizen to perform any work at any place of its own choosing. 33

In 1920, Lenin, who had long held these views, put Trotsky, who had already abolished soldiers' soviets in the army, in charge of the commissariat of transportation. Trotsky immediately instituted martial law over railway personnel and replaced all old union leaders who disagreed with his policies.

Lenin and Trotsky logically and consistently carried out a strategic conception within which the dynamics of the structure of the army and of industry *were not nearly so important as who ruled over them and how effective that rule was.*

In 1921, after the New Economic Policy was enacted, Lenin took the logic of his strategy to its conclusive stage. He admitted and basked in the fact that what he was building in Russia was state capitalism.

> State capitalism in a land in which capital is the governing authority and state capitalism in a proletarian state are two different things. State capitalism in a capitalistic state means capitalism controlled by the state for the benefits of the middle class as opposed to the proletariat. In a proletariat state this process benefits the working class and enables it to defend itself against a middle class that is too powerful. 34

Rosenberg explains the motivations at work nicely:

> ... the main concern of the Bolshevik Party during this period was not how the taking over by the workers of management of production be facilitated? It was, what is the quickest way to develop a layer of managers and administrators for the economy? 35

As the Bolshevik Tomsky said in one of the clearest descriptions of the Leninist internal 'power struggle':

> -- it was the task of the communists first to create well-knit trade unions in their industries, secondly to take possession of these organizations by tenacious work, thirdly to stand at the head of these organizations, fourthly to expel all non-proletarian organizations, and fifthly to take the union under our communist influence. 36

The task was to transfer power from indigenous, *spontaneously* controlled worker's committees and give it to the more *bureaucratic and manageable* trade unions, so that it might then finally be completely held by *managers* and other *party bureaucrats.*

At the close of the process in 1922 Lenin delivers one final blow to any chances for even minimal worker's power:

> It is absolutely essential that all authority in the factories should be concentrated in the hands of management -- under these circumstances any direct intervention by the trade unions in the management of enterprises must be regarded as positively harmful and impermissible. 37

Lenin and the Bolsheviks believed firmly in the rightness of their approach. There were no excuses, no protestations that the policies were brought on by hardship, no excuses that they were necessary evils. In fact the Bolsheviks glorified their tactics as the only model for socialist revolution -- they didn't think creatively about other alternatives, they ruled them out as foolhardy or counter-revolutionary.

But they also felt from the start that the success of their revolution depended in large part upon world events. They wanted European revolution and European support. During the early years Lenin tried to 'export' the revolution through the Third International.

Broad masses of workers in Europe saw what had been accomplished in Russia. They were willing to sacrifice democracy in their organizations if it would get them as far. They didn't know or particularly care about the middle-class aspects of the Russian revolution nor were they interested in hearing such things. As we show later they misperceived what were misrepresented events. Lenin wanted to consolidate European revolutionary forces around coteries of professional leaders who would exercise authority at the behest of the Russian Central Committee. He was trying to resolve the need for a revolution in another country by choosing between various poor but necessary tactics. Centralization and participation in reactionary parliaments were two things he 'forced' upon the European revolutionaries. But there was also submission to his ultimate authority as the head of the Bolshevik Party, and the use of expulsion against those who dissented.

Leninist world strategy was formulated in the context of Lenin's understanding of Classical Marxist theory and his Classical Marxist analysis of the conditions in Europe and the possibilities within Russia itself. Leninist models were quickly pushed outwards beyond Russia's borders and even beyond her specific kinds of conditions.

Classical Leninism is then a strategic perspective that was formulated in the context of Lenin's Classical Marxist world view and the experiences of a group of intellectuals in peasant Russia. It was elevated to the status of an ultimate strategy on the wings of the Bolshevik victories. It was turned into dogma by the fact that it was 'forced' upon Europe as the road to socialism.

It stresses the need to take and maintain power by means of the correct employ of a small party of professional revolutionaries, or at least a small central committee of professional revolutionaries, leading the revolutionary working class and the masses, in the name of the proletariat. It takes power and then employs it to new ends. It stresses a Classical Marxist analysis of tactics to determine their value -- and on the basis of such analysis, it stresses the importance of some organizational forms (centralism, the party, the dictatorship of the proletariat,) and the relative unimportance of others (decentralism, spontaneity, etc.). To understand it more fully and to begin on the road to a critique of it and of Classical Marxism, we must now spend some time critically examining the actual Bolshevik practice of the Russian Revolution up through the year of Lenin's death.

FOOTNOTES

1. Lenin, *What Is To Be Done,* International Publishers, New York.
2. Keynes quoted in E.F. Schumacher, *Small Is Beautiful,* Harper Torchbooks, New York.
3. Lenin, *Left Wing Communism: An Infantile Disorder,* International Publishers, New York. 34
4. Lukacs, *Lenin,* MIT Press, Cambridge, Mass. 17.
5. Lenin, *Left Wing Communism*, op. cit. 46
6. ibid. 11.
7. Marx in Avineri, *Marx and the Intellectuals,* Journal of the History of Ideas, xxviii, no. 2 (April-June 1967)
8. Avineri, *Marx and the Intellectuals,* op. cit.
9. ibid.
10. Lenin, *Left Wing Communism,* op. cit. 53.
11. Lukacs, op. cit. 79.
12. Lenin, *Left Wing Communism,* op. cit. 52.
13. ibid. 47.
14. See for example Arthur Rosenberg's *A History of Bolshevism,* Doubleday Inc. Garden City, New York.
15. ibid.
16. Lenin, *Left Wing Communism,* op. cit. 26.
17. Rosenberg, op. cit. 29.
18. Lukacs, op. cit. 29.
19. ibid. 35.
20. Lenin, *What Is To Be Done,* op. cit. 31-32.
21. Luxemburg, "The Organization of the Social Democratic Party in Russia," *Rosa Luxemburg Speaks,* Pathfinder Press, New York.
22. Rosenberg, op. cit. 71.
23. ibid. 111.
24. ibid. 137-138.
25. Lenin, *Left Wing Communism,* op. cit. 9.

26 ibid. 9.
27. ibid. 10.
28. Lenin in Lukacs, op. cit. 75.
29. Lenin in Maurice Brinton, *The Bolsheviks and Workers' Control*, Solidarity, London. 46.
30. Lenin in Lukacs, op. cit. 86.
31. Trotsky quoted in Brinton, op. cit.
32. Trotsky quoted in Daniel Cohn Bendit, *Obsolete Communism: A Left Wing Alternative*, McGraw Hill Book Company, New York. 229.
33. ibid. 229.
34. Lenin quoted in Rosenberg, op. cit. 177.
35. Rosenberg, op. cit.
36. Tomsky quoted in Brinton, op. cit.
37. Lenin quoted in Brinton, op. cit. 63.

CHAPTER FIVE

A CRITIQUE OF BOLSHEVIK PRACTICE

"Incapacity of the masses." What a tool for all exploiters and dominators, past, present, and future, and especially for the modern aspiring enslavers, whatever their insignia -- Nazism, Bolshevism, Fascism, or Communism. "Incapacity of the masses." The is a point on which the reactionaries of all colors are in perfect agreement with the "communists." And this agreement is exceedingly significant. 1

Voline

It is necessary to abolish completely in principle and in practice everything that may be called political power, for as long as political power exists, there will always be rulers and ruled, masters and slaves, exploiters and exploited. 2

Mikhail Bakunin

Even 'successful' revolution is problematic. It is necessary to think twice not only about how one goes about winning but also about what exactly winning is.:

The crushing of the Paris Commune in 1871 -- or of the Budapest up-rising in 1956 -- showed that proletarian revolts face immensely difficult problems of organization and politics. They showed that an insurrection can be isolated and that the ruling classes will not hesitate to employ any violence or savagery when their power is at stake. But what happened in the Russian Revolution compels us to consider not only the conditions for working class victory, but also the content and the possible fate of such a victory, its consolidation, its development, and the seeds that it might contain of a defeat, infinitely more far reaching than the ones inflicted by the troops of the Versailles or by Kruschev's tanks. 3

102

We see the Soviet Union in 1972 as an exploitative society with a ruling bureaucracy that furthers its own vested interests at the expense of the people's welfare. If it has some advantages over western society it also leaves much to be desired. Where did the revolution go wrong? Was it Stalin? Was it the contingencies of backwardness and Civil War? Was it isolation? Or was it perhaps the weakness of Lenin, Trotsky, the whole Bolshevik strategy, and even the Classical Marxist theory underneath it all?

> But the essential question is not whether there has been progress, as progress itself is not too difficult to achieve, but whether there has been the maximum possible degree of progress in existing conditions. In other words one must consider the point of departure, all the alternatives and their results, (real and potential), then combine all this into a whole, compare the various alternatives, and only then evaluate the results. 4

From an historical perspective the important question is whether or not an alternative and superior form of development was possible. From our perspective the most important questions are what does the Bolshevik experience say about Marxism Leninism, and what are the implications for our own political options in the advanced west? In this chapter we examine the revolution's practice with an eye toward critiquing its strategy and then its theory.

The revolution was sparked by government inability to meet any demands of the masses. The Bolsheviks didn't organize it, they appropriated it. As Trotsky says in his version of the history:

> The soldiers lagged behind the shop committees... the committees lagged behind the masses .... The Party also lagged behind the revolutionary dynamic -- an organization which had the least right to lag, especially in a time of revolution... The most revolutionary party which human history until this time had ever known was nevertheless caught unawares by events of history. It reconstructed itself in the fires, and staightened out its ranks under the onslaught of events. The masses at the turning point were a

hundred times to the left of the Party. 5

Trotsky goes on and says firmly that "the Central Committee was unable to give directions for the coming day." 6 According to his history the Bolsheviks usually tried to slow things up but the masses paid little or no attention and spontaneously pushed ahead. "The movement had begun from below irrespective of the Bolsheviks -- to a certain extent against their will." 7

Further, according to Trotsky, Lenin was the only one who knew what was going on, and what to do, and he pushed everybody else along. Trotsky even says that things were so chaotic that Lenin had to bypass the central committee and break discipline over and over in order to get things into line and that "Lenin did not decide easily on such steps, but it was a question of the fate of the revolution and other considerations fell away." 8

At the uprising's crucial point the Petrograd garrison transferred their allegiance to Lenin and Trotsky and the revolution was carried out successfully and easily. But even with victory in sight certain Party members pressed for a coalition government with the Mensheviks and others. They could conceive only of a middle-class revolution led by a coalition, but Lenin stuck to his anti-imperialist position and fought successfully for his conception of a Bolshevik Democratic Dictatorship.

The Soviets brought the masses liberty, the Bolsheviks pursued peace, the peasants were authorized to dispossess the landowners, and the workers to run the factories. But the workers went further and dispossessed the capitalists as Trotsky had predicted they would. In the early stages of his victory Lenin had no choice but to reconcile himself to this fact. The Bolsheviks had to recognize the workers' spontaneous 'extreme' actions and plan within the constraints they imposed, but they didn't have to admire or try to further those actions. They could and did view them as adventurist, and struggled,eventually successfully, to undo them.

> ...once in control of the government the Communists saw that the Soviets threatened the supremacy of the State. At the same time they could not destroy them arbitrarily without undermining their own prestige at home and abroad as the sponsors of the Soviet system. They began to

shear them gradually of their powers and finally to subordinate them to their own needs. 9

In the revolution's early years it was true only that the "equality of man was achieved through communism in starvation." 10 But because of the new equality and a land redistribution and hopes for a
continually improving future, the working class and the Red Army had
relatively good morale: they supported the revolution enough for it to
achieve victory in the Civil War.

So right from its commencement the revolutionary project was viewed
in two almost opposite ways. On the one hand, Trotsky felt that the upheaval
caught the Bolsheviks somewhat unprepared, but he also felt that it was
then successfully led by the Bolsheviks lest it become misdirected and revert
under counter-revolutionary pressures. On the other hand in the view of
Rosa Luxemburg and seemingly of at least some elements of the 'Russian
Masses', too, the upheaval was a *spontaneous revolutionary upsurge of the
masses pregnant with immense possibilities, but steadily undermined by
the Bolsheviks' bureaucratic, coercive authoritarianism:*

> Finally we saw the birth of a far more legitimate offspring of
> the historical process: the Russian workers' movement,
> which for the first time, gave expression to the real will of the
> popular masses. Then the leadership of the Russian
> revolution leapt up to balance on their shoulders, and once
> more appointed itself the all powerful director of history, this
> time in the person of his highness the Central Committee of
> the Social Democratic Workers' Party. This skillful acrobat
> did not even realize that the only one capable of playing the
> part of director is the collective ego of the working class,
> which has sovereign right to make mistakes and to learn the
> dialectics of history by itself. Let us put it quite bluntly: the
> errors committed by a truly revolutionary workers'
> movement are historically far more fruitful than the correct
> decisions of the finest Central Committee. 11

Lenin said in late 1918, "...we passed from worker's control to the
creation of the Supreme Council of National Economy..." 12, the function

of which, according to E.H. Carr, was to "replace, absorb, and supersede the machinery of worker's control." 13 And as Carr went on to say:

> Those who paid most lip service to worker's control and purported to expand it were in fact engaged in a skillful attempt to make it orderly and innocuous by turning it into a large scale, organized, public institution. 14

It is clearly true that in 1917 the main desires of the workers and the Bolsheviks converged. The government was overthrown. The Bolsheviks were installed. The workers expropriated the capitalists without directives but then the Bolsheviks expropriated the revolution -- with Lenin directing the whole way. Despite the fact that rhetoric pointed to the new state as "worker-led," the convergence of worker and Bolshevik interest was only fleeting and essentially opportunist. Luxemburg's description (see above) was far closer to truth than Trotsky's, and Maurice Brinton's even fuller still:

> During the middle of 1917 Bolshevik support for the factory committees was such that the Mensheviks were to accuse them of abandoning Marxism in favor of Anarchism. "Actually Lenin and his followers remained firm upholders of the Marxist conception of the centralized state. Their immediate objective, however, was not yet to set up the centralized proletarian dictatorship, but to decentralize as much as possible the bourgeois state, and the bourgeois economy. This was a necessary condition for the success of the revolution. In the economic field therefore, the factory committee, the organ on the spot, rather than the trade union was the most potent and deadly instrument of upheaval. Thus the trade unions were (temporarily) relegated to the background"...
>
> This [continues Brinton] is perhaps the most explicit statement [by a favorable Marxist commentator] of why the Bolsheviks at this earliest stage supported workers' control and its organizational vehicle the Factory Committees. Today only the ignorant -- or those willing to be deceived -- can still kid themselves into believing that proletarian

power, 'at the point of production' was ever a fundamental tenet or objective of Bolshevism. 15

Emma Goldman, who was in Russia at the time, and who first compassionately and then critically evaluated revolutionary events, had this to say about the same early dynamics:

> ...[a] spirit of mutual purpose and solidarity swept Russia with a mighty wave in the first days of the October-November revolution. Inherent in that enthusiasm were forces that could have moved mountains if intelligently guided by exclusive consideration for the well-being of the whole people. The medium of such effective guidance was on hand: the labor organizations and the cooperatives with which Russia was covered as with a network of bridges combining the city with the country; the soviets which sprang into being responsive to the needs of the Russian people; and, finally, the intelligentsia whose traditions for a century expressed heroic devotion to the cause of Russia's emancipation.
> But such a development was by no means within the program of the Bolsheviki. For several months following October they suffered the popular forces to manifest themselves, the people carrying the revolution into ever widening channels. But as soon as the communist party felt itself sufficiently strong in the government saddle, it began to limit the scope of popular activity. All the succeeding acts of the Bolsheviki, all their following policies, changes of policies, their compromises and retreats, their methods of suppression and persecution, their terrorism and extermination of all other political views -- all were but the means to an end: the retaining of the state power in the hands of the communist party. 16

Right from the beginning the Bolsheviks were concerned to eventually establish centralized iron rule. To the extent they initially supported certain aspects of decentralization it was because conditions made all other courses less desirable. There is no other rational way to interpret the history of their intervention, very briefly on behalf of, and from then on in strict opposition to, all forms of worker's self management.

Lenin's first major policy act against considerable opposition from all sides, was to push through the Brest Litvosk treaty. He was convinced it was impossible to fight the imperialist war and experiences at the front eventually proved him quite correct. However when Germany was finally defeated, pressures, instead of easing up, actually got much worse. The allies doubled their efforts to overthrow Lenin by way of supplying the White Armies. As a result the Civil War was almost historically unparalleled for its violence and brutality, but the masses loved the party that gave them freedom from the Czar and the hope of a soviet state, and the Red Army fought to eventual victory.

During the war the Bolshevik ideology polarized Russia into pro- and counter-revolutionary factions. All opposition was considered seditious. The army and economy were centralized, and the soviets were weakened until they had no power and the Central Committee had all.

During the Civil War all Russians suffered immeasurably but they continued to support the revolution, because, despite the absence of democracy and despite other hardships, there was still a new equality and an abiding fear of returning to the past. Everyone *looked forward* to the fruits of the *soviet communism* they were fighting for.

But socialist freedom was not to be what many anticipated, and some Anarchists even had the foresight to see the coming 'reaction' relatively accurately. Voline, for example, in 1917 made a dire prediction:

> Once their power has been consolidated the Bolsheviks as
> state socialists, that is as men who believe in centralized and
> authoritarian leadership -- will start running the life of the
> country and of the people from the top. Your soviets... will
> gradually become simple tools of the central government.
> You will soon see the inauguration of an authoritarian
> political state apparatus.... "All power to the soviets" will
> become "all power to the leaders of the party." 17

Repression did in fact begin in 1918 and it centered around the issue of workers' management and the nature of the army. The party worked methodically through both administrative and directly coercive channels.

"...Within a year of the capture of state power by the Bolsheviks, the relations of production (shaken for awhile at the height of the mass movement) had reverted to the classical authoritarian pattern seen in all class societies. The workers as workers had been divested of any meaningful authority in the matters that concerned them most." 18

And it was no wonder that it took such a short time for transition, for as E.H. Carr reports,

> It was indisputable that the soviet bureaucrat of these early years was as a rule a former member of the bourgeois intelligentsia or official class, and brought with him many of the traditions of the old Russian bureaucracy. 19

And these facts were not accidental but instead fit quite nicely with Bolshevik strategy. Brinton's pamphlet explains the effects of the reversion in social relations:

> The capitalist world is one of fetishism, where interpersonal relationships tend to disappear behind relationships between things. But the very moment when the masses revolt against this state of affairs, they break through the smoke screeen. They see through the taboo of 'things' and come to grips with people, whom they had 'respected' until then in the name of the all holy fetish known as private property. From that moment on the specialist, manager, or capitalist, whatever his technical or personal relationship to the enterprise, appears to the workers as the incarnation of exploitation, as the enemy, as the one with whom the only thing they want to do is to get him out of their lives. To ask the workers at this stage, to have a more balanced attitude, to reorganize in the old boss the new 'technical director', the indispensable 'specialist', is tantamount to asking the workers at the very moment when at last they are confident in themselves, they are asserting their autonomy, -- to confess their incompetence, their weakness, their insufficiency, -- and this in an area where they are most sensitive, the field encompassing their daily lives from childhood on -- the field of production. 20

The implication is clear -- the practices of the Bolsheviks and most especially the return to old authoritarian modes of local leadership depoliticized the workers by stifling them -- *it led to regimented hierarchy where there was the potential for self-management.* In early revolutionary Russia, the use of old institutions, old capitalist forms, old 'personnel', and 'new' centralized bureaucracy/discipline forms, and especially, as we shall see, one-man management forms, the militarization of labor, and the creation of party dictatorship were all critical in the process of recreating, perpetuating, and newly creating, oppressive modes. Worker opposition was plentiful but ultimately, as we'll see, quite futile.

Repression began in earnest in 1918 around worker's management issues, and by March of 1921 all opposition party factions were wiped out and efforts were underway to repress the Kronstadt sailors, the Makhnovites, and the Petrograd workers.

To take it a step at a time: in 1919 Trotsky published his thesis on the militarization of labor. In his own history of the period he points out that "militarization of the trade unions and the militarization of transport required an internal ideological militarization too." 21 But he draws no conclusions about whether this was a cost of the process or a valuable side effect. His mentality of the moment, and the Bolshevik mentality of the moment, is revealed somewhat in a number of his statements about one man rule in factories and about the militarization of the railroad economy:

> It is a general rule that man will try to get out of work. Man
> is a lazy animal. 22

> Those workers who contribute more than the rest to the
> general good have every right to receive a larger share of the
> socialist product than layabouts, idlers, and the undisci-
> plined. 23

Trotsky sounds much like a modern capitalist. Perhaps he was referring to the railway workers; perhaps they weren't enthusiastic enough concerning his decisions about their unions and their lives. Perhaps their work grew tedious and fell off -- unjustifiably of course. But perhaps they just didn't like oppression ... no matter what package it came in.

Lenin also had some interesting, pertinent thoughts on similar topics at the same time:

> Unquestionably submission to the single will is absolutely
> necessary for the success of labor processes based on large
> scale machine industry.... Revolution demands, in the
> interests of socialism, that the masses unquestioningly obey
> the single will of the leaders of the labor process. 24

> Large scale machine industry which is the central produc-
> tive source and foundation of socialism calls for absolute
> and strict unity of will... How can strict unity of will be
> ensured? By thousands subordinating their will to the will of
> one. 25

Not by education, not by solidarity, not by a community of interests
and experiences, but by *enforced external discipline* -- this was, and
remains, the practical Leninist approach.

This was not an approach held defensively, for Lenin continually
pointed out that only the petit bourgeois and the counter-revolutionary
could be so backward as to not understand immediately the true thrust of
what he was saying. Anyone who suggested that discipline and organization could spring from political consciousness and collectivity was
simply naive -- and objectively counter-revolutionary. Clearly there is
indication of a narrow strategy and perhaps even theory, creating sectarianism and laying the seeds for self-justifying repression.

Corroborating our implication that militarization of political and
economic life was no hated necessity, but a well thought-out, believed-in
universal policy Trotsky said:

> I consider that if the Civil War had not plundered our
> economic organs of all that was strongest, most independ-
> ent, most endowed with initiative, we should undoubtedly
> have entered the path of one-man management much
> sooner and much less painfully. 26

Perhaps Trotsky is exact and the Bolsheviks would have got the same
results without the war's divergences and perhaps he is not and the
peasants and workers would have clung more effectively to their soviets.
From our point of view it doesn't matter insofar as we admit what the
Bolsheviks would have tried to do, not because they were 'evil', but because

they were consistent, competent Classical Marxist Leninists. The 'proof' is that the whole process of transfer of power began and was well under way before the Civil War broke out and that, as we'll soon see, it was in no way rectified when that war ended.

The implication is that we should examine Classical Marxist Leninist theory and strategy and see how they affected views, programs, and even perceptions, and we should look with a special eye toward trying to describe the kind of dynamic that Louis Cardan describes:

> Trotsky for example, described the anonymous workers of Petrograd in glowing terms when they flocked into the Bolshevik Party or when they mobilized themselves during the Civil War. But he was later to call the Kronstadt mutineers "stool pigeons" and "hirelings of the high command" when they were moved by the same motivations in directions that opposed his will. 27

In almost all his declarations Lenin called for unquestioning obedience to the will of a *single representative* of the Party. He said over and over again that this was crucial to the development of socialism and that those who couldn't understand why, were laggards or worse. In 1918 the 'Left Communist' paper *Kommunist* said, "laggingly":

> The introduction of labor discipline in connection with the restoration of capitalist management in industry cannot really increase the productivity of labor, but it will diminish the class activity, initiative, and organization of the proletariat. It threatens to enslave the working class. It will rouse discontent among the backward elements as well as among the vanguard of the proletariat. In order to introduce the system in the face of the hatred prevailing at present among the proletariat for the "capitalist saboteurs," the Communist Party would have to rely on the petit bourgeoisie, as against the workers, and in this way it would ruin itself as the party of the proletariat. 28

This is fine tactical analysis. It is obviously generated by an understanding of the dynamics of oppression and an understanding of the likelihoods for more to come. It does not seem similar to the work of the abstract Leninists, but to a group with *populist insight*. Lenin didn't share the Left Communists' experiences or their views. He was in power, he was incorruptible his path was the only one he knew, and from the evidence it was the only one he was capable of believing in. It seems reasonable to say that his consciousness simply didn't allow him to fully understand the Left Communist position.For he responded to it violently, calling it a "denunciation of communism," a "disgrace," and a "desertion to the camp of the petit bourgeoisie."29 This seems to have been the only way that he knew to argue these issues, precisely because they lay outside his own awareness. He verbally linked the leaders of the Left faction to other people who were openly admitted enemies of the revolution. He didn't address their critique.

The Left Communists broke under the assault, but *Kommunist* kept up its attacks and during 1918 pointed out that the end result of Bolshevik practice would only be bureaucratic centralization and the loss of all soviet power, worker freedom, and worker initiative. The new articles were written by members of the Democratic Centralist faction of the Party;

> We stand for the construction of a proletariat society by the class creativity of the workers themselves, not by the ukases from the "captains of industry"... We proceed from the trust in the class instinct, and in the active class initiative of the proletariat. It cannot be otherwise. If the workers themselves do not know how to create the necessary prerequisites for the socialist organization of labor -- no one can do this for them, nor can the workers be forced to do it. The stick if raised against the workers, will find itself either in the hands of another social force ... or in the hands of the soviet power. But then the soviet power will be forced to seek support against the proletariat from another class, and by this it will destroy itself as the dictatorship of the proletariat. Socialism and socialist organization must be set up by the proletariat itself, or they will not be set up at all; something else will be set up; state capitalism. 30

These were impressive ideas -- Lenin militarized labor and dissolved the Democratic Socialist faction.

The last Party battle around the militarization of labor was fought in 1920-1921 between the 'party regulars and the 'Worker's Opposition'. Lenin called them "a menace to the revolution" and Trotsky took up the club in deliberated earnestness:

> They turn democratic principles into a fetish. They put the right of the workers to elect their own representatives above the Party, thus challenging the Party's right to affirm its own dictatorship, even when this dictatorship comes into conflict with the evanescent mood of the worker's democracy. We must bear in mind the historical mission of our Party. The Party is forced to maintain its dictatorship, without stopping for these vacillations, nor even the momentary falterings of the working class. This realization is the mortar which cements our unity. The dictatorship of the proletariat does not always have to conform to formal principles of democracy. 31

This must simply be called astounding. Now there was a Party dictatorship and, though it couldn't hurt the workers and did things only in their interest, it could be hurt by them and, of course, it had to defend itself. It sounds almost like destroying cities to save them -- and it is quite important to think later if the roots of this position lie only in Trotsky's brain, or also in the sets of theoretic and strategic beliefs to which he cleaved.

The facts:*the Party bent the revolution and not vice versa,* and as the dynamic unfolds, the leaders become more and more enamored of their own virtuosity. Trotsky said that others took democracy as a fetish -- but his words indicate that he lost sight of the nature and purposes of real democracy. The realization of the Party's right to repress became the mortar of the revolution -- not solidarity, shared experience, shared consciousness, and freedom. It seems that Trotsky believed, and at a very minimum Marxism Leninism did nothing to stop him from coming to believe, that in the workers' best interests they should be organized around their own impotence and undeservingness.

And Lenin was certainly no better:

> the militarization of labor.. is the indispensable basic

method for the organization of our labor forces... is it true that compulsory labor is always unproductive? ...This is the most wretched liberal prejudice, chattel slavery too was productive...compulsory slave labor...was in its time a progressive phenomenon. Labor, obligatory for the whole country, compulsory for every worker, is the basis of socialism. 32

In another context he says:

A producers' congress! What precisely does that mean? It is difficult to find words to describe this folly. I keep asking myself can they be joking? Can one really take these people seriously? While production is always necessary, demo-cracy is not. Democracy of production engenders a series of radically false ideas. 33

Perhaps there is an obvious reason why it was difficult to find words to whitewash libertarian impulses -- certainly rational arguments wouldn't work. Lenin ridiculed his left opponents' arguments. The evidence suggests that he didn't respond to them directly precisely because he didn't fully understand them. He was unable to; if he had still had the breadth of insight to understand the workers' opposition he would have joined it, but no, it was not in his interests, it didn't relate to what he saw through his own slightly shaded eyes, it *didn't correspond to the flow of history he had internalized.* He reiterated Trotsky's position in one of his later declarations on the topic:

The decisions on the militarization of labor etc. were incon-trovertible and there is no need to withdraw my words of ridicule concerning references to democracy made by those who challenged these decisions... we shall defend demo-cracy in the workers' organizations but not make a fetish of it. 34

But the history of the revolution shows graphically that it was never democracy that was in danger of being fetishized, quite the contrary, it was democracy that was from the first opposed at all levels, lest the workers' own

initiatives and desires rise to supremacy above even the desires of the
Bolshevik Party itself.

The Worker's Opposition had a weak perspective about many issues but
about one key one they did ask the right question and give the right answer:
In a worker's state who should manage the factories? The workers! Such a
position does not represent a fetishization of democracy, but rather a wise
realization of democracy's central place in any real socialist process.
Further the position was not attacked for being impractical, but for being
irrelevant, incorrect, and destructive. It is at least doubtful it was any of
these things and it's enlightening that Marxist Leninists thought that it was.
Malatesta, in 1919, made the following relevant succinct analysis:

> General Bonaparte defended the French Revolution a-
> gainst the European reaction, and in defending it he
> strangled it. Lenin, Trotsky and their comrades are surely
> sincere revolutionaries and they will not be traitors; but
> they are preparing the government cadres who will come
> later to profit from the revolution and assassinate it. They
> themselves will be the first victims of their methods, and I
> fear that the revolution will crumble with them. 36

Not all Russian opposition was situated inside the Party itself. In 1918
to 1921 the Makhnovites fought against the White Guard Armies and then
against the Red Army with little respite. The main Makhnovite
programmatic leaflet is especially informative:

> 1-Who are the Makhnovites and what are they fighting for?

> The Makhnovites are workers and peasants who in 1918
> rose up against the brutality of the German, Hungarian,
> and Austrian interventionists and against the Hetman of
> the Ukraine.

> The Makhnovites are the workers who have carried the
> battle standard against Denikin and against every form of
> oppression and violence, who have rejected lies from
> whatever source.

The Makhnovites are the workers who by their life's labor have enriched and fattened the bourgeoisie in the past, and are today enriching new masters.

2-Why are they called the Makhnovites?

Because during the greatest and most painful days of reactionary intervention in the Ukraine they had within their ranks the staunch friend, comrade Makhno, whose voice was heard across the entire Ukraine, challenging every act of violence against the workers, calling for struggle against the oppressors, the thieves, the usurpers and those charlatans who were deceiving the workers. That voice still rings among us today, and unwaveringly calls for the liberation and emancipation of workers from all oppression.

3-How do you think you will obtain this liberation?

By overthrowing the coalition of monarchists, republicans, social democrats, communists, and bolsheviks. In place we call for the free election of worker's councils which will not rule by arbitrary laws because no true soviet system can be authoritarian. Ours is the purest form of socialism, anti-authoritarian and anti-government, it calls for the free organization of the social life of the workers, independent of authority, a life in which each worker in a free association with his brothers, can build his own happiness and well-being in accordance with the principles of solidarity, amity, and equality.

4-What do the Makhnovites think of the soviet regime?

The workers themselves must choose their own councils to express the will and carry out the orders of those self-same workers.
The soviets will be the executive organs of, and not authorities over the workers. The land, the factories, the

businesses, the mines, transport etc. must belong to those
who work in them. All that the people inherit must be
socialized.

5-What are the paths that will lead to the final goals of the
Makhnovites?
A consistent and implacable revolutionary battle against all
the false theories, against all arbitrary violence and power,
no matter from what quarter, a struggle to the death. Free
speech, justice, honest battle with guns in our hands.
Only by overthrowing all governments, every representative
of authority, by destroying all political, economic, and
authoritarian lies, wherever they are found, by destroying
the state, by a social revolution, can we introduce a true
system of workers' and peasants' soviets, and advance
towards socialism. 37

The Makhnovites wanted to transfer ownership and control of the
factories to democratically elected soviets. They believed in the slogan 'all
power to the soviets' and in the dissolution of all state power. They were an
immense threat to Lenin and Trotsky because no matter what Lenin and
Trotsky sometimes said about power in the soviets, they no longer believed
in it as a first principle and they had no intention of ever allowing it to
come about. Trotsky fought the Makhnovites personally by first denying
them any rights of assembly and then waging war on them. Neither he nor
Lenin thought it might be worth while to let them proceed on their own in
the Ukraine, that they might either succeed and then be emulated
throughout Russia, or fail, and then be convinced of the Bolsheviks'
pragmatism and follow their leadership peacefully. Indeed it seems that
unconsciously or otherwise the Bolsheviks disliked and destroyed the
Makhnovites not because they thought of them as naive, *but because they
thought of them as a direct threat; not to the whole revolution but to
themselves, and to their own particular view of the revolution.*
    For Cohn Bendit "Makhno's defeat spelled the defeat of the revo-
lution, Trotsky's victory the victory of the bureaucratic counter
revolution." 38 In the course of the last battle of the war the Maknovites
issued the following leaflet to the Red Army men who had come to destroy
them:

STOP, READ, AND THINK:

Comrades of the Red Army!

You have been sent by your commissars to fight the revolutionary Maknovites.

On the orders of your commander you ruin peaceful villages, you will raid, arrest, and kill men and women whom you do not know but who have been presented to you as enemies of the people, bandits and counter-revolutionary. You will be told to kill us, you will not be asked. You will be made to march like slaves. You will arrest and you will murder. Why? For what cause?

Think comrades of the Red Army; think workers, peasants, suffering under the task of new masters who bear the high sounding name of 'worker peasant authorities'! We are revolutionary Makhnovites. The same peasants and workers as you our brethren in the Red Army. We have risen up against oppression and slavery, we fight for a better life and a more enlightened one. Our ideal is to build a community of workers without authorities, without parasites, and without commissars. Our immediate aim is to establish a free soviet regime not controlled by the Bolsheviks, without the pressure of any Party.

The government of the Bolsheviks and the communists have sent you out on a punitive expedition. It hastens to make peace with Denikin and with the rich Poles and other rabble of the White Army, the better to suppress the popular movement of the revolutionary insurgents, of the oppressed, of the rebels against the yoke of all authority. But the threats of the White and Red commanders do not frighten us. We shall reply to violence with violence. If necessary we, a small bandful of people shall put to flight the divisions of the Red Army because we are free and love our liberty. We are revolutionaries who have risen up in a just cause.

> Comrades think of whom you are fighting and against
> whom! Throw off your shackles you are free men!
>   The Revolutionary Makhnovites 39

Is it too much to say that in these incidents we have the forerunner of the Hungarian and Czech invasions? Who were the real hypocrites? Who was blind to the real truth? Who evidenced loyalty to leftist values and who evidenced compromise in the name of personal ambition and power or in the face of potential repression?

The Makhnovite appeal went unheard, the Red soldiers felt too indebted to their Bolshevik leaders to understand, they had too many personal beliefs at stake, too many rationalizations for their past behaviors and for their hardships. The Bolsheviks won; they wrote the accepted histories of the battles, causes, and results much as they wrote the accepted histories of the entire revolution. One wonders whether they had the objectivity to do the job well -- indeed one even wonders if they had the breadth of insight and awareness to do it well at all?

But the Makhnovista was not the only nor even the last rebellious episode. With conclusion of the Civil War, rationales for wartime stringencies had passed. If the strict repressiveness of war had been only a contingency, certainly it should have rapidly been undone. The policies of forcibly taking the peasants' surplus produce and even their food necessities and of strict discipline in industry no longer had the obvious (though actually only mystifying) justification of being necessary for the anti-White effort.

Peasant and other rebellions were by no means confined to the Ukraine. -- According to Cheka reports, in 1921 alone there were 118 uprisings throughout Russia, and other reliable sources cited up to 60,000 guerillas in only one of many rebellions in the Siberian districts. 40 The main peasant demands were aimed at ending the hated forced food requisitions and forced creation of State farms.

Further, post Civil War feelings in the cities were described as follows:

> For the rank-and-file workmen, the restoration of the class
> enemy to a dominant place in the factory meant a betrayal
> of the ideals of the revolution. As they saw it, their dream of
> a proletarian democracy, momentarily realized in 1917,

had been snatched away and replaced by the coercive and bureaucratic methods of capitalism. The Bolsheviks had imposed "iron discipline" in the factories, established armed squads to enforce the will of management, and contemplated using such odious efficiency methods as the "Taylor system." That this should be done by a government which they had trusted and which professed to rule in their name was a bitter pill for the workers to swallow. 41

With the Civil War's conclusion the last possible justification for centralized coercive excesses was gone and the workers grew more and more restive.

Most massively in February of 1921 the famed Petrograd workers went on strike demanding economic revival, free soviets, and an end to repressions in and out of the factories. The Russian Bolshevik government declared a state of seige and sent in troops. They broke the strike but not before the stage was set for a climax to libertarian opposition.

For before the strike fell, the neighboring Kronstadt sailors sent representatives who saw the repression and then returned to their ship where mass meetings passed a 15-point resolution demanding: free elections to new free soviets with secret ballot and free electioneering; freedom of speech and press for workers, peasants, anarchists and all other left socialist parties; right of assembly for trade unions and peasant organizations; organization of a conference of non-Party workers, soldiers, and sailors in Kronstadt, Petrograd, and the entire Petrograd district no later than March 10, 1921; liberation of all left political prisoners; election of a commissar to review cases of those held in prison camps; abolition of all Party detachments in military units, factories and other institutions, because no party should have special privileges; elimination of country-side roadblock detachments; equalization of rations except in unusual circumstances requiring dispensations; abolition of Communist guards in fighting units, factories and mills, but if such guards were really necessary, appointment of them by the local units affected; freedom of action on their own soil for peasants not employing others; support for the resolution from all military units; wide press coverage of the resolution; institution of a mobile workers' control group and authorization of free handicraft production by individuals. 42

The demands were clearly doubly-directed, on the one hand toward relieving economic problems especially among the peasantry, and on the other toward returning the revolution to its original mass-based free soviet ideals. The very fact that workers and sailors had to demand freedom to assemble, free press, and so on is a clear indication of the gravity of the situation Bolshevik repression had created. The eventual government response was, as we'll see, the final indication necessary for our overall argument.

Bolshevik reaction grew swiftly. The economic demands were no real problem as Lenin and other central authority figures had already seen the necessity for alleviating peasant tensions by embarking on just such proposals.43 The political thrust of Kronstadt was, however, a whole different matter. For the Bolsheviks couldn't possibly admit that the soviets weren't representing peasant and worker interests, couldn't admit to having arrested people wrongfully and couldn't recognize the advisability of popular initiatives and general worker-managerial influence, without renouncing their entire ideological orientation and also the bulk of their power. This tack was never in the offing; compromise with the rebels was never really considered. This is the key point in understanding the Kronstadt affair. For no matter how much Lenin, Trotsky et. al. were afraid Kronstadt could aid White enemies, surely the fastest way to alleviate the tension was to compromise. For the sailors were adamantly anti-bourgeois and pro-revolution. That the Bolsheviks eventually, indeed, as quickly as possible resorted to force instead of dialogue was clear indication that their real worry was the persuasive power of the Kronstadt program's inherently anti-dictatorial thrust and some White Guard or other counterrevolutionary plot.

Further the Kronstadt sailors had a long history of devotion to revolutionary principles. They'd lent decisive support during the 1917 uprising and fought valiantly during the Civil War, at the same time, however, they'd never really adopted Bolshevik methodology, always preferring decentralization to centralization, always fearing dictatorship rather than pursuing "iron discipline," and always praising the "free initiatives of the masses" rather than the efficiency of bureaucracy. Their demands and rebellion were thus a natural culmination to their entire revolutionary experience.

Under the slogan 'All Power to the Soviets', they sought to democratize their society. "They had no use for representative government, but wanted direct mass democracy of and by the common people through free soviets." 44 They wished to continue guarding against White Guard plots and ruling over landlords, ex-capitalists and so on, but they also wanted real freedom for the peasant and worker toiling masses.

Their strategy was simple even if somewhat naive:

> What then was to be done? How could the revolution be returned to its original path? Until March 8, when the Bolsheviks launched their initial assualt, the insurgents continued to hope for peaceful reform. Convinced of the rightness of their cause, they were confident of gaining the support of the whole country -- and Petrograd in particular -- in forcing the government to grant political and economic concessions. 45

In response to the courageous efforts of the sailors the Moscow Bolsheviks and many of those in Petrograd went into a period of great activity. The threat of spread of the revolt (which is to say the threat of spread of the demands) in a time of grave peasant and worker dissatisfaction was very real. The Kronstadters, contrary to their expectations, had to be rhetorically undermined and also physically combated.

Although it was true that White emigres and other counter-revolutionaries rejoiced in all Russian uprisings, and especially in the Kronstadt one, and were even seeking to find ways to exploit it to their own benefit, it was completely false that they'd had anything to do with planning it or that they'd actually succeeded in in any way supporting it. Nonetheless the Bolsheviks always labeled opposition "White counter-revolutionary" and the Kronstadt case could be no exception. For the revolutionary legitimacy of the sailors had to be severely undermined by any conceivable means lest their programs gain a real and sympathetic hearing in Petrograd and elsewhere. Thus the Bolshevik calumny that the uprising was led and planned by White Generals. 46

Lenin and Trotsky seemed simply to not understand the true roots of the uprising. On the one hand they primarily cursed it as a White Guard conspiracy and on the other as a work of petit bourgeois deviance. Although all the evidence pointed clearly, the Bolshevik leaders simply couldn't fathom that the revolt was profoundly socialist. To see and admit such a thing would have been too alien and too detrimental to their own ways of thinking.

Under Trotsky's direct and Lenin's indirect leadership Red forces were gathered for an assault. But even this was no simple task for the 'revolution's leaders'. For no matter how much propaganda they released the Kronstadt position was still quite available for all to evaluate: they wanted to restore power to the soviets and undermine the power of party officials. In the army and in the party itself many were affected by the Kronstadt plea. Despite the personal and political difficulties many party regulars and troops sided with the sailors and deserted the Bolsheviks. To stem this dangerous tide and ensure a reliable striking force it was necessary to call upon highly seasoned Red Army troops, on armed party cadres and even on foreign troops, and to also continually expand the attacks upon the Kronstadter's motivations:

> Struggle against the White Guard plot... Just like other White Guard insurrections the mutiny of ex-General Kozlovsky (who in reality had literally nothing significant to do with the insurrection) and the crew of the Battleship Petropavlovosk has been organized by entente spies... 47

As shelling of Kronstadt began and persisted, naive non-violent strategic hopes faded and political lines hardened.

> Our cause is just. We stand for the power of the soviets not for that of the party. We stand for freely elected representatives of the toiling masses. Deformed soviets, dominated by the party, have remained deaf to our pleas. Our appeals have been answered with bullets. 48

The conflict grew and the following threat appeared in the Kronstadt *Izvestia*:

> Be careful Trotsky! You may escape the judgement of the people, you may shoot down innocent men and women by the score, but even you cannot kill the truth. 49

Nonetheless Trotsky's troops successfully quashed the rebellion;

Lenin's socialist state prevailed. Not a single rebel political demand was met. The NEP was initiated, true, but only to consolidate Bolshevik monopoly power: while dealing with many peasant dissatisfactions it did so in bourgeois bureaucratic ways that boded badly for the future.

Indeed the whole post-Civil War and Kronstadt experience puts the lie to present Marxist Leninist assertions that repressive excesses were only a hated wartime necessity. For with the war's close there was an immense popular outcry for freedoms to the people and power to the soviets even including concrete programmatic demands, but it was all met with fierce hostility rather than a spirit of reform. Moreover even after all rebellious elements were smashed there was no let up but rather a further tightening of dictatorial controls. Thus "all pretense at a legal opposition was abandoned in May 1921, when Lenin declared that the place for rival socialists was behind bars or in exile, side by side with the White Guards."50 Anarchists, Mensheviks, Socialist Revolutionaries and all other opposition groups were hounded, jailed, exiled, and finally wiped out. And even within the party too, the screws had to be tightened anew; for the Kronstadt affair certainly had its effects even if not those desired. As Lenin put it, "The time has come to put an end to opposition, put a lid on it; we have had enough opposition." 51 He ordered a top to bottom party purge that soon eliminated nearly one fourth of the party's total membership.

At Kronstadt the rebels had aimed at a new type of socialism -- "At Kronstadt the foundation stone has been laid for the third revolution. This will break the final chains that still bind the working masses and will open up new paths to socialist creation." 52 -- but had found only further authoritarianism. Alexander Berkman, the American Anarchist, who was in fact on the scene in Petrograd, summarized the lessons he took from the events:

> Kronstadt destroyed the myth of the worker's state; it provided the proof of an incompatibility between the dictatorship of the Communist Party and the revolution. 53

Trotsky of course managed to preserve a different perception of the same realities:

> It has been said more than once that we have substituted the

dictatorship of the Party for the dictatorship of the Soviets. However we can claim without fear of contradiction that the dictatorship of the soviets was only made possible by the dictatorship of the Party... In fact there has been no sub- stitution at all, since the Communists express the funda- mental interests of the working class... the Communists become the true representatives of the working class as a whole. 54

Trotsky's kind of rationalizing is about as transparently self-serving as Adam Smith's assertions that Capitalist pursuit of profit motivated by naught but greed serves all human needs equally and in the best possible ways. Further Trotsky's and Lenin's ideological machinations are quite comparable to Smith's in form and motive: each develops rationales for their interests and activities and then bends their perceptions of reality to fit those rationales rather than vice versa. They believe what they say and often struggle valiantly to pursue its implications, but of course that has never been the surest sign that something is either true or particularly worthwhile. Rudolf Rocker describes the type of dynamics that lead to such perverse justifications of inequities as those of Smith and Trotsky:

Dictatorship is the negation of organic development, of material building from below upward; it is the proclama- tion of hardship over the toiling people, a generalship forced upon the masses by a tiny minority. Even if its sup- porters are animated by the very best intentions, the ironic logic of the facts will always drive them into the camp of extremist despotism.... Such a thing as the dictatorship of a class is utterly unthinkable, since it will always involve merely the dictatorship of a particular party which takes it upon itself to speak in the name of a class, just as the bourgeoisie justified any despotic proceeding in the name of the people. 55

We've seen thus far that Bolshevik tactical analysis was narrow to the point of being lies, that their authoritarianism ran rampant, that they used force even against the very groups they were supposedly representing, that they avoided real debate, ignored real worker sentiment, employed ridicule, text book plans, and force. In 1920 Kropotkin wrote to Lenin:

> One thing is indisputable. Even if the dictatorship of the party was an appropriate means to bring about a blow to the capitalist system (which I strongly doubt), *it is nevertheless harmful for the creation of a new socialist system.* What are necessary and needed are local institutions, local forces; but there are none, anywhere. Instead of this, wherever one turns there are people who have never known anything of real life committing the gravest errors which have been paid for with thousands of lives and the ravaging of entire districts. 56

THE BOLSHEVIK HERITAGE

Despite Classical Marxist Leninist protestations to the contrary, the Russian workers actually did have their own revolutionary consciousnesses. They developed them in the course of struggle during their society's revolutionary ruptures. In 1917 they moved earlier and further than the Bolsheviks. In 1918, 1919, and 1921 they formed opposition factions within the party. Every time they were defeated by the iron discipline of the Bolsheviks, and by the heritage of revolution that belonged solely to the Bolsheviks due to their expropriation of the revolutionary uprising. In 1921 Errico Malatesta wrote:

> However much we detest the democratic lie, which in the name of the 'people' oppresses the people in the interests of a class, we detest even more, if that is possible, the dictatorship, which, in the name of the 'proletariat' places all of the strength and the very lives of the workers in the hands of the creatures of a so-called communist party, who perpetuate their power and in the end reconstruct the capitalist system for their own advantage. 57

In 1968 Daniel Cohn Bendit wrote:

> The defeat of all the opposition groups inside the party -- the Left Wing Communists in 1920, the Centralist Communists

in 1919, and finally the Worker's Opposition in 1921, -- are
so many nails in the coffin of the Russian Proletariat ... As
far as we are concerned there is no break between the ideology of the Old Bolshevik Party and that of the new
bureaucracy. 58

Paul Cardan draws his conclusions from similar views:

We may therefore conclude that, contrary to established
mythology, it was not in 1927, nor in 1923, nor even in 1921,
that the game was played and lost, but much earlier, during
the period between 1918 and 1920. 59

As did Emma Goldman:

It is now clear why the Russian Revolution, as conducted by
the Communist Party was a failure. The political power of
the party, organized and centralized in the State, sought to
maintain itself by all means at hand. The central authorities
attempted to force the activities of the people into forms
corresponding with the purposes of the Party. The sole aim
of the latter was to strengthen the state and monopolize all
economical, political, and social activities -- even all
cultural manifestations. The revolution had an entirely different object, and in its very character was the negation
of authority and centralization. It strove to open ever-larger
fields for proletarian expression and to multiply the phases
of individual and collective effort. The aims and tendencies
of the Revolution were diametrically opposed to those of the
ruling political party. 60

One might agree with Cardan and Goldman's assessment; or think
that if the Bolsheviks had taken any other course, even more chaotic events
would have resulted. But in any case, even given the fact that the revolution's
degeneration in one form or another might have been inevitable, the *actual
form the degeneration took, bureaucratic and repressive, was a result of
Bolshevik policy.* If there was ever a coincidence between Bolshevik
programs and the needs of the Russian people it was due to chance and the

influence of the people themselves, and not to the scientific methods of the leadership. They didn't choose tactics in response to the pressures of grotesque conditions; they got away with using the tactics they inevitably picked because of the grotesqueness of conditions. Their tactics were the distillation of their theoretic, strategic analysis. Alternatives weren't carefully analyzed -- alternatives were completely beyond Bolshevik thought, they called for more subtle awarenesses than Bolshevik ideology allowed. The Leninists didn't warn anyone that their tactics had weaknesses, they themselves didn't understand the weaknesses, they forced their tactics upon everyone as the one right road to socialism.

In 1899 Malatesta wrote the following prophetic words:

> If some people will have assumed the right to violate any-body's freedom on the pretext of preparing the triumph of freedom, they will always find the people are not sufficiently mature, that the dangers of reaction are ever present, that the education of the people has not yet been completed. And with these excuses they will seek to perpetuate their own power -- which could begin as the strength of a people up in arms, but which if not controlled by a profound feeling for the freedom of all, would soon become a real government no different from the governments of today. 61

Emma Goldman later described the reality in retrospect:

> It is at once the great failure and the great tragedy of the Russian Revolution that it attempted (in the leadership of the ruling political party) to change only institutions and conditions, while ignoring entirely the human and social values involved in the Revolution. Worse yet, in its mad passion for power, the Communist State even sought to strengthen and deepen the very ideas and conceptions which the Revolution had come to destroy. It supported and encouraged all the worst anti-social qualities and systematically destroyed the already awakened conception of the new revolutionary values. The sense of justice and equality, the love of liberty and human brotherhood -- those

fundamentals of the real regeneration of society -- the
Communist State suppressed to the point of extermination.
Man's instinctive sense of equity was branded as weak
sentimentality; human dignity and liberty became a
bourgeois superstition; the sanctity of life, which is the very
essence of social reconstruction, was condemned as
unrevolutionary, almost counter-revolutionary. This fear-
ful perversion of fundamental values bore within itself the
seed of destruction. With the conception that revolution
was only a means of securing political power, it was
inevitable that all revolutionary values should be subor-
dinated to the needs of the Socialist State; indeed, exploited
to further the security of the newly acquired governmental
power. "Reasons of State," masked as the interests of the
Revolution and of the People, became the sole criterion of
action, even of feeling. 62

*The Bolsheviks created a transfer of power but not an all-sided rev-
olution.* They did not comprehend their own policies' dynamics and they
gave birth to a state that they themselves would undoubtedly now rebel
against were they to come back again as workers and not as commissars.
The Bolsheviks, and especially Lenin and Trotsky, bent the realities to suit
their conception; they bent the revolution to fit their needs, rather than
those of the masses.The important example is basically a lesson in what is
not to be done. Further, we can certainly say that though Bolshevik
practice might not be the only approach consistent with Classical Marxist
Leninist ideology, it is one of the approaches consistent with it and
therefore Classical Marxist Leninist ideology must at least have very little
within it to offset the kinds of errors the Bolsheviks made or the
'parallel' kinds of errors we might make in our more modern circumstances. It's thus important to find the roots of Bolshevik weaknesses
in Leninist strategy and in Classical Marxism, first to shatter the myths of
the invincibility of the old ideology and second because good criticisms of
it can help in efforts to revise or even to build a significantly new ideology.

FOOTNOTES

1. Voline, *The Unknown Revolution,* Free Life Editions, New York. 190.
2. Bakunin in *Bakunin*, edited by Maximov, Collier MacMillan Limited, London.
3. Cardan in the Solidarity pamphlet, "From Bolshevism to the Bureaucracy" -- see also his other Solidarity pamphlets.
4. Gajo Petrovic, *Marx in the Mid Twentieth Century*, Doubleday Anchor Book, Garden City, New York.
5. Trotsky quoted in *Obsolete Communism: A Left Wing Alternative,* McGraw Hill Book Company, New York. 202.
6. ibid. 203.
7. ibid. 205.
8. ibid. 206.
9. Emma Goldman, *Red Emma Speaks,* Vintage Books, New York. 344.
10. Rosenberg, *A History of Bolshevism,* Doubleday and Company, New York. 126.
11. Luxemburg, "The Organization of the Social Democratic Party in Russia."
12. Lenin as quoted in Maurice Brinton's *The Bolsheviks and Workers' Control,* Solidarity. 22.
13. E.H. Carr as quoted in Brinton, op. cit. 22.
14. ibid. 18.
15. Maurice Brinton, op. cit. 14.
16. Emma Goldman, op. cit. 338-339.
17. Voline in Cohn Bendit, op. cit. 218-219
18. Brinton, op. cit. 48.
19. E.H. Carr quoted in Brinton, op. cit. 49.
20. Brinton, op. cit. 54-55.
21. Trotsky in Cohn Bendit, op. cit. 230.
22. ibid. 231.
23. ibid. 231.
24. Lenin in Brinton, op. cit. 41.
25. ibid. 41.
26. Trotsky in Brinton, op. cit. 66.
27. Cardan, op. cit.
28. In Brinton, op. cit. 38.
29. Lenin in Cohn Bendit, op. cit.

30. Quoted in Brinton, op. cit. 39.

31. Trotsky quoted in Brinton, op. cit. 232.

32. Trotsky in Maurice Brinton, op. cit. 64.

33. Lenin in Cohn Bendit, op. cit. 232-233.

34. Lenin in Maurice Brinton, op. cit. 71.

35. See Brinton and Emma Goldman, op. cit.

36. Malatesta quoted in *Quotations From Anarchists,* edited by Paul Berman, Praeger Paperbacks.

37. From *Obsolete Communism*, op. cit. 220-222.

38. Cohn Bendit, *Obsolete Communism,* op. cit. 224.

39. ibid. 223-224.

40. Paul Avrich, *Kronstadt 1921*, Princeton University Press. 14.

41. ibid. 29.

42. ibid. 73-74.

43. ibid. 75.

44. ibid. 162.

45. ibid. 166.

46. ibid. 126.

47. Cohn Bendit, op. cit. 236.

48. ibid. 238.

49. ibid. 239.

50. Avrich, op. cit. 226.

51. Lenin in Avrich, op. cit. 227.

52. Cohn Bendit, op. cit.

53. Alexander Berkman, *What is Communist Anarchism?*, Dover, New York, N.Y.

54. Trotsky, *Terrorism and Communism*, Ann Arbor Paperbacks.

55. Rocker, *Anarcho-Syndicalism*, London.

56. Kropotkin in *Quotations From The Anarchists,* op. cit.

57. Malatesta in *Malatesta: His Life and Ideas* by Vernon Richards, London.

58. Cohn Bendit, op. cit. 243.

59. Cardan, op. cit.

60. Emma Goldman, op. cit. 344.

61. Malatesta, op. cit.

62. Emma Goldman, op. cit. 354.

CHAPTER SIX

CRITIQUE OF LENINIST STRATEGY

... who would exercise the dictatorship of the proletariat? 1
Charles Peguy

The idea of soviets, that is to say, of councils of workers and peasants, conceived first at the time of the revolutionary attempt in 1905, and immediately realized by the revolution of February, 1917, as soon as Czarism was overthrown, -- the idea of such councils controlling the economic and political life of the country is a great idea. All the more so since it necessarily follows that these councils should be composed of all who take a real part in the production of national wealth by their own efforts. 2
Peter Kropotkin

Classical Marxism Leninism is a revolutionary ideology -- it provides its practioners with a framework for thought, a long-term goal, a set of strategic imperatives, and a number of tactical rules. A Marxist Leninist is ostensibly fully armed to participate in revolutionary struggle.

Classical Marxist Leninists first determine the mode of production, then the forces and relations of production and their interrelations, then the class character of on-going social conflicts, and then what form the primary and subsidiary contradictions are taking and how they are affecting one another. The Classical Marxist Leninists determine which forces are propelling class struggle and which are hindering it. And with all this done they establish goals and strategies for reaching them. They form a party, institute discipline, and begin establishing leadership over all other already existent revolutionary groups.

To achieve these ends Classical Marxists Leninists choose tactics by studying their potential effects on all class alignments -- they organize successful tactics into programs, and they carry out programs in the name of the oppressed classes, until such time as they achieve victory over the old ruling classes.

But none of this occurs in a historical vacuum. All Classical Marxist Leninists are well versed in the views of their forebears -- each does not redevelop Classical Marxist dogma from its roots. Organizatonal tactical rules are not reviewed, they are *accepted and employed. One doesn't look to see if there is a well-defined mode of production -- one looks to see what* the *necessarily existing* mode of production is. One doesn't look to see if classes are struggling and if that struggle is of central importance, one looks to uncover the characteristics of *the* centrally important class struggle. One doesn't just look for potential forces to be employed in the revolution, one looks at the political economy and at interrelations of classes to find *the* forces that can ultimately be employed by the working classes in their revolution. Finally, one doesn't look to see · what the superstructure is and how strongly it affects things, one looks to see the composition of the *already well understood and well defined* superstructure, and attempts to understand how exactly it is carrying out its tasks.

If it is true, as Cardan says, that "in the last analysis, the ideas that inspire men are as much an objective factor in history as the material environment in which they develop and as the social reality which they seek to transform," 3 then it is crucial to come to a full understanding of all the weaknesses of the Classical Marxist Leninist ideology. We have already discovered gross inadequacies in Bolshevik practice. These directly intimate weaknesses at the strategic level and in this chapter we explore those in somewhat more detail.

Lenin thought that it was simple and clear that classes should be led by parties and parties by individuals. His overall perspective emphasizes the efficient use of ignorant class forces, and at the same time it excludes from consideration any of the dynamics of his party's organization. As he put it:

> To a Russian Bolshevik, who is acquainted with the mechanism and who for twenty five years has watched it growing out of small, illegal, underground circles, all talk about 'from above' or 'from below', about the dictatorship of the leaders and the dictatorship of the masses etc. cannot but appear to be ridiculous and childish nonsense, something like discussing whether the right leg or the left leg is more useful to a man. 4

We agree with Lenin that the Bolshevik will be incredulous when confronted with our criticisms -- so incredulous that, like Lenin, he probably wouldn't even bother to respond. In fact we even accept Lenin's explanation for the whole phenomenon. We see, as Lenin seems to see, that Bolshevik thought is made circumspect by Bolshevik experience. We see that, as Sartre puts it, action and thought are not to be separated from organization since one always thinks in terms of the structures he or she finds him or herself in and acts according to the organizations to which he she belongs. 5 We just say these things differently than Sartre or Lenin.

We say an individual works in the context of his or her consciousness which in turn derives in reasonable part from the person's surroundings and work groups. It is impossible for a person to see beyond the bounds of his or her own consciousness. A person cannot even be fully aware of possibilities or criticisms generated outside his or her domain. Lenin didn't put much credence into criticisms about his tactical thoughts because he was unable to accept or understand them -- he usually didn't think them deserving of anything more than a flippant reply. Later we will come to understand how the narrowness of his theory led to this kind of sectarian stance on these matters.

If the proletariat as a group controlled economic life and was a majority, if it became increasingly more and more oppressed, and if the group considered its oppression unjust, its members would probably not need any substantial political consciousness to initiate some kind of revolution. But none of this is the modern-day case: workers do not control the society, they do not think of themselves as a powerful, deserving majority, and they are not constantly being forced into what they perceive to be worse and worse conditions of life. They are not "immiserated," and so long as they are lacking in political consciousness they will tend to accept their hardships as necessary concomitants of the rewards their society also produces. *Modern workers require high levels of political awareness to move from reactionary political ideologies to revolutionary ones.* They must overcome racist, sexist, authoritarian, and liberal obstacles, see beyond fascist alternatives, and overcome all kinds of political inhibitions. Revolutionary organizations can't solely be premised on the fact that workers or anybody else will move solely because starvation compels them to -- instead it must foster conditions of motion in the workers' environment and in his and her consciousnesses. As we will see, modern Leninists don't ponder these things deeply enough before choosing their organizational forms.

Two quotes from Rosa Luxemburg set the stage for our discussion of

Leninist organization, and also help to remind us that not all Marxists
were oblivious to the dynamics we will soon discuss:

> But Socialist Democracy is not something that begins only
> in the promised land after the foundations of socialist
> economy are created, it does not come as some sort of
> Christmas present for the worthy people who, in the
> interim, have loyally supported a handful of socialist
> dictators. 6

> The ultra-centralism asked by Lenin is full of the sterile
> spirit of the overseer. It is not a positive and creative spirit.
> Lenin's concern is not so much to make the activity of the
> party more fruitful as to control the party -- to narrow the
> movement rather than develop it, to bind it rather than
> unify it. 7

Paradigmatically, parties are generally supposed to bring the
masses together around revolutionary political actions dictated by
Marxist Leninist analysis. They become hierarchical because of the
dynamics of democratic centralism. Their goal is efficiency, their means is
centralization, and their product is all too often primarily leftist *'law and
order'.*
Parties are not aimed at developing the political effectivenesses of
their members but *at directing the activities of their members.* Decision
making goes *unshared;* information and experience is *monopolized* by
those at the top.
Party leaders function according to their ideological views and try to
mold everyone else's in compliance. They see themselves as being at the
top due to their knowing more than anyone else, and so they feel responsible for enforcing their views upon everyone else. With time leaders asso-
ciate their own interests with the interests of the entire revolution -- this is
their way of rationalizing their position, influence, and power.
Efficiency couples with Classical Marxist dictates and creates blind
discipline. The party is initially well motivated. It considers itself a servant
of the people. But eventually, due to its own 'good' desires it begins sub-
merging the will of the people in its own plans and needs. The party
comes to see the revolution's future and its own future as inseparable -- the

party acts to strengthen its own scope in the belief that it is thereby broadening the strength of the base of the revolution. But as time passes the analysis is done more and more in terms of the party's welfare and less and less in terms of the revolution's though of course they are always described as inextricable.

The hierarchical party disciplines the revolution so that its patterns follow those of the party, and so that party people will be in the vanguard. One is reminded of the story of the old peasant in southern Russia, about 1923, who was standing with some other villagers watching a loud speaker being put up on the main street. A young party official said to the peasants, "Just think! With this, you'll be able to hear Lenin all the way from Moscow!" "Good!" replied the old peasant. "And will Lenin be able to hear us?"[8]

The leaders project their styles and views upon the party -- the party projects upon the whole revolution. The revolution is supposed to look like the Communist vision and not vice versa. In time and since the party is the revolution, those who disagree with it are counter to the revolution. They must be dealt with as enemies, or as Lenin put it in an address to a Party Congress in young revolutionary Russia: "The time has come to put an end to opposition, to put the lid on it; we have had enough opposition."[9]

The results are only too clear. If a Classical Leninist Party achieves power, the leaders' and Party's interest, *the maintenance of their own essentially absolute dominance, leads to dictatorial bureaucracy.* If a Party does not seize power, but only a position of influence within the old system, then again the leaders' and Party's interests are in defending the Party's role in society-as-it-is, and thus counter to the workers' interest in overthrowing the society-as-it-is. And even if the leaders are relatively incorruptible when in opposition, and thus capable of moving from electoral participation to militant opposition, they will nevertheless continue to enforce their own conceptions, *stifling creativity* and foreshadowing their even more dictatorial days to come. Whether in opposition as militants or reactionaries, or in power as dictators, the Classical Marxist Leninist Party and leader characteristics are essentially the same: hardening of the political arteries, theoretic myopia, and organizational sclerosis, all brought about by steadily worsening effects of the dreaded disease 'vested interesto-authoritosis', and certainly unhampered, if not furthered by continual feeding by Classical Marxist Leninist analysis.

Rosa Luxemburg has a decidedly more instructive approach to the same problems Lenin so counter-productively 'solved':

> Freedom only for the supporters of the government, only for
> the members of the party -- however numerous they may be
> -- is no freedom at all. Freedom is always and exclusively
> freedom for the one who thinks differently. Not because of
> any fanatical concept of justice but because all that is
> instructive, wholesome, and purifying in political freedom
> depends on this essential characteristic, and its effective-
> ness vanishes when freedom becomes a special privilege. 10

In short, revolution depends upon creation and creation upon
freedom -- *creation and "strictly imposed discipline" are antithetical.*
Further, in the modern context, even allegiance and hierarchical discipline
are antithetical.

The Leninist model is perhaps not so bad if one wants a transfer of
power in an environment of chaos, or if one wants merely to run a
bourgeois factory effectively. But for an all sided revolution or any kind of
broadly humanitarian endeavor it is terrible. As Cohn Bendit says ,
"Democracy degenerates into the ratification at the bottom of decisions
taken at the top." 11 And under such conditions the Marxist Leninist
ideology becomes eternally stagnant. It doesn't grow with passing time. It
forces itself upon its surroundings. It develops a *sectarian life of its own.* It
acts contrary to real interests of revolution. Initiative disappears, new
ideas are submerged and old ideas are repeated endlessly -- freedom dies in
the dictatorship of ideological leaders.

In talking of the two-way dynamic of disciplined centralization,
Rudolf Rocker's criticism is very like our own:

> Power operates only destructively, bent always on forcing
> every manifestation of life into the straitjacket of its laws.
> Its intellectual form of expression is dead dogma, its
> physical form brute force. And this unintelligence of its
> objectives sets its stamp on its supporters also and renders
> them stupid and brutal, even when they were originally
> endowed with the best of talents. One who is constantly
> striving to force everything into a mechanical order at last
> becomes a machine himself and loses all human feeling. 12

The preceding chapter's study of Bolshevik practice suggested still another of Leninism's weaknesses: it ignores hierarchical organizational long run tendencies towards bureaucracy and towards the undermining of revolutionary goals. But at least here the Leninist view is quite consistent. For if their Party is as effective as possible, then in their view any minor costs its practice creates can be dealt with easily enough after the productive mode is altered. Changing the mode is the central historical problem; all others need only be addressed in relation to it. Those that persist or that must even be exacerbated during struggle can be handled easily enough when power is attained. But there are other perspectives on this same issue as, for instance, Murray Bookchin's:

> This remarkable susceptibility of the left to authoritarianism and hierarchical impulses reveals the profound roots of the radical movement in the very society it professes to overthrow. In this respect nearly every revolutionary organization is a potential force for counter-revolution. Only if the revolutionary organization is so 'structured' that its forms reflect the direct, decentralized forms of freedom initiated by the revolution, only if the revolutionary organization fosters in the revolutionist the life-styles and personality of freedom, can this potential for counter-revolution be diminished. Only then is it possible for the revolutionary movement to disappear into its new, directly democratic, social forms, like surgical thread into a healing wound. 13

And of course this describes a process almost exactly opposite to the one which characterized Bolshevik relations to Russia's freely created soviets. For rather than the Party becoming one with the soviets, *the soviets were altered and made to become 'one' with the Party.* They dissolved into the Party's form rather than vice versa. The potential for a real alteration of all productive relations as well as of ownership relations disappeared. The interests of the leadership, molded by their 'domination roles' and their narrow ideology, overwhelmed the interests of the people and even the workers.

The essence of the criticism is that *capitalist societies inculcate in their citizenry oppressed and oppressing modes of behavior which are*

aggravated rather than overcome by hierarchical forms -- so that such
forms rather than being temporary measures that overcome oppressions,
virtually inevitably become ends in themselves which in fact continually
recreate the dynamics they were supposedly aimed at conquering. The
ability to understand and relate to such analysis is an obviously
important success criterion for any political consciousness to be used in a
capitalist society. The fact that Classical Marxism Leninism can't relate to
the analysis is rather critically important. The reasons are twofold: first,
relating to this analysis doesn't correspond well with Classical Marxist
Leninist needs to lead and have loyal followers, and second, the thinking
involved is somewhat outside the Classical Marxist theoretical methodology. There is thus a kind of 'unhappy' coincidence between a lack in
theory and a vested interest in behavioral arrogance and elitist
self-conceptions, and it is just the kind of coincidence that we know often
leads to sectarian narrownesses that prevent one's seeing one's own
shortcomings.

Lenin thought that principled rejection of compromise was stupid. As
he said, "There are compromises and compromises. One must be able to
analyze the situations and the concrete conditions of each compromise, or
of each variety of compromise." A leader must "be able to attack
ruthless compromises and sellouts, while at the same time using those that
help the cause." 14

But the problem was and always is how one does actually determine
which compromises are good and which are bad. One of our main
criticisms of Classical Marxism Leninism is that it is not well suited to this
type of critical determination.

For example: Lenin defended participation in reactionary parliaments against those who said that it was the place where the bourgeoisie
was always most successful in deceiving workers. He said simply, that the
Party should overcome its own weaknesses in functioning in Parliament,
and then participate.

It is hard to tell whether he truly understood the reasonableness of the
fears of the Parliamentary critics but it's not too important to speculate
about. The real problem was that his analysis of the parliamentary tactics
ignored its possible internal effects on the cadre who would become
'statesmen' and on the movement of which they would still constitute a
part. Lenin's major question was, will there be a sell out or not?

He didn't have the more reasonable tack of trying to ascertain both the benefits and costs at all levels. For example: will acting in Parliament hinder or foster left growth? Will it have good or bad psychological effects upon the people who do it and the party which supports them? Will the new ways of acting affect our old ways of acting, feeling, and thinking, favorably or otherwise? It seems that our analysis of the concerns of Leninist strategy and of practice of the Bolsheviks gives us ample evidence that these type questions were never considered, precisely because the *Classical Marxist Leninists never really concern themselves with understanding the internal dynamics of their own movements.* We'll later try to find roots for this in the methodology of Classical Marxist theory.

It seems reasonable to surmise, even at this point, that Classical Marxist Leninist tactical weaknesses have their roots in theoretic narrownesses or errors. Lacks of strategic insight into the dynamics of elitism, authority, and bureaucracy suggest that we should later examine Classical Marxist theory for flaws which would contribute in these directions. This is our whole presentation's logic. We move from describing Classical Marxism and Leninism to viewing practice and then to critiquing first strategy and then finally theory. We do it in a loose flow, not causal so much as suggestive, and we do it in our order because our general understanding of the interrelations of theory, strategy, and practice suggest that such an approach is the best way for generating new insights and for correcting, perhaps working out old ones.

In this light consider Lenin's view of the need for "efficiency and discipline" in all things and especially in the economy. In *One Step Back: Two Steps Forward* Lenin glorifies the effects of factory life on accustoming "the proletariat to discipline and organization." Rosa Luxemburg responded quite forcefully:

> The discipline which Lenin has in mind is driven home to the proletariat not only in the factory, but in the barracks, and by all sorts of bureaucracies, in short by the whole power machine of the centralized bourgeois state... It is an abuse of words to apply the same term 'discipline' to such unrelated concepts as the mindless reflex motions of a body with a thousand hands and a thousand legs, and the spontaneous coordination of the conscious political acts of a group of men. What can the well ordered docility of the former have in common with the aspirations of a class struggling for its emancipation. 15

Lenin felt that his answer concerning efficiency was enough -- if he ever even considered Luxemburg's question at all. Why else would he have maintained that it was fine to use capitalist forms to build a socialist state? His words are instructive enough as to his mentality and they at least suggest something about the shallowness of his theoretical tools:

> A single huge state bank, with branches in every rural district and in every factory -- that will already be nine-tenths of a socialist apparatus. 16

> We must raise the question of piece-work and apply and test it in practice... we must raise the question of applying much of what is scientific in the Taylor system... 17

> Socialism is nothing but state capitalist monopoly made to benefit the whole people. 18

Lenin didn't make such forceful statements simply because he was compelled by circumstance -- one can be compelled to use tactics but not to extol them and push them on others as if they were universally correct dogma. And if such views were only unworshiped responses to situations of the moment they would not have lived on as part of the overall approach of virtually all Classical Marxist Leninist groups. No, we should expect a reasonable likelihood that the inadequacies of Classical Leninist strategy are endemic to the processes of its creation by real people in real circumstances, struggling for power using Classical Marxist theory as a guide. Classical Marxist theory in the first place simply doesn't have sufficient understanding of the effects of shop level productive relations as a whole, and in the second hides that ignorance from its practitioners.

> The Bolshevik leaders saw capitalist organization of production as something, which, in itself was socially neutral. It could be used indifferently for bad purposes (as when the bourgeoisie used it for the aim of private accumulation) or good ones (as when the 'workers state' used it for the 'benefit of the many') .... What was wrong with capitalist methods of production in Lenin's eyes, was that it has in the past served the bourgeoisie. They were now

going to be used by the workers' state and would thereby become 'one of the conditions of socialism'. It all depended on who held state power. 19

At one stage Lenin pointed out that Communism was like a contagion -- it sprang from every side of life and if one channel of the invasion was blocked up another side would open. This was quite true, but what Lenin and the Leninists didn't perceive was that capitalism and authoritarianism were also contagious -- even though one aspect of one or the other might be overcome, the other aspects could go on fighting so strongly that they could succeed in resuscitating the old disease and holding off the communist contagion for ages and ages.

Given Leninism's attitudes about organizational forms, the importance and unimportance of various economic considerations, and tactics in general, we might well be tempted to suggest that it was Lenin, and not the workers, *who was never able to rise above a trade union consciousness.* He was the one who always thought in terms of bourgeois motivations and bourgeois forms of organization, precisely because and not in spite of the fact that he was the most creative and confident of all the Classical Marxists. For as we saw in our earlier chapter on Classical Marxist theory the Classical Marxist theory of knowledge and the Classical Marxist theory of classes lead together quite naturally to the Leninist perspective on capabilities of workers and to the Leninist belief in the supreme value of 'efficiency' in all things.

A quotation from Lenin and one from a Solidarity pamphlet contrast interestingly and outline a part of our overall theses:
In *State and Revolution* Lenin said:

We want the socialist revolution with human nature as it is now, with human nature that cannot dispense with subordination, control, and managers. 20

In the Solidarity pamphlet on the Bolsheviks and workers' control we find the explanatory postulation:

The concept that society must necessarily be divided into leaders and led, the notion that there are some born to rule while others cannot really develop beyond a certain stage

have from time immemorial been the tacit assumptions of
every ruling class in history. 21

Our assertion is not so much that Lenin wouldn't ideally agree with the
second statement as that he ignored its implications, and fell victim to the
logic of that deficiency.

Classical Marxism Leninism roughly says: 1-formulate all plans
toward furthering class struggle, 2-do all strategic thinking with regard for
the contradictions propelling oppressed classes toward revolt, and 3-do all
analysis in the context bounded by the Classical theory of Marxism and
the concrete realities of concrete experiences.

Practitioners overlook or minimize forces lying outside the class
categories of Marxism. They don't fully understand and are not able to
cope with the changing import of old contradictions. They don't
understand how and why old modes of class struggle are assimilated into
the system, especially when such understanding might threaten some of
their more fervently held beliefs. They don't relate well to issues of
property and power. They don't understand the full gamut of forces that
add to worker restlessness and so they have little understanding of how
their tactical choices affect those forces. They don't understand, and have
no real tools for even trying to understand the interrelations between
consciousness, revolutionary practice, and societally given or adapting
material or cultural conditions. They don't understand the full importance of racial or sexual oppressions nor how they affect and are affected
by other even more capitalist dynamics. Perhaps most damning from
their own perspective, they don't even understand the effects of productive
relations and most particularly of firm level productive relations on
workers and on society's overall dynamics as well. They aren't prepared to
address the full gamut of worker's needs, nor even the material needs most
effectively; and they are not even sufficiently aware of all the other
important groups of people whose needs they should also address. They
don't seem to realize the importance of a fully outlined goal, or of the many
aspects of life such an outline must relate to, and as a result they can't
really address people who have no necessity to act but rather only potential
desires to do so. But to really fully understand these assertions *in practical
terms* one must do a broader analysis of the Bolsheviks than ours, and even
more importantly an equally broad analysis of present day Classical
Marxist Leninist groups in the U.S. and Europe. Not having space or time

for such tasks here we will move on to instead immediately consider Classical Marxist theory, -- but from the specific orientation of understanding the theoretical roots of Classical Leninism's and Bolshevism's weaknesses. Thus this chapter's brevity is not for lack of more things to say but in anticipation of saying at least some of them still more persuasively in the next two chapters.

FOOTNOTES

1. Peguy quoted in Preface to Rosenberg, *A History of Bolshevism,* Doubleday.
2. Peter Kropotkin, *Kropotkin's Revolutionary Pamphlets,* Dover Publications, New York. 254.
3. Cardan in "From Bolshevism to the Bureaucracy," Solidarity, London.
4. Lenin, *Collected Works,* International Publishers, New York.
5. Sartre, *Search for a Method,*-------
6. Luxemburg in Cohn Bendit, *Obsolete Communism: A Left Wing Alternative,* McGraw Hill. 215.
7. ibid. 216.
8. There are countless quotes and examples in Brinton's book which demonstrate these dynamics.
9. Lenin in Paul Avrich, *Kronstadt 1921,* Princeton University Press. 228.
10. Luxemburg, op. cit.
11. Cohn Bendit, op. cit. 249.
12. Rocker in *Anarcho-Syndicalism,* London.
13. Bookchin in "Listen Marxist," in *Post Scarcity Anarchism,* Ramparts Press.
14. Lenin in *Left Wing Communism: An Infantile Disorder,* International Publishers, New York, N.Y.
15. Luxumberg in Cohn Bendit, op. cit. 215-216.
16. Lenin in Brinton, *The Bolsheviks and Workers' Control,* Solidarity. 12.
17. ibid. 40.
18. ibid.
19. Brinton, op. cit.
20. Lenin in *State and Revolution,* International Publishers, New York, N.Y. 22.
21. Brinton, op. cit. xii-xiii.

CHAPTER SEVEN

CRITIQUE OF CLASSICAL MARXIST THEORY

How many care to seek only for precedents? How many fiery innovators are mere copycats of bygone revolutionaries? 1
Peter Kropotkin

I cleave to no system, I am a true seeker. 2
Mikhail Bakunin

Classical Marxism is built upon the theory of dialectics, the theory of knowledge, the Classical Marxist description of human nature, the theory of classes, and the Classical Historical Materialist theory of history. It is for use by revolutionaries who are attempting to understand and change the world. Based upon the last two chapters' criticisms and upon our own experiences with more recent Classical Marxist Leninist practice, there are a number of weaknesses we perceive whose roots we hope to now uncover:

1-Classical Marxism doesn't generate an organic enough understanding of *racism, sexism, or even classism.* These oppressive forms do not get a high enough analytic priority. At motivation and human interaction levels they are simply not well enough understood. As a result Classical Marxism doesn't help practitioners sufficiently with related strategic problems. It doesn't adequately predict or even explain sex, race, or even class related behavioral events.

2-Classical Marxism's level of abstraction is too high to deal well with a whole variety of important historical and day to day situations. While its largely implied methodology is well suited to studying historical contours, it is not so well suited

146

to studying the dynamics of separate institutions, groups of people, or even of revolutionary tactical plans or revolutionary acts themselves. Classical Marxism relegates too much that is critical to the category 'accident of history' or to the non-theoretically supported common sense of its users. While giving brilliant broad outline understandings of macro trends *it leaves out or even misleads about too much that is relevant to day to day local practice.* It is not applicable in constructive enough ways to small scale but still critically important situations. Its methods are better suited to understanding decades than days; and when applied to the latter lead to error or confusion just as often as to success.

3-In line with point two, Classical Marxism says very little about *revolutionary organizational dynamics, bureaucracy, violence, and the adverse effects of severe discipline.* It says very little about how revolutionary efforts affect their own initiators. Indeed it says very little about how any *relations of production, be they those of the revolutionary party or those of the bourgeois factory, affect 'workers' functioning within them.* Further, in paying little attention to the effects of relations of production on producers, Classical Marxism also says very little about contradictions between varying relations of production and even within a given set of relations in a given mode. It focuses instead almost entirely on the more economic contradictions between growing forces and fettering relations.

4-In fact, though Classical Marxism says people of any one class will either share a consciousness or gravitate towards sharing one, it says little about precisely how such processes occur, and even less about how they might be propelled or why they are frequently hindered. In what it does say it sticks pretty much to issues of material well being, minimizing the obviously also important issues of authority, race, sex, and even age. With reference to the

Proletariat, for example, Classical Marxism says very little about how their consciousnesses change on the road to socialist awareness, or when they reach it, and it doesn't go very far in explaining the *actual tendencies in concrete initial proletarian consciousnesses that foster or that hinder revolutionary possibilities.*

5-Classical Marxism focuses so much on classes that it tends to forget individuals, both as components of classes and other groups, and as separate people unto themselves. For Classical Marxists the statistically expected (but often not forthcoming) average over the whole large group becomes the reality, while the real underlying basis, the social individual person both alone and in concert with other individuals, somehow largely disappears. Statistical expectations become dogma and the individual realities that could set them right become lost to sight. The focus of attention never swerves from the mass; it becomes dehumanizingly large, abstract, and often even alienated from real people's real personal needs and desires.

6-Thus Classical Marxism is generally narrow in its under-standings of the forces lying behind class struggles; it says little about the many forces entering into the formation of class consciousness and class interests. *It does not deal at all adequately with the dynamics between relations of production and the consciousnesses of producers.* It doesn't really explain how or why ruling class ideologies are at least in part adopted and defended by non-rulers, it doesn't even really explain how they are adopted by rulers. It doesn't explain how or why they are so deeply rooted, and it doesn't explain why workers often become oppressors and often even support their own enemies. *It gives a solid explanation of why workers should revolt but it doesn't say why, in concrete situations, they will or they won't.* In general Classical Marxism simply doesn't *translate awarenesses at the material level to awarenesses at the consciousness and behavioral levels* well enough for proficient strategizing.

7-Classical Marxism doesn't adequately explain third world revolution, or even the history of Russia since 1905.

8-Classical Marxism gives an inadequate view of the dynamics of advanced capitalist societies. It is weighted too heavily to the economic, not comprehensive enough, and not convincing enough. It does not predict well enough. It does not understand the actual variety of day-to-day life or even of the more subtle aspects of long term living. *It does not provide guidance for local work or tools well suited to fully analyzing a local situation's dynamics. It does not allow for an understanding of people's thoughts and emotions and so it does not sufficiently help one evaluate potential effects of alternative tactical approaches.* It does not understand the factory well enough in its day-to-day functioning, and hardly understands many of society's other institutions and dynamics at all -- thus the family, the athletic institutions, the media, the state, and so on.

9-And finally, when used by real normal active people, *Classical Marxism becomes dogmatic, exclusionary, and self-defeatingly blinding.* It has nothing within itself to offset modern day tendencies towards polarizing and over-abstracting, and dogmatizing -- and indeed we might even expect to find some aspects within it that foster these tendencies. Thus Classical Marxism in *action* suffers from all the theory's problems and then some, due to harmful dynamics between practitioner and theory.

Of course we haven't yet given any evidence that these weaknesses really are endemic to Classical Marxist theory. However, on the basis of our study of Bolshevik practice and Classical Leninist strategy we've posited 2,3,4,5,7, and 9 above. And on the basis of our own experiences with modern Classical Marxist Leninists we've posited 1,6, and 8. Keeping all these areas of potential weakness in mind as a guide, we will now look at the historical context of Classical Marxism, its basic tenets, and its useability in search of the roots of whatever weaknesses it does in fact turn out to have.

Classical Marxism developed in the context of scarcity, the need to overcome metaphysics, the need to have a revolutionary transfer of power, and the need to counter bourgeois liberalism. The backward political, psychological, and technical awarenesses of its times are responsible for many of its weaknesses. For example, as we already saw in the 'presentation' chapter, the more varied Marxist understandings of human behavior, need, and thought never made it into the pragmatically oriented Classical theory precisely because there were no psychological awarenesses sufficient to give them any practical concrete implications for strategy or even for analysis.

Marx was thus highly aware of all kinds of human needs while Classical Marxism as an ideology of practical revolution is not. For in practice as opposed to rhetoric, it recognizes only material needs backed up by scarce conditions, competition, or forceful exploitation. It almost completely ignores human potentialities related to fulfillments more than to survival, precisely because it contains no meaningful ways to incorporate the former, no ways to understand how they affect behavior and consciousness, and thus no ways to understand how they affect revolutionary potentials. These weaknesses, rooted in some sense in the scientific lacks of Marx's age, have still to this time been hardly at all rectified, at least insofar as practical application of theory is concerned, and will thus certainly demand considerable amounts of our attention.

Similarly Marx understood the inevitability of imperialism but he did not fully understand, nor could he have, *the depths of capitalism's abilities to reorganize itself in the face of its own weaknesses.* He couldn't foresee the ways contradictions could alter over time, nor the ways in which they could be continually reresolved through *displacement* into new spheres with new defining characteristics. Working in a time of relative scarcity when it seemed quite clear that the driving motivations for revolution would be survival needs, Marx laid his main emphasis on the revolutionary potentials of the *continually more and more impoverished* working classes. He did not and could not fully foresee the effects of economic growth on diminishing the previous overriding importance of material needs, while increasing the influence of *power, sexual, racial, community, identity, ecological,* and other such 'higher' needs. In Marx's context there was no obvious impetus to fully understand the inner dynamics of racism or sexism (at least none for a white male to do so); there were no on-going forces pushing him to such understanding or to an understanding of the revolutionary potentials of women or minorities. Classical Marxism reflected and still reflects these biases.

Further there was no obvious impetus for Marx or Engels to carefully analyze their own motivations -- they were right and that was that. The times did not fully recognize the absolute corruptibility of all people's thoughts, and so the times did not make Marx adequately self-critically cautious. Moreover, the times did nothing to suggest that the theory itself should have self-critically cautious dynamics of its own.

Since Marx opposed the decentralization of his time, since he felt that scarcity was the main factor of revolutionary motivations, and since he opposed the power of the bourgeoisie, he constantly emphasized the need for centralization and discipline among workers. He didn't foresee that motion in exactly *the opposite direction* would eventually be far more important. He developed a theory that revolved around the working class potentials of his own time (or at least his perceptions of those potentials); he ignored the need to analyze the intellectual dynamics of revolutionaries themselves -- people who in a manner of speaking lived outside of class constraints. He didn't understand, or at least could in no way pragmatically deal with needs for theories of *'micro'* rather than just aggregate motivations. His theory, at least as it was taken by the Classicists, was thus understandably narrow. It took off from a desire to explain only what was necessary for a revolutionary *transfer* of power. It didn't address needs to overcome all *authoritarianism*, and it didn't address itself very deeply or clearly to the nature of the society that revolution was going to create. While talking about power at the top it didn't talk enough about power throughout societies and especially in their productive and other institutional relations. It didn't talk enough about revolutionaries' given weaknesses resulting from their various backgrounds and it didn't talk sufficiently or convincingly enough about a newly revolutionized society's potential strengths.

Classical Marxism understandably but incorrectly thinks that revolution is motivated by material needs and consciousness of material oppression alone -- not by other needs and by political consciousnesses of new alternatives as well -- and so it is quite content in leaving descriptions of future social forms to the future.

In the seventies and perhaps for a long time past this has been a serious error. People are not suffering so much that they are motivated to move from pain alone (have they ever been?) or even from pain and an awareness of that pain's unjustness. They want to know precisely what radicals are suggesting and precisely *how new programs will affect their lives*. They will not be motivated to risk by need alone, but only by combinations of need and desire both resting on deep political insights about present conditions and about future possibilities. Modern citizens won't trade their present positions for new ones that are substantially the same (or unknown) save for the costs of transition. The whole context in which Marx thought about revolution is very different from our own. The analysis of revolution from *feudal class society to bourgeois class society* in times of scarcity is certainly not a good jumping off point for developing a theory which can help modern activists understand their present realities fully, engage in revolutionary activities based on their own needs and expectations, and aimed at meeting all and not just a few of those needs and expectations.

But what is most striking and what we must come to understand most clearly is how the dictates of Marx's historical context manifested themselves in the roots of his theory and thus pervaded its later interpretations; and how they manage to *persist* in those interpretations (for use) throughout the years rather than being altered as new insights grew. This means we must turn to Classical Marxism's dialectics, theory of people and knowledge, and theory of history, in search of the manifestations already suggested, as well as of possible explanations for why such weaknesses were never rooted out. (We should be very clear here lest the reader rebel in justified anger. We are not implying that Marx's original efforts had all the weaknesses we attribute to Classical Marxism, but rather, as we have already said often before, that it had many wider, better insights, which were left behind by those who were looking only for a core theory with immediate use value, and that even Marx's own practical suggestions were tinged by his inability to translate implications from many of his more important, more flexible awarenesses. Further, when we say 'never rooted out', we mean out of the body of thought that still exists called Classical Marxism Leninism. We are perfectly aware that many scholars, and a few activists have gone beyond such weaknesses in their own more flexible and better interpretations of Marx's work -- and that those people who are trying to create a new consciousness for the seventies are frequently Marxists who have gone well beyond the kind of weaknesses this book finds in Classical Marxism, and who indeed share the bulk of our criticisms of it and are even implicitly employing such a set of criticisms in their present efforts.)

THE CLASSICAL MARXIST THEORY OF DIALECTICS

As we've seen, the Classical theory of dialectics is essentially implicit. It is confined to understanding historical motion; it looks solely at contradictions insofar as their resolutions intimate or in fact demand the *dissolutions* of their constraining historical systems. Our criticism is directed not so much at any outright error in this approach, as at its narrow inadequacy and at its tendency to mislead further analysis.

The method focuses practitioners on broad aspects of history's propensities towards major change and on epochally critical struggles enmeshed within those propensities. It overthrows the 'progressivisms' and 'metaphysicalisms' that continually thwart revolutionary analyses but there is considerable 'side cost.'

The practitioner, insofar as he or she uses the methodology, focuses on broad tendencies to historical change. He or she looks for contradictions that throw up the conditions of dissolution of whole societies. He or she looks for imminent change. The methodology orients his or her attention and strategic thought away from considerations of smaller scale relations, away from considerations of changes that are not dissolving of past totalities, and away from considerations of tendencies toward prolonged continuities.

The dialectician, as Classical Dialectician, indeed focuses admirably on historical revolution but at a great cost. Attention swerves from and methodology is insufficient for *other issues of smaller scale changes and tendencies towards absences of change.* Thus the Classical dialectician hardly ever moves to analyze questions of party change or party tendencies not to change, questions of class changes or class tendencies not to change, and so on. The question "Why will one society eventually transform its nature?" is at least seemingly comprehensively asked and analyzed. The question "Why doesn't it happen more quickly?" or "Why hasn't it happened at all in near the proportions we expect?" are not so well asked, discussed, or answered. And similarly, the posing and answering of questions about day-to-day tendencies toward change or stability at local levels, in workers, in party members, and so on are also not so well asked or dealt with -- and in any case to the extent that they are, the methodology used lies outside the Classical theory itself.

Thus the classical dialectical method is weak due to narrow applicability and one sided (change as opposed to stability) orientation. We might now suggest, in anticipation of the rest of our analysis, that those biases will show up in varying forms throughout the theory, and thus help explain many of the weaknesses outlined, one to eight, above. However, consider its theory of human nature. For certainly it is reasonable to guess that some of its narrowness in tactical analysis and in understanding racism, sexism, authoritarianism, and its so-called accidents of history, likely stem from basic weaknesses in its understandings of human nature.

But here again we should include our oft repeated proviso: we will not critique the most general Marxist understandings of people and their potentials. Rather, we will examine that understanding that was most easily translatable to pragmatic results, and thus that understanding that was taken from Marx's wider body of thoughts precisely for its pragmatic useability, and not that understanding that was deeper and more subtle but unable to be immediately translated into concrete theoretic and strategic results.

THE CLASSICAL MARXIST VIEW OF HUMAN NATURE

Classical Marxism emphasizes that human nature is *not innate but transitional*-- that it is determined by environment and individual history, and that it changes and develops as productive modes change and as man's interrelations with nature change. We could agree easily enough if these views were applied only to human personality or character structure. When one goes further, however, as the Classical Marxists do, the picture becomes sorely lacking for its excess simplicity.

Classical Marxism doesn't describe human nature fully enough. It *abstracts* out too much that is critically important. That this occurs because of needs to counter metaphysics and because of lacks of psychological ideas for dealing with more complete views is at least a viable justification for the weakness occurring in Marx's time, but not a full critique of that weakness and its effects, and with reference to our own present efforts, certainly not a justification at all.

People often doubt the legitimacy of the question "what is man?" in its general form. This question, they say, is sometimes posed by certain philosophies, but it is a false question and it cannot be asked by Marxism. Different special sciences explore different aspects of man's activity; no aspect remains unexplored; and all "special" sciences together give a complete picture of man. On the other hand, man in general, man as such, does not exist; there is only a concrete man of a concrete society; slave owner or slave, landlord or serf, bourgeois or worker.

Man is not, however, the sum total of his parts or aspects, but an integral being; and no special science does or can answer the question of what he is as an integral being, that is, what makes him man and each of his activities or aspects human. Although man is not always and everywhere the same, although he historically changes, there is something that allows us to call a proletarian as well as a capitalist, a landlord as well as a slaveowner, a man. 3

If people can be greedy, that must be an internal potential; if they can be bourgeois, then that must be a potential; and if they can be socialist, that too must de a potential. Human character structure is as much a 'product' of the interactions of human nature as it is innately at birth and in the genes, with its environment. To what extent there are innate traits or drives or tendencies is still an open question but that there is in a person something given which then interacts is known, and that that given is something more than just an empty slate is also known. And finally, that such assertions in no way contradict materialism is a direct and obvious result of the fact that 'people at birth' are not ideas or products of ideas, but material entities caused in the first place by material rather than idealistic interactions. Saying that people have as part of their reality a given-at-birth nature, including two arm-and legness, bilateral symmetry, a powerful but not too powerful brain, *and other more psychological features* is by no means the same as saying that autonomous ideas create realities.

Human character structure changes over small time spans precisely because human nature is complex and contains many potentialities. Human beings are like all other systems, not simply slates upon which external causes can have any and all effects. They have on-going internal *natures* at the basis of their changing personalities. And those natures include biological constitutions, given needs, tendencies, and creative potentials, and perceptual and cognitive apparatuses. Social, political, and economic interactions in the real world from birth on are the *cause* of any moment's personality, but human nature is the *basis* for it. And further, human nature evolves over long time periods -- it too is 'material' and not somehow outside the processes of reality. Over the long haul human nature and human interaction with environments each cause and are affected by the specific character structures endemic to changing time periods.

Although it is unnecessary for our critique, perhaps we can go a bit further in trying to say something about what the knowledge of human nature is needed for, and about what it might be like. Wilhelm Reich worked hard on precisely these questions and decided that the main purpose of the psychological model was to explain the *mediations between the economy and its people,* and to explain precisely how it is that "ideas form themselves in people's heads." 4 Further, he felt that the psychological model was the only way to explain the "irrational ways of behavior (such as every kind of religion and mysticism)... because psychoanalysis alone is capable of investigating the instinctual reactions of the unconscious. But it can do this in the right way only if it does not merely 'take account of the economic factors', but is clearly aware that the unconscious structures which are reacting irrationally are themselves the product of historical socio-economic processes, and that, therefore, they cannot be ascribed to unconscious mechanisms as opposed to economic causes, but only viewed as forces mediating between social being and human modes of reaction." 5

It seems reasonable to agree with Reich that a knowledge of human nature, or what he calls the psychology of human behavior, *is essential to an understanding of how people form their consciousnesses, how they react in changing circumstances, why they have the personalities they do, and how those personalities might change with time, or be affected by varying revolutionary policies.* It is thus critical knowledge for understanding how events affect people's behaviors and their personalities, and of course that is the critical calculation of the revolutionary policy maker.

In trying to augment Classical Marxism with a psychological insight Reich postulates a model in which human nature has two essential attributes, the instinct for self preservation and the instinct for sex, and in which these two needs interact with the environment by way of man's mental and bodily facilities, to co-motivate all of his behavior. And even this 'simple' model was enough different from Marx's total 'relativism' to lead to results that were significantly new enough for Reich to be thrown out of the party for espousing them. Nowadays it seems a little more reasonable to go somewhat further than Reich and say that people have innate tendencies to need food, shelter, safety, sex, self-esteem, companionship, knowledge of their environment, and the fulfillment of these innate capacities for expression, and that all these 'needs' interact with one another and with external causes to create the multiplicity of human personalities that exist throughout history and throughout any given society.

But far short of the above statement, even just admitting the existence of something called human nature which changes over evolutionary time spans, and admitting that it's important to understand because such understanding would help us explain personality, consciousness, and motivation, is a big step from the Classical Marxist approach. It leads to a more balanced, broader theory and it opens up a difficult problem that we only barely began dealing with in the above paragraphs: what is human nature, how much of a factor is it in personality, and how do its various aspects struggle and interpenetrate with one another and with external causes?

Classical Marxism's extreme abstractness about psychology and its ignorances about human nature are at the base of its greatest weakness: its inability to cope with psychological aspects of either oppression or liberation and its resulting tendency to overemphasize the 'material' side of things, thus incorrectly understanding dynamics of human interactions, human consciousness, and human motivation, and thus *even of human political struggle.*

As we've seen, Classical Marxism, as a theory used by pragmatists who require concrete analyses, regards people almost totally in context of their needs for material sustenance, -- in the prevalent formulations there is little mention of other needs or desires or of the paramount importance of sex and race or for that matter ego and self-image. The theory of alienation, again as we've mentioned earlier, arises only with the description of capitalism and on a basis of the more varied Marxist humanist insights into human behavior. It plays only a small role in

Classically oriented theory, strategy, or practice. That Marx was more aware than Classical Marxism is clear enough. The critical point, as we've suggested elsewhere as well, is that while the whole body of any Marxist's thoughts contain much about racism, general human behavior, et al, the practical core of it that actually guides activity does not: there is an absence of a useable theory of behavior and consciousness that can translate observations at the psychological, personality, need levels into concrete perscriptions at the practical level. Regrettably over time the reason has been pushed to the background and the effect has gained independent life -- the Classical Marxist view of human nature, as narrow as it is, and as obviously a product of intellectual lacks as it is, is nonetheless held up as truth and even defended against critical improvement: thus the extensive length of this part of our discussion.

Perhaps a new view of people and history would take the position that instead of being passive recipients of their character structures, people are *active engagers* in a process that creates character structure from a combination of *internal human nature and external social cause.* Perhaps it would assert that innate human needs, desires, potentials, and weaknesses are just as instrumental in unfolding history as are material and productive dynamics. It might find that the former provide the *basis* for change and the latter the cause, and that that was true not because of some metaphysical postulation but because of the real interrelations between people and their environments. The new view would still be materialist precisely because people's innate natures are part of the real material world just as much as anything else is, but at the same time it would be altered from an old approach stressing the dominance of material production, to a new approach stressing the interrelated causal and effectual framework formed by the interactions between human nature and the fulfilling/oppressing characters of productive and social organizations.

In any case it is fair to make the minimal assertion that if the rest of our study shows that Classical Marxism's psychological narrowness is a severe debit, then attempts to build a new ideology with a broader psychological model would be a good thing, to the extent that it could show up such weaknesses, at no new costs.

THE CLASSICAL MARXIST THEORY OF CONSCIOUSNESS

We should now consider the Classical Marxist theory of knowledge in the light of our overall intuitions about Classical Marxism as a whole, and in the light of our analysis of the Classical Marxist view of human nature, and finally also in the light of our own modern insights into the problems of consciousness formation. For given our earlier analyses of Classical Leninist strategy and practice and our recognition of Classical Marxism's inability to understand and prevent sectarianism, or to say much about the formation of oppressor and oppressed consciousnesses, it is reasonable to think we'll find some weaknesses in its root conceptions concerning consciousness formation.

To review: Classical Marxism says knowledge derives from practice, guides it, and is either verified or transformed by it. It says production is at the root of people's consciousnesses but it doesn't say much about precisely how. It doesn't go into details of how productive influences manifest themselves in consciousness and thus overlooks the extents to which they often do not. It doesn't tell how emotional needs, creative potentials, previously arrived at knowledge, and previously adopted thought habits all subjectively affect new perceptions and analyses. It doesn't deal sufficiently with the ways people's subjective weaknesses affect their consciousness formation processes.

Like the classical dialectical methodology, the classical understanding of consciousness formation sees the forest, or at least one aspect of it, but directs attention away from the trees, thus often completely misunderstanding the interrelation. It overcomes many idealist errors but in doing so pays only lip service to the fact that thinking is a process involving on-going interactions between various aspects of people's natures, of their personalities, and of the contexts or things they're thinking about. It overlooks the fact that each contributes to the resultant knowledge and that each is somewhat changed by the contributory process. It correctly recognizes that people's consciousnesses are largely determined by interactions with their environments, but it overemphasizes the import of purely production related environments, and underestimates the import of *human nature and personality in both affecting and impeding* final results.

Human nature and previously developed personality provide the basis for human changes and external effects provide the causes. Perception, the process of thought, and the development of theory are human changes that are based on people's natures and personalities and are bounded by their interactions with their environments.

Beyond its 'narrowness' problem there is a very simple fact that Classical Marxism doesn't seem to adequately understand. "Practice, knowledge, practice" is a far from fool proof approach to consciousness development. Sometimes it leads to good results, sometimes and perhaps even more often than not, it leads to a kind of perversely correct result which is in fact unrelated to the whole truth or to human welfare. For example, capitalist practice usually achieves its ends but in no way leads to a full understanding of reality -- it simply functions in a peculiar constricted environment where its inadequacies go 'unnoticed'. Classical Marxists probably understand this phenomenon on some level but they have never developed that understanding to its fullest or incorporated the results into their theory. For if they did they would understand Classical Leninism's authoritarian drawbacks much more than they do. The explanation for the lack lies in the coupling of vested interests, authoritarian personalities, and narrow constraining methodology.

Therefore we have two criticisms, each of which suggest that the Classical theory of knowledge is not aptly suited to understanding the pitfalls of human perception and thought. First, it does not understand the ways people subjectively alter perceptions and thoughts to fit needs, and second, it does not understand that oftentimes wrong or at least narrow knowledge can lead to successful practice and therefore go uncorrected over time. These root weaknesses explain at least something about why Classical Marxism in use is almost always sectarian.

Further it seems not unreasonable to say that in certain circumstances useful ideas might even be *'latent'* in people due to the *material basis* all people have in reality. In such cases ideas might be released from inside us rather than adopted or constructed. In any case ideas are not products of human thought alone; various aspects of *human nature and character structure* always enter into the process. A person's world view depends a good deal more on his or her upbringing and social situation than on just job, class, or even past work experience, though of course these are all critically important too. In any repressive country men have different consciousnesses than women and Blacks have different consciousnesses than whites. Even in a class or caste there can be vast divergences in the ways people view things. One cannot just abstract out as relatively unimportant the non-class related factors, as Marxists tend to do. In Classical Marxism there is, despite all protestations, an excessive and unhealthy overemphasis on the productive realm.

Further, consciousness actually changes in a variety of ways. Sometimes an individual acquires new views through *introspection*, or even *spontaneously* when all his or her old ones are severely undermined and conditions favor free human development and the strengthening of what were previously only latent ones at other times education or changing conditions, or new experiences weaken old ways or enforce new ones, and so on.

In any case a good understanding of knowledge would have to include an awareness of all the ways that *subjectivism* affects consciousness, all the ways that ideas are *held* and why, all the ways that they can be *changed* and why, all the ways that they affect behavior and vice versa, and all the ways that all these things occur both in groups as well as in an individual. Classical Marxism accomplishes very few of these tasks and as a result doesn't understand the dynamics of subjectivism or of consciousness change. Thus it is very weak with regard to adapting over time, seeing its own subjective inadequacies, and understanding how events affect people's views and behavior.

Marx said that it is not men's consciousnesses that determine their existences but, on the contrary, their existences that determine their consciousness. What we've been suggesting is that it is not the consciousness of people that determines their being or vice versa, but on the contrary, it is both which, through their interaction, determine each other and only then in the contexts of their whole on-going histories.

People and their beliefs are not abstractly outside the economic and social systems that are torn by contradictions, but in fact, are an integral part of those systems, a part whose own potential is one of the determining factors in the nature of the whole. And thus we tend to agree with Paul Cardan's remarks in the Solidarity pamphlet *History and Revolution*:

> The famous phrase about "consciousness lagging behind reality" is no more than a phrase. It represents an empirical assertion, valid so to speak for the right half of any phenomenon and false for the left half. 6

In our view, effects of consciousness on history are not so clearly secondary to history's effects on consciousness. Further, influences of production in consciousness formation are not so obviously always in accord with or dominant over other socialization influences, family influences, race or sex influences, and so on. For us the awareness that might logically arise out of any one set of relations can be easily forestalled or at least altered by the effects of the other sets even when the first set is productive and the latter only familial or otherwise superstructural. Finally we expect that to understand such dynamics one must understand the *totality of people's active needs* and their relations to perception and behavior rather than simply their material needs and their effects. Thus we can say that because the Classical Marxist theory skimps in its understanding of human need and behavior, and because it focuses dogmatically on mode-of-production dynamics, it overlooks many sides of the process of human consciousness formation and subsequent use.

Finally, we can also point out that the Marxist theory of knowledge underestimates the importance of secondary information gained by the analysis of the experiences of others. People in 'backward' countries often learn from the experiences of people in more 'advanced' countries. People can and often do transcend the intellectual content of their personal environments by reading about other people's environments. The interaction of ideas found in books and in intrinsic dynamics of human nature and need can lead people to world views that go far beyond those they might be expected to have, both in richness and in depth of knowledge. Further, it is even possible for people to make very educated guesses about conditions that no one has actually experienced.

People have latent intellectual and other potentials due to their material make-ups and their evolutionary development, and these can be *uncovered or thwarted* by any of many different processes. We agree with Cardan when he recognizes the importance of living ideas: "*The Sermon on the Mount* and *The Communist Manifesto* belong just as much to historical practice as any technological invention. And their real effects on history have been infinitely weightier." 7

Having looked at least briefly at the roots of Classical Marxism, we are now prepared to examine its view of history as a whole, and to thereby better understand just what its weaknesses really are, and just how they are manifested.

CLASSICAL HISTORICAL MATERIALISM

To review: Classical Marxists say that societies undergo constant processes of change centering around development of their productive forces, and the conflicts between those forces, and the relations within which those conflicts are constrained to operate. Classical Marxism is centrally based in the belief that at any time in history the overall nature of any society is determined by the nature of the primary aspect of the principal contradiction of the society's main historical process -- that is, it is determined by the society's mode of production.

Classical Marxism goes on to say that modes of production change during revolutions which are brought on by the aggravation of a society's primary contradiction to its most extreme *antagonism*. This all rests on the belief that in any society forces of production are expanded to their limits within old relations of production while at the same time new relations of production are foreshadowed at many levels until finally the growing forces of production compel a change in the relations and then in society's whole superstructure.

Classical Marxism says that the contradiction at work in all revolution comes into existence precisely because *people must work to survive* and because they invariably seek the best possible material conditions for themselves. Human labor is necessary to produce and reproduce the conditions of human existence. But at the same time it also produces and reproduces large groups of people who share the same relationship to the productive mode of their society, and who therefore also share roughly the same consciousnesses. According to Classical Marxism these groups, called classes, inevitably have different interests from one another -- in times of rupture the landed and then the capitalist classes try to maintain the old modes of production, *while the working and other disenfranchised classes try to promote new ones.*

So emerges the Classical Marxist view of history: class conflict, built upon contradictions between forces and relations of production, 'creates' history -- men themselves have been impotent to prevent class struggle and thereby create their own long term and material fulfillment. Over and over, men's long term desires fall prey to the 'demands' of on-going class struggle -- the dynamics of history are, at least up to now, essentially the dynamics of material scarcity and class struggle.

Though this view far surpasses those of the liberals and the metaphysicians and others, it is still far too abstract and far too steeped in economic biases to be really useful for revolutionaries. It doesn't really engender an understanding of the dynamics of individual or caste oppression, not recognizing the non-material, psychological effects of many social roles. It doesn't concern itself significantly with the dynamics of upbringing. It doesn't recognize that people are most often both *oppressors and oppressed* and that their character structures are therefore full of complexities that go well beyond simple class governed expectations.

Classical Marxism doesn't explain the preponderance of *economically irrational behavior* that various individuals and social groups exhibit. It doesn't even explain why classes don't always pursue their own best material interests. Though it uses the phrase "false consciousness," it doesn't define it adequately or give any significant insights into how the condition it is applied to arises and persists. It recognizes that certain traits created by one's relations to work can be repeated over and over from person to person and thus achieve a societal importance. It doesn't, however, recognize that the same can be true for traits acquired through upbringing, experiences due to race, sex, or religion, the dynamics of interpersonal relations, or the dynamics of various forms of oppression. Certainly it is true that people must work to survive, but it is also true that they must have safety, and intermingle with other people, and that in most cases they must have families that relate to people of other sexes and races etc. Certainly there is no a priori reason to postulate that these other influences will necessarily have only secondary effects upon consciousness formation. In fact, what will determine the relative importance of various kinds of experiences upon people's consciousnesses are *people's past experiences and their human natures.* And it seems at least reasonable to suggest that human nature and people's collective experiences are generally such that under many conditions things relating to sex, race, self-image, self-management, and creative fulfillment are at least as important, if not much more important to consciousness change than things concerned with only material fulfillment.

By and large in its real-world application, Classical Marxism simply ignores the likelihood that many times individuals in one class will form different consciousnesses from one another in understandable patterns. It underestimates the importance of *internal class conflicts* and so it doesn't deal with them effectively. It doesn't adequately understand the dynamics of class collaboration based on fear, insecurity, racism, and other psychological motives, and so it does not provide adequate directions for overcoming it.

Classical Marxism doesn't perceive that classes are not necessarily always a given society's best defined groups -- it denies that contradictions between other sorts of groups could be more important than class struggle and eventually overwhelm it as causal agents in history. It denies this possibility because of its *fetish for one principal contradiction in history and for the idea that only classes are in a position to mediate the dynamics of that contradiction.* Classes over all: for all its protestations to the contrary, Classical Marxism does give more weight to the importance of the productive mode than is justified. This stems directly from the biased nature of Classical Marxist dialectics, the absence of an understanding of psychology, and the narrowness of the Classical Marxist theory of knowledge.

Classical Marxism doesn't understand the dynamics of *revolutionary collectivities.* It finds the problem unimportant, in fact it doesn't even seem to recognize its existence. Each revolutionary is left to do what he or she will about understanding his or her own motivations, weaknesses, and strengths. It doesn't incorporate an understanding of its practitioners into its 'dogma'; it doesn't provide any real tools for the development of such an understanding, or even for realizing the importance of such understanding. Here is a fairly strong analogy to the way capitalist ideology allows its practitioners to overlook the existence of classes, exploitation, oppression, etc. *Classical Marxism has categories which allow its practitioners to ignore their own weaknesses and to overlook their own oppressive tendencies and authoritarian interests.*

At its roots Classical Marxism's categories are self-sustaining of certain oppressive tendencies. This problem becomes most apparent in the modern age, when we're trying to create a revolution that really will lead to a *classless society* -- we are forced to consider how to change from class consciousnesses that are oppressive to revolutionary consciousnesses that are liberating, and therefore we must understand what exactly a revolutionary consciousness is, how it evolves, and how it can be reached. It no longer suffices for Classical Marxist leaders to say that working-class consciousness becomes objectively revolutionary when capitalist contradictions become antagonistic; this is obviously untrue. People's consciousnesses are very complex; it is true that under pressures they change, but it is not necessarily true that they always change to the left. If nothing else is sufficient to prove this, the lesson of post-World War One Germany certainly is. *A useful theory must take into account the multiple realities of consciousness.* It must understand what is necessary for consciousness to move left and stay there, and in understanding that, it's not unreasonable to believe that such a theory would reverse many of the weaknesses we uncovered in Leninist strategy. If nothing else such a theory would likely explain why it is that authoritarian approaches, though they may create motion, in the end do not create truly revolutionary consciousnesses in their practitioners or in the affected masses. It is probable that it would also explain the role sexism and racism play in maintaining reactionary consciousnesses and the roles struggles against such oppressions could play in developing revolutionary consciousnesses.

No social systems are closed. Frequently external pressures, knowledge, models of previous experiences, and/or coercion can outweigh any social system's purely internally expected dynamics. Thus what seems like a backward country's primary productive contradiction can be made relatively unimportant by interactions with an intervening external environment.

Classical Marxism does not adequately explain the emergence of bureaucratic social forms in third world countries. The new class in these countries is not created by new modes of production and it does not develop in the 'womb of the old society'. On the contrary, *the Chinese bureaucracy creates the new mode of production rather than vice versa. The bureaucracy emerges from the incapacity, rather than the growth of the productive forces.* Its roots lie in the 'future' rather than in the past. These are all facts that the actual logic of the Classical model precludes at least insofar as that model is applied consistently. Indeed the reality is that there has never been a revolution corresponding to the simplistic model of growing forces bursting fettering relations.

Certainly, for example, one can say that consciousness and practice in China, Cuba, and other parts of the world, have outstripped mode-of-production developments there and perhaps anywhere, and further, this has occurred not because of any mystical metaphysical miracle, but because of the dialectical interaction of the human (material) base and the productive and social boundary.

Our criticism's essence is that Classical Marxism's unbalanced dialectics forces its practitioners into dogmatic incorrect understandings of the roles of social classes and the nature of social change. Classical Marxism excludes from consideration the potentials and peculiarities of human nature, which prove crucial to understanding day to day work, and to understanding something more about the finer details of history's flow.

It isn't sufficient when the Classical Marxist rejoins that over the long haul historical 'deviations' due to chance occurrences, and the dynamics of revolutionary thought, race, sex, etc., will all even out in the welter of events so that the overall flow becomes consistent with Classical Marxist expectations. For even if the assertion were true, and it would certainly be a hard one to prove, it would still say very little with regard to offsetting our actual criticisms of Classical Marxism.

When we make strategic determinations we are not so much interested in *eventual success* as we are in *hastening success* by exploiting every available opportunity for skillful activity. We must be able to understand as many situations and so called accidents as possible, we must know more about history's main contours, and we must be able to apply all our awarenesses effectively in local contexts. Finally any theory that could accomplish such ends should also and, to be fully worth while, constantly grow in light of new experiences so that it can continually do its tasks better even as circumstances significantly alter.

Classical Marxism doesn't fill the obvious criteria for a good theory of history and revolution, and yet most revolutionaries passively accept it as a kind of revolutionary gospel. No doubt if Marx were alive, despite whatever personal weaknesses he might have had, he would frown on our fealty, toss aside the errors of old, and work toward a new updated workable ideology. The reasons many people don't try doing the same probably lies in the ease with which they attach themselves to tried ideas, the beauty of those ideas, the extent to which the ideas superficially fill present needs, and the latent fear that in trying to do better one would likely do worse or discover too many of one's own weaknesses or too many obstacles to success. It is not excessive hubris to say that ideas over a hundred years old can no longer be sufficient, *but it is irrational to face the realities of the Russian revolution and of Classical Marxist dogmatism and continue claiming that an extensive overhaul is unnecessary.*

Classical Marxist methodology focuses on contradictions between forces and relations of production, thus missing the fact that significant changes always involve contradictions between *aggravated human desires and restraining 'external' impediments.* Refocusing perceptions on oppression versus liberation might help a new theory demystify the at least highly influential position of human nature and human personality in history. We might then see that social change always derives from human struggles occurring in varying contexts, that the contexts and struggles are mutually affective, and that the crux around which to understand each is their interactions is *fulfillment and oppression,* and most particularly the contradiction between desires for increased fulfillments and the existence of recognized and recognizably eliminable obstacles.

Thus in contrast to Classical Marxism we might say that economic developments provide *constraints,* at times motivate changes, and are at times *necessary* if a particular thing is to actually occur, but that they are neither necessary nor sufficient alone for much of anything -- except insofar as they are viewed as an inextricable part of a totality of forces and contradictions. With such a perspective we would recognize that most events are multiply caused and *overdetermined.* We would understand why it is so easy to postulate many different theoretical explanations for why any single event has occurred, each of which has a certain amount of validity (because were it acting alone it could have been a sufficient cause), and none of which has a complete validity (because none was acting alone and thus when viewed as if they were sole or even primary causes are misleading). Thus arguments about what causes particular occurrences often go on interminably with no one recognizing that each pinpointed cause was in fact sufficient but that since they were all acting at the same time none was really necessary or more important than any other.

More correct approaches would probably stress the *totalistic interaction* of many contradictions at many different hierarchical levels. They would recognize that in complex situations most often one cause is *paralleled and supported by others,* where each in itself is sufficient and none really alone necessary. It becomes important to realize that in real situations causes hardly ever appear separately from one another so that dealing with only one or another but not with all is hardly ever a good strategy for affecting their common activity.

Dialectics can easily encompass this type view when formulated in more balanced manners. But when used in its old Classical forms dialectical approaches cause people to give dominance to one part of any multiple set of contradictions, and thus lead to more simplistic views than are actually required. For example a Classical Marxist analyzes a situation and determines that if he or she could resolve a certain productive contradiction it would create a newer better situation precisely because the old dominant aspect of that contradiction was defining the old situation. Sometimes the Classical Marxist will get his expectations fulfilled but more often even if his or her focused approach does resolve the favorite contradiction, others will intervene to affect the final outcome and make it different from expectations. In such cases the Classical Marxist would have been right in suspecting that the aspect was sufficient to define the old situation but wrong in thinking it was necessary, and so would have overlooked other contradictions that were also critical and continued to affect the situation adversely. So Classical Marxists often overlook the psychological for the material, or the interpersonal for the bureaucratic. They concern themselves with changes in forces and sometimes relations of production but not enough with changes in interpersonal relations, political relations, sexual relations, racial relations, etc. and as a result *they often overlook crucial sides of revolutionary problems.* In Bolshevik practice, for example, they missed immense problems of the total strategy of creating a new society and also shorter run problems of organization, day to day living, the employment of coercion, the effects of sexism, and the effects of interpersonal interactions. Certainly it's not enough for the Classical Marxist apologist to shrug and say that such errors occur only because practitioners are incompetent at using what is actually quite correct theory. For theories are irrelevant in isolation from their use. When their correct use requires essentially herculean efforts, their usefulness to revolutionaries becomes nearly nil. And even further no Classical Marxist would claim that Lenin himself was incompetent, but as we've amply seen, he made precisely the types of errors our above analysis pins to the inadequacies of Classical Marxist theory. It is an unhappy coincidence of error laden possibilities: The practitioner generally starts with certain vested interests to protect, (or acquires them in the course of struggle), and with certain bad habits of mind, and the theory fosters those weaknesses rather than illuminating or opposing them. Thus, most clearly with the problems of authoritarianism, the 'leader' starts with an interest in not fully understanding, and the theory serves well by fostering exactly that form of ignorance.

Classical Marxists say that though political relations influence economic movement, they are first created by it, and that while the superstructure influences the base, it is first called into existence by it. We ask the Classical Marxist whether hills are created by valleys or vice versa, and go on to say that the human emerges due to interactions of nature with itself, that the economic emerges due to interactions of the human with the natural, that the political emerges due to interactions of the human and the economic, and that as they all achieve existences of their own, they create, recreate, and change one another all on an essentially equal basis.

A Classical Marxist says that large scale changes in human character structure are determined by changes in the mode of production. We wonder about knowledge based on observation of the experiences of others. We wonder about the innate characteristics of human nature. We wonder about the effects of movements concerned with race, sex, and authority. And we also wonder about the fact that changes in the Classical Marxist mode of production don't necessarily change human character that much. Out of these questions come many of our criticisms and many of our new intuitions.

We see that social structures do perish before all the productive forces for which they have room have developed.

We see that thought can outstrip the material base in a given society and that external factors can be crucial to the development of a society's internal contradictions.

We see that the Classical Marxist theory of classes is wrong, that it overlooks much that is important, and that it ignores forces that can effectively pervert consciousness potentials.

We see that in practice the overall Classical Marxist theory is dogmatic and that it forces its practitioners to subjectively alter their perceptions, to develop fetishes, and to dichotomize according to their preconceptions. We see roots of these maladies within the theory's methodology as well as within practitioners' personalities and role requirements.

We see accidents crucial to our understanding and practice passed off as unimportant to theory. We see the whole area of human motivation and need ignored despite the fact that knowledge of it is crucial to any rational decision-making about tactics, strategy, and program.

And finally we see that Classical Marxism does very little to develop an understanding of the dynamics of a future revolutionary society or of the kinds of people who would populate it. We see that Classical Marxism deals only inadequately with the problems of oppressing and being oppressed, with the problems of consciousness and personality change, and with the problems of knowledge, ideology, and sectarianism, and as a result we see that it creates strategies and goals that are illsuited to the realities of the present human condition, and to the realities of where that condition might eventually go.

Classical Marxists know much more about history's dynamics than anyone who preceded them but are nonetheless quite ignorant of many of its most important aspects. Further their ignorance is of a critical kind that must interfere with their chances for successful practice. Material conditions help create possibilities for societies but contrary to Classical historical materialist injunction, they do not dictate final choices between possibilities. Objectively revolutionary conditions can often be diverted into non-revolutionary directions by people with inadequate or peculiarly self-interested ideologies. *In history, people's actions make choices and people's actions are related to their needs and beliefs, which are in turn factors in history and which are therefore deserving of careful scrutiny, most especially when they claim to be something which history shows them to not be.*

We've begun seeing that the Classical Marxist theory of historical materialism as we've outlined it is lacking at a number of levels, and our findings have gained considerable force from the fact that they seem to explain the weaknesses we earlier found in Classical Leninist strategy and Bolshevik practice. We haven't yet proven any of our assertions but we have given some considerable evidence. It is likely that the only real proof that Classical Marxism Leninism is a sorely deficient ideology will be the development of a new and better political consciousness at some future time. Perhaps our efforts will help give people the confidence that efforts in that direction are called for and quite likely to be successful. For now it must suffice to continue somewhat further with discussions of historical materialism and the use of Classical Marxism, in the hopes of further tracing its multiple weaknesses and of thereby developing at least a few intuitions concerning how a new formulation might improve upon the past one.

Classical Marxism says that any society has a base and an associated superstructure, and that the superstructure's main content is determined by the will of the ruling classes and the nature of the class struggle of the time. Classical Marxism says that once there is revolution at the base, the superstructure is also "more or less quickly" revolutionized. And this flows straight from the Classical Marxist belief that human character inevitably changes with a change in the mode of production; with changes in human character classes also change and exert new pressures upon society. The new ruling class changes the superstructure of the society it comes to lead. But in fact this is all quite faulty. For as we've come to see, *the economic is not only not the sole cause of changes, it is not even the sole sufficient cause of changes.* Old political, interpersonal, or social forms can 'dominate' changes in the mode of production and can reverse or alter them at least as easily as the opposite can occur. Many of humankind's superstitions, myths, religions, and even warring tendencies would have been done away with ages ago if the only causes for their continuation had been material. Leaders and systems are not corrupt *solely* because someone is able to pocket some extra cash. History's religious, racial, and even imperial wars were all undoubtedly fought for economic reasons at least in part, but none of them can be explained solely or even largely in purely economic terms. Often ideology has held back productive change rather than vice versa, often people have fought and died in wars for 'higher glories' despite the losses they would incur, and often people have been moved to barbarism with no visible material reward available whatsoever. Classical Marxism, as opposed to today's better neo-Marxist practitioners and to Marx himself at times, is almost oblivious to the socio-political dynamics of social change despite continual lip service to its importance. Classical Marxism is just not encompassing enough, *it has too narrow a framework for an understanding of interpersonal relations and personal or group psychologies -- it doesn't even give an adequate perspective for understanding the history of the Russian Revolution itself.* It doesn't adequately account for the fact that *even revolutionaries' consciousness can change adversely.*

Marxism states that ruling class ideas always dominate but all Classical Marxists actually investigate real situations more closely to determine exactly what the interplay between various kinds of thought and culture is at any given time. The trouble isn't that they do this, but that their theory provides no good framework for doing it -- it just doesn't adequately discuss cultural development or consciousness interaction. It has no provision for understanding the different world views and ideologies associated with political versus repressive work, statespeople versus cops. *There is no real attempt to provide tools for understanding day-to-day life, or movement activity, or consciousness alteration; the resulting deficiencies are profound.* Classical Marxist disagreements are most severe in this area; each practitioner postulates his or her own conceptions and virtually none actually works from a theoretical framework that can answer questions like those raised here.There is no commonality and only a little success. We come full circle; good modern Marxists frequently better their theory, though often with misgivings lest their creativity be called *infidelity.*

Finally, the Classical Marxist analysis says that when contradictions become profound the oppressed classes line up with the revolution and the oppressor classes defend the old order. Would that it were always so! Classical Marxism doesn't explain why this should always occur and how the personal decisions of various kinds of individuals are likely made -- it doesn't include an understanding of the many ways the expected process can break down. And as a result it doesn't include an adequate understanding of *how revolutionary activity can make the hoped for process most likely occur.* Classical Marxism doesn't even give us a concrete understanding of why Marx, Engels, Lenin, or Mao transcended their class backgrounds and became revolutionaries, if that is indeed even what they in fact did.

It doesn't explain why the totally immiserated classes of some countries are passive or reactionary, while the comparatively well off classes of other countries or even of the same countries are quite radically active. To say that some people see beyond their immediate situations, or that they are more sensitive or that it is an accident or whatever, totally begs a fundamentally important set of questions. Why don't the oppressed constantly rebel against their oppressors? Why do they often even support them? What can revolutionaries do to affect the involved dynamics? Why does increased oppression more often push people to the right and not the left?

Beyond these questions, the crucial issue is not what is Classical Marxism in its isolation, or what was it at some time past, but what is it in the hands of its practitioners. What is important about a social theory is not so much whether it is right or wrong in the abstract, as whether it is right or wrong in application, whether it is used correctly or incorrectly, to advantage or to disadvantage. A theory which fosters modes of thought that play into the weaknesses of its practitioners can easily become practically counter productive no matter what its 'isolated intellectual value' might be.

And indeed problems do arise due to the interactions between

Classical Marxist tneory and people whose characters were largely formed in class-stratified racist, sexist, authoritarian societies.

Experience shows that when people accept the overall tenets of Classical Marxist theory *and no other offsetting ones*, they become unable to use dialectical analysis in a way that avoids dogmatism. Their complete emphasis on major contradictions leads Classical Marxists inexorably toward putting a bias on the importance of dichotomizing and polarizing. As a result they become unwilling and even unable to realize that most dichotomies are false and arise from unnatural conditions imposed from without. Classical Marxist patterns of analysis do nothing to alter what seem to be most people's normal tendencies toward exaggeration and extremism. In fact, if anything, it is probably reasonable to say that Classical Marxism pushes people further in the direction of sectarianism than in the direction of science because its dynamics suggest that it would, and because our experience seems to suggest that it does.

Classical Marxism seems to have been adopted and to have prevailed partly for its correctness but also for the way it fills people's needs to have a clear ideological explanation for all things. In a way, then, it is an animist theory accepted like most religions for its size and shape rather than for its verifiable use value. And that is why Classical Marxists put the lid on the scientific work of geneticists in much the same way that earlier religious folk put the lid on the works of other kinds of scientists. Classical Marxists have a vested psychological interest in the unalterability of their theory precisely because of the ways they adopt it and because of the ways it serves them by giving them an unassailable identity. *As a result they are more interested in preserving its form than they are in altering it for the better* -- and thus the explanation for decades of sectarian resistance to any broadening of the theory as a whole.

The Classical Marxist employ of dialectics is dogmatic. The Classical Marxist emphasis on class is dogmatic. Classical Marxism perceives reality in terms of a materialistic class bias -- i.e., Classical Marxists order their perceptions in accordance with their past ideas and past experiences, unwittingly but almost inevitably. Some do it through habit, some do it because their identities depend upon it, some do it because the social pressures of their environments compel it, some do it simply because it seems quite right to them. But as a result most Classical Marxists are *unable to transcend* the appparent contradictions between the communal and the individual, work and play, equality and excellence, study and participation, objectivity and participation, leadership and democracy, violence and love, feeling and rationality, and culture and political economy. In practice they always go to one extreme or to the other, frequently to their own and to almost everyone else's detriments.

Classical Marxist thought occurs in essentially the same framework as bourgeois thought -- that of *worship of authority, awe of scarcity and a lack of self-awareness.* It has little understanding of the dynamics of elitism, sexism, and egotism. Indeed it actually precludes each of these areas of concern from any kind of independent understanding in its own right -- they either fit into a class view of history and can be so understood or they are irrelevant to revolution. No matter how sound much of what Classical Marxists suggest is, in practice all is frequently lost due to the same kind of dynamics that plague all capitalists and bureaucrats. Classical Marxists fit everything to their views lest those views be somehow upset; they see things in terms of previous beliefs, they do not grow wiser with each new experience. Classical Marxists end up by manipulating people, movements, and ideas, because their identities depend upon their doing so. It can only be a largely unsupported guess but it certainly wouldn't be very surprising to discover that Marx and Engels were egotistical, authoritarian, male supremicists in their everyday lives.

Perhaps we can move toward concluding with an example. When Classical Marxists consider the problem of spontaneity and organization they are unable to conceive that the seeming dichotomy might be imposed and thus one which can be overcome. They don't bother to think about the possibility of *spontaneous organization* or of *organized spontaneity*; they don't think about the fact that organized activity in isolation from spontaneity suffers as much as spontaneity isolated from organization; and what they do do is wipe out spontaneity because it seems to be less scientific. Then they go on to the opposite extreme. They correctly realize that nihilist spontaneity is destructive but they employ extreme versions of organization to isolate themselves from value considerations and to justify the most unjust activities. In essence they simply miss some reasonably obvious truths while picking up on a few others -- they are extremist and it goes back to the nature of their whole approach to analysis and history. Their world view is constricting and narrow in a way difficult if not impossible for its own practitioners to fully perceive. In a recent *Liberation* article on the German movement, Michael Schnieder characterized Classical Marxist Leninist sectarian psychological problems:

Since the dialectic of many comrade's emotional universe seems locked in a neurotic syndrome, the reservoirs of libidinal energy from which they might draw strength and inspiration in their political work are constantly shrinking. And so, in them, Marxist Leninist theory, instead of being the'intellect of the passions' becomes a 'mere passion of the intellect'. In a way these comrades are like the sinner in the second circle of *Dante's Inferno*, who carries his head before him as if it were a lantern: "The severed head, held by the hair, hangs from his head like a lantern.. So the wretch carried his brain, cut off from the source of life in his body." The brains of our cadre, filled with quotations from Marx and Lenin, often seem likewise to be cut off from their source of life, the emotional and erotic wellsprings which they have repressed and dismissed as so much "non-political rubbish."If on the one hand, they enlighten themselves and the masses with the beacon of Marxism Leninism, on the other hand they estrange themselves from the masses insofar as they are estranged from their own needs and feelings, which they denounce as 'petty bourgeois'. Under these circumstances how can a cadre awaken liberatory needs and feelings in young workers and apprentices when for himself these feelings exist only on paper; how can you believe him when he says socialism develops not only the material production forces but also "the creative imagination of the masses." (Mao) when he himself articulated his political beliefs as if he were reciting a liturgy? 8

And as Fidel Castro has said about the degeneration of Classical Marxism in practice:

These are the paradoxes of history. How, seeing sectors of clergy become revolutionary, can we resign ourselves to seeing revolutionary forces become ecclesiastical forces. 9

THE CLASSICAL MARXIST VIEW OF CAPITALISM

Classical Marxism centers people's thought processes around groups and masses. *It objectifies individuals or even ignores them and sets a manipulative tone,* rather than personalizing individuals and setting a liberating tone. It makes a fetish of content and largely ignores form, rather than understanding the full intricacies of both, and as a result, its understanding of capitalism is as misleading as its understandings of the rest of history's major creations.

Classical Marxism does not understand capitalism's resiliency. It formed in a time when no one knew much about advanced technics and so it couldn't be fully aware of capitalism's immense capacities for growth. It couldn't predict that contradictions between forces and relations would manifest themselves in very different spheres in capitalism's later days than in its earlier ones.

Classical Marxism emphasizes class consciousness and class struggle but has only a very shallow understanding of how consciousnesses form and change, and of what the consciousnesses of workers or bosses are really like. Classical Marxism *identifies wholes but pays little attention to fine structure;* it addresses the qualities of masses but not of individuals, of economies but not of economists. It doesn't understand deviations from its own expectations and it usually simply ignores them. It doesn't adequately understand inner-class divisions, it says little about capitalist bureaucracy's pervasive effects and it doesn't really understand very much about dynamics of the consciousnesses of capitalism's leaders -- especially when those dynamics are derived from desires other than simple considerations of material self-interest.

Classical Marxism doesn't provide tools for understanding subsocietal environments. It doesn't help the hospital nurse to decide what courses of action might best affect other hospital workers' consciousnesses. It doesn't allow community movement people to understand their own interactions with one another or to formulate the best possible inter-group work relations. It doesn't help activists figure out how to talk to people, how to write leaflets, how to plan demonstrations or strikes, how to run meetings, etc. All this and more simply because it doesn't give sufficient insight into how and why people act the ways they do, not decade by decade, or class by class, but day by day, and group by group, or even person by person.

Classical Marxism doesn't understand modern culture. It looks for racism's and sexism's roots in the monetary requisites of capitalism, rather than in the *weaknesses* of people who have lived through ages of competitive struggles, and who had innate potentials for irrationality and injustice in the first place. And with regard to elitism the situation is even worse. Classical Marxists don't only not understand modern autoritarianism and the importance of anti-authoritarian ways; they sometimes glory in the dynamics of authority and take them for a virtue, thus crippling themselves, oppressing others, and making countless irretrievable errors with regard to day to day programs and even long term strategy.

Classical Marxists as Classical Marxists don't understand human needs or motivations that arise on a basis of reasonable material fulfillment. They try to fit all drives into a framework of class explanation, they say that Black movements are generated mostly by economic factors and that wealthy students rebel mostly because they are worried about future job possibilities. Generally speaking Classical Marxists are simply poorly prepared to understand the *multiplicity of forces* that go into determining what modern people do and why they do it, and when they go beyond that poor preparation to good results, it is usually because they have also gone beyond the bounds of Classical Marxist dogma.

In essence the Classical Marxist view of capitalism, as might be expected, given its roots in Classical Marxist views of change, history, and human nature, is much too *narrow* to be very useful. When it does work it is usually at too high a level of abstraction to be relevant to day to day practice. It overemphasizes class forces and misunderstands racism and sexism. It underestimates the importance of non-material human needs and desires. It completely misjudges the importance of authoritarian and anti-authoritarian dynamics. It oversimplifies the state's role and doesn't adequately explain the mentalities of society's administrators. It understands parts of modern society but it misses the whole and the relatively fine detail; it just doesn't give us a really convincing explanation for why modern capitalism functions the ways it does, or for why its citizens act as they do. It finds what seems to be sufficient causes for most things it addresses but it doesn't find the *full panoply of interacting forces that we all intuitively know to be there . It doesn't help us to understand fully the factory and other work environments and their effects on us all. Mostly it does not provide us with adequate tools for understanding the dynamic effects our activities have on ourselves and others.*

Classical Marxism goes further in its explanations of history and revolution than any other widely accepted system of thought, but it overlooks a great many relatively simple truths, and in this lies its ultimate revolutionary counter productivity. It is not an accurate gospel though it is often taken as one. Its errors begin in its historical roots but they spread through the totality of its major announcements. As Marcuse said:

> The petrification of Marxian theory violates the very principle which the New Left proclaims: the unity of theory and practice. A theory which has not caught up with the practice of capitalism cannot possibly guide the practice aiming at the abolition of capitalism. 10

It is a relatively simple fact, that should occasion little surprise, that Classical Marxism, Classical Leninism, and the body of thought and practice called Classical Marxism Leninism, are all quite outmoded. Much can be learned from them, but it is simply undeniable that they must sooner or later be largely transcended.

FOOTNOTES

1. Kropotkin in *Quotations from the Anarchists,*edited by Paul Berman, Praeger Books,New York.
2. Bakunin, *Bakunin,* edited by Maximov, London. 34.
3. Gajo Petrovic, *Marx in the Mid Twentieth Century*, Doubleday Anchor Books, Garden City, New York.
4. Wilhelm Reich, *Sex Pol*, edited by Lee Baxandall, Vintage Press, New York. 66.
5. ibid. 66.
6. Cardan in the Solidarity pamphlet *History and Revolution.*
7 ibid.
8. Michael Schniedre in *Liberation Magazine,* 1973.
9. Castro, *Fidel Castro Speaks,* Grove Press, New York.
10. Marcuse, *Counter Revolution and Revolt,* Beacon press, Boston. 34.

CHAPTER EIGHT

CRITIQUE OF CLASSICAL MARXIST LENINIST IDEOLOGY

Nevertheless there comes a time when a detour ceases to be a
detour, when the dialectic is no longer a dialectic... 1
Maurice Merleau-Ponty

At this point we shall do a summary review of the past three chapters
in an order that is more conducive to seeing causal relations than to slowly
working out an analysis.

Classical Marxism is a powerful social theory that gives people a
compelling understanding of history's dynamics and uncovers a great
many of its hidden but important attributes. Nonetheless it has numerous
weaknesses which are highly consequential precisely because of the ways
they affect Classical Marxist practitioners' abilities to fully understand
their surroundings and to consciously change them for the better.

Classical Marxism is based on a dialectical approach that is
somewhat unbalanced and quite narrow and that thereby causes excessive
dichotomizing and fixating.

It is based on a theory of knowledge that is narrow, that does not
understand the full dynamics of thought processes, that overemphasizes
the dominating importance of material needs, that does not understand
the dynamics of defensiveness and sectarianism, and that therefore
postulates no powerful methods for dealing with either.

It is based on an unenlightened understanding of human behavior
that largely ignores the importance of many human needs, tendencies, and
desires, and as a result has almost no understanding of the full complexity
of human motivation, believing all such issues in any case to be secondary
and 'unmaterial'.

As a result of these weaknesses *Classical Marxism is not well suited to
analyzing tactics with regard to their likely effects on real concrete
in-the-world people.*

Further Classical Marxism develops a theory of history, Classical historical materialism, that is also so lacking.

It is based on an unbalanced view of historical forces that underestimates and misunderstands the relevance and the dynamics of racism, sexism, authoritarianism, and even classism.

It is based on a non-psychological highly abstracted theoretical basis, and so does not understand the dynamics of short run events and day to day occurrences, all of which it most often dismisses as simply accidents or irrelevancies of history.

It is based on a view of people that stresses scarcity almost entirely and that therefore creates a theory that overemphasizes the importance of class, and underestimates the importance of other groups, and of 'ideas'.

It is based on a theory of contradictions that makes classes dominant but ignores the reality of 'revolutionaries' who are no longer explicable as solely class motivated people. It is not self-critical and does not promote self-criticism among the people it selects for creating change.

It doesn't really understand oppressive dynamics in their totality and it gives no very powerful understanding of why oppression is and has always been so prevalent. It abstracts away much that has been important to history's course and then protects itself against understanding its own resulting deficiencies.

It doesn't provide any means for postulating goals because it doesn't really talk about human fulfillment. It does not really say where the 'good' will come from or what it will look like, merely that it will arrive.

Perhaps most important of all, because of the peculiar dynamics of its weaknesses and because of the ways it affects its practitioners and the ways they affect it, Classical Marxism does not change over time. It becomes a kind of *religion* in which people have an on-going interest causing them to worship it rather than to try to critically understand its tenets. *Classical Marxism gives believers a vested interest in stability rather than in change;* and it creates a strategy that reflects all these weaknesses in a variety of ways.

Classical Leninism exaggerates the importance of immiseration and underestimates the importance of a knowledge of viable future alternatives.

It has no capacity to understand the dynamics of tactics as they affect practitioners or 'recipients' and so its decisions about such issues are highly problematic, and quite often wrong. It doesn't arm people to effectively compose or evaluate their own programmatic efforts.

It makes a fetish of discipline and hierarchy to the absolute detriment of real revolutionary potentials in the people who use it and in the people they encounter.

It overemphasizes the importance of class conflict and underemphasizes the importance of struggles around race, sex, dignity, freedom, and alienation.

It compels people to be 'protestantly workerlike' at exactly that moment in history when they are struggling to be free of old identities and definitions in order to adopt newer better ones. It pushes people to submit to new authorities at exactly that moment when it is most critical that they *confront all authority.*

It makes a fetish of whatever it first finds important and hardly ever flexibly adapts to changing conditions -- it is sectarian to an extreme that increases as its practitioners have more and more power.

It is a poor blueprint for a power take over -- it says almost nothing important about the dynamics of an *all-sided revolution* that would successfully eliminate exploitation, much less all other modern forms of oppression.

And it leads to practice that reflects all these weaknesses in their most brutal imaginable forms. Practice that ignores most human needs, tramples opposition, learns almost nothing from experience, and becomes progressively more and more despotic as its practitioners gain power, or more and more irrelevant as they encounter insurmountable difficulties they can't really understand.

Classical Marxist Leninists don't grasp what revolution really is -- they limit themselves to a less than full picture of the society they wish to change, they have only a minimal sense of the people they expect to do the changing, and they have almost no vision of what the new society should be like.

They don't perceive the importance of a clearly outlined goal. They don't really understand that revolution doesn't come because a situation is totally intolerable but because of a clash between what is, and what people want and realize could be. They don't see that misery alone usually produces only demoralization and competition, while political understanding of viable alternatives produces action. They don't know the dynamics of oppression; they refuse to acknowledge the oppressive behavioral baggage they have been given by their capitalist backgrounds.

Modern movements must open up new potentials through their *practice* and through their *demeanor* for their 'practitioners' and for the 'masses.' Classical Marxist Leninists don't see that revolutionizing all people's thoughts is the priority, while revolutionizing just the thoughts of a few leaders is impossibly counter-productive. And they don't realize these things not because they are stupid but because the weaknesses of Classical Marxism Leninism steer their consciousnesses away from understanding -- and because the dynamics of Classical Marxist Leninist revolutionary practice and their own bad traits give them *vested interests* in this 'ignorance.'

Classical Marxist Leninists can not see that a revolution to a classless society can't arise from a traditional class conflict over power, but only from the dissolution of all oppressed sectors and the emergence of a *revolutionary collectivity*. A modern revolution will be carried out against the ruling classes, not by oppressed classes, but by masses of democratically organized revolutionaries no longer primarily identifiable as 'class people.' Classical Marxist Leninist understanding is based on a revolution wherein people are concerned with power transfers; but people are now (and perhaps always?) concerned rather with an all-sided revolution that would deal with every aspect of the social question.

Workers and others develop revolutionary ideologies precisely to the extent they throw off their old traditional patterns of thinking and of acting. Classical Marxist Leninists don't realize that the worker must become less (capitalistically) workerlike and more revolutionary, that the doctor must become less doctorlike and more revolutionary, that each remains worker or doctor though each may also develop new skills, but that both become in the first place, revolutionaries. And Classical Marxist Leninists don't understand that the same is true for women, service employees, youths, Blacks, etc. Classical Marxist Leninists have yet to realize that work *under capitalism* inculcates more bad habits and more bad ways of thinking and acting than good -- and that that is a large part of why it is so oppressive. They have yet to sense that it is necessary for people to step outside the dictates of their present roles so as to construct new ways of being, more suitable to their own needs and to the needs of people around them. Though people must preserve what is good in their old ways, they must also drop what is bad; make fetishes of nothing.

Classical Marxist Leninists don't realize that when they cynically exploit the nature of the hierarchical factory's effects to bring people into hierarchical parties they are doing more harm than good. They don't have any idea of what it takes to create an environment that will allow people to escape from reactionary world views into revolutionary ones. They don't even address many of the major forms of oppression workers and others feel.

The Classical Marxist Leninists' problem isn't even that they will lead an abortive American revolution but that *they will lead no American revolution at all.* Americans won't risk comparative comfort and security because a central committee so orders them. Those Americans who are at the point where they might move spontaneously and then be coopted as happened in Russia, know that they are too few and too weak alone. No one is too interested in taking risks for a central committee that is part racist, part sexist, and authoritarian and bourgeois; it looks more promising and less dangerous to take lesser risks for fascists or capitalists who offer substantially the same rewards and have the same attributes. But there are exceptions. Some people do rapidly feel their injustices and further recognize that socialism of some kind is the only possible remedy. They then try to function in existing socialist movements but more often than not are unable to grow there. The movement dynamics foster the movement's members' own worst tendencies -- people become slaves of their movements, or they become immobile and despondent and drop out, or they rise in its hierarchy and make other members miserable. Classical Leninist parties, Classical Leninist centralism, and Classical Leninist narrownesses just can't sustain revolutionary activism over long periods in people who are struggling for freedom, integrity, and an end to illegitimate authority.

Modern western revolutionaries are confronted by a situation that the Classical Marxist Leninists have yet to fully appreciate:

> ...the process of the disintegration (of old forms) now becomes generalized and cuts across virtually all the traditional classes, values, and institutions. It creates entirely new issues, modes of struggle, forms of organiza-tion, and calls for an entirely new approach to theory and praxis. 2

The Classical Marxist Leninists rely on *economic* crisis even though it doesn't appear likely for the U.S. and isn't essential to revolutionary success. They aim at only workers even though many strata are in motion. They focus entirely on poverty when the distribution of centralized wealth is a major problem. They have a negative approach that attacks existing conditions when what is needed is a positive approach that aims at new conditions. They centralize and demand obedience when decentralization and anti-authoritarianism are critical. They prove incapable of understanding racism and sexism and of relating honestly to anti-racist and anti-sexist struggles even though these are growing more and more important. They cling to old tactics, old thoughts, and even old culture, and they do it because their identities, their interests, and their ideology demand that they do it. And though the best Classical Marxist Leninists quite obviously often get beyond many of these weaknesses, a little study usually shows that they are simultaneously and to the same extent getting beyond Classical Marxist Leninist dogma.

Classical Marxism is supposedly a philosophy of change and yet Classical Marxist Leninists do almost nothing to overcome the most pressing reactionary philosophic belief of our times: the belief that most if not all people are essentially lazy, dumb, evil, and greedy; the belief that no one can ever form a societal organization that is significantly better than that now existing in the United States. Classical Marxist Leninists damn just about anything and everything but they do almost nothing to constructively suggest new possibilities. There is very little in Classical Marxist ideology that can convince people things can get better and there is almost nothing in their practice that can convince people of the same thing. In fact their practice usually does more to prove the reverse. Perhaps Maurice Brinton is not going too far when he writes:

> In the struggle for these (truly humanitarian) objectives Bolshevism will eventually be seen to have been a monstrous aberration, the last garb donned by a bourgeois ideology as it was being subverted at the roots. Bolshevism's emphasis on the incapacity of the masses to achieve a socialist consciousness through their own experiences of life under capitalism, its presumption of a hierarchically structured 'vanguard' party and of 'centralization to fight the centralized state power of the bourgeoisie', its proclamation of the historical birthright of those who have accepted a

particular vision of society (and of its future) and the
decreed right to dictate the vision of others -- if necessary at
the point of a gun -- all these will be recognized for what
they are: the last attempt of bourgeois society to reassert its
ordained division into leaders and led, and to maintain
authoritarian social relations in all aspects of life. 3

Or Svetozar Stojanovic when he suggests:

It would seem that the theory of the unconscious should be
applied more broadly than it has been to include
revolutionary groups as well. The phenomenon of the
inversion of ends and means leads one to suspect that from
the very first there were subconscious goals underlying the
conscious ones, and that great differences existed between
them. The conscious goals, centered upon a society without
classes or a state, in circumstances like these only serve to
conceal the movement's subconscious desire to absolutize
itself once it reaches power. Individual Marxists have also
contributed to this tendency, albeit unintentionally, by
giving simplified and ultimately vague definitions of the
goal of socialist revolution, which in their view is the seizure
of power. 4

In any case Classical Marxism Leninism does not provide a suitable
basis for truly revolutionary activity. It rules out too much that is
important, emphasizes things that aren't as crucial as they might have
been, makes a fetish of organizational and behavorial forms that are destructive and totally unappealing, and creates a dynamic which leads
seemingly inexorably to dogmatism. It is not a growth ideology. The
relations between theory, strategy, and practice, and practitioners, are not
such as to lead to constant improvements. Marxism Leninism's
weaknesses have been made worse over time if they have changed at all. Its
latest practitioners have no real choice: they bend reality to suit their
conceptions, rather than bending their conceptions to suit reality. They
are not very self-conscious. They bend revolutionary impulses and
movements to fit their desires rather than vice versa or some middle
course.

The Russian revolution has given us a lesson in what is not to be done. It killed the soviets, it bombarded the Kronstadters, it destroyed the Makhnovites, it trampled opposition and reestablished capitalistic authoritarian dynamics, and then later and quite consistently it unleashed Stalin upon the peoples of the Soviet Union and the world.

There is a tremendous amount we can learn from Marx and those who followed, but a great deal of care should be taken lest we turn out as the Bolsheviks did. Being part right and cocksure is at least as bad as being all wrong but humble about it.

Kurt Vonnegut has a passage in a book essentially about Fascism's roots in human capacities for self-deception, that with some literary license, provides a fitting close to our present somewhat similar discussion:

I have never seen a more sublime demonstration of the totalitarian mind, a mind which might be likened unto a system of gears whose teeth have been filed at random. Such a snaggle toothed thought machine, driven by a standard or even substandard libido whirls with the jerky, gaudy, pointlessness, of a cuckoo clock in Hell.

Jones wasn't completely crazy. The dismaying thing about the classic totalitarian mind is that any given gear, though mutilated, will have at its circumference unbroken sequences of teeth that are immaculately maintained, that are exquisitely machined.

Hence the cuckoo clock in Hell -- keeping perfect time for eight minutes and thirty three seconds, jumping ahead fourteen minutes, keeping perfect time for six seconds, jumping ahead two seconds, keeping perfect time for two hours and one second, then jumping ahead a year.

The missing teeth of course are simple, obvious truths, truths available and comprehensible even to ten year olds, in most cases.

The willful filing off of gear teeth, the willful doing without certain obvious pieces of information --

That was how a household as conspicuous as one composed of Jones, Father Keely, Vice-Bundesfuehrer Krapptauer,

and the Black Feuhrer, could all exist in relative harmony --
That was how my father-in-law could contain in one mind
an indifference toward slave women and a love for a blue
vase --
That was how Rudolf Hoess, Commandant of Auschwitz,
could alternate over the loudspeakers of Auschwitz great
music and calls for corpse carriers --
That was how Germany could see no important differences
between civilization and hydrophobia. 5

And perhaps that was also how the Russian Bolsheviks could simultaneously proclaim revolution and repress all worker and peasant initiatives toward real self-management freedoms.

FOOTNOTES

1. Maurice Merleau-Ponty, *Humanism and Terror,* Beacon Press, Boston Mass. 150.

2. Murray Bookchin, *Post Scarcity Anarchism,* Ramparts Books, San Francisco.

3. Maurice Brinton, *The Bolsheviks and Workers' Control,* Solidarity, London. 85.

4. Svetozar Stojanovic, *Between Ideas and Reality,* Oxford University Press, London. 185.

5. Kurt Vonnegut, Jr., *Mother Night*, used with permission of Seymour Lawrence/Delacorte Press.

CHAPTER NINE

THE LIBERTARIAN ANARCHIST ALTERNATIVE

I believe that Anarchism is the finest and biggest thing man
has ever thought of; the only thing that can give you liberty
and well being, and bring peace and joy to the world. 1

Alexander Berkman

The Anarchist heritage provides one of many reactions to
Classical Marxism Leninism. It rebels against economism and central-
ism/authoritarianism, but often to a distorting extreme. As we'll see, it
makes many significant contributions while also regrettably creating some
new problems and leaving many old ones unaddressed.

Anarchism is a set of libertarian ideas, strategies, goals, behind which
no one has yet constructed an encompassing theory. It overlaps Classical
Marxism in many places while going beyond and falling short of it in
others. It diametrically opposes Leninism at almost all points. It is
constructed largely upon a basis of *anti-authoritarian impulses.* In this
chapter we examine it, as espoused by its most famous 'believers', trying
throughout to gather positive insights rather than to do a really thorough
critique.

Anarchists believe that evolution is largely driven by people's
tendencies toward *mutual aid* and the self-assertion of individual and
social needs. They feel that the fulfillment of each brings sequentially ever
greater moral goodness and joy, but they also warn that the process has
countless pitfalls. They argue that history's ugliness arises when things
interfere with people's otherwise natural tendencies toward sociability,
thereby causing painful conflicts. The things they put highest in causing
oppressive diversions from what would be an ideal flow of history are the
influences of property, religion, government, heirarchy, and the existence
of nation states and patriotism. And so Bakunin said:

Until now all human history has been only a perpetual and
bloody immolation of millions of poor human beings in
honor of some pitiless abstraction -- God, country, power of
State, national honor, historical rights, judicial rights,
political liberty, public welfare. 2

While Malatesta said:

We believe that most of the ills that afflict mankind stem
from bad social organization, and that man could destroy
them if he wished and knew how. 3

People are *naturally good*; they have tendencies to *sociability* and
they want health, liberty and well being. History is an evolutionary flow
toward a condition of political and economic freedom wherein social
instincts are free to reign and people have the capacities to meet their
own needs. The flow is exceptionally long and rocky precisely because
when an impediment arises the ensuing bad conditions of "existence
suppress and stifle the instincts of kindness and humanity in us, and
harden us against the need and misery of our fellow man." 4 In essence the
*Anarchists believe that when oppression exists it is because some people's
natures have become maligned by their positions in society, while other
people accept their plight because they become convinced it is either just
or necessary.* The oppression persists because the warped people continue
their unjust behavior and the downtrodden people more or less accept it
ad-infinitum, or at least until they, through the reality of their situations,
understand its unjustness and rebel against it.

Anarchists believe that the accumulation of property and power are
one of the means by which people have almost timelessly warped their own
instincts toward goodness and so have oppressed others. They feel that
property and the products of human labor are all social goods which owe
their existence to nature and to the social labors of countless individuals
and so they feel that private ownership is a kind of theft, wherein what
should really be communal is appropriated for the individual, to the
detriment of all other individuals. They believe that once people have appropriated what should be owned communally, they have gained unjust
advantages which they then automatically seek to defend and justify. By a
vicious dynamic *property and wealth* become central to such people's

identities and lead them to oppress others precisely in efforts to defend or to gain more power and wealth. So Bakunin says:

> Much more seriously than they themselves realize, property is (their) God, their only God, which long ago replaced in their hearts the heavenly god of the Christians. And, like the latter, in days of yore, the bourgeois are capable of suffering martyrdom and death for the sake of this God. The ruthless and desperate war they wage for the defense of property is not only a war of interests: it is a religious war in the full meaning of the word. 5

Power, wealth, and authority once they appear in history march through hand in hand, creating people who oppress, and then justify and defend that state of oppression. As Berkman says:

> Authority tends to make its possessor unjust and arbitrary; it also makes those subject to it acquiesce in wrong, subservient, and servile. Authority corrupts its holder and debases its victim. 6

And so Bakunin shows the relations of power and wealth to each other:

> Political power and wealth are inseparable. Those who have power have the means to gain wealth and must center all their efforts upon acquiring it, for without it they will not be able to retain their power. Those who are wealthy must become strong, for, lacking power, they run the risk of being deprived of their wealth. The toiling masses have always been powerless because they were poverty stricken, and they were poverty stricken because they lacked organized power. 7

The anarchists feel, then, that the devil in history is the "power principle," the reality that once inequalities appear they tend to persist, to create and to recreate themselves over and over to the detriment of the whole of humanity's real potentials for rewarding sociability. For the anarchists once inequity arises it creates rationalizations that twist people's characters making some into oppressors and some into more or less acquiescent oppressed.

> Power operates only destructively, bent always on forcing every manifestation of life into the straightjacket of its laws. Its intellectual form of expression is dead dogma, its physical form brute force. And this unintelligence of its objectives sets its stamp on its supporters also and renders them stupid and brutal, even when they were originally endowed with the best of talents. One who is consistently striving to force everything into a mechanical order at last becomes a machine himself and loses all human feeling. 8

So in the anarchist view people have *instinctively good tendencies* that are often sidetracked by the development of inequities and by the persistence of ignorance of the true state of things. For the anarchists law plays a very important role in the whole dynamic. It is used by those who have, to justify their relative good fortune, and to convince those who have not, that their plight is a *necessary* one that should be made the best of, but not actively opposed. Thus law justifies the accumulation of wealth and power, gives legitimacy to those who have it, and puts reins on those who don't. And law is believed because it is high sounding, because it appeals to what is good in people by preaching its own equity, and because within its totality it also includes all those common sense precepts of behavior that people normally accept anyhow. As Kropotkin points out:

> Such was law and it has maintained its twofold character to this very day. Its origin is the desire of the ruling class to give permanence to customs imposed by themselves for their own advantage. Its character is the skillful comingling of customs useful to society, customs which have no need of law to insure their respect, with other customs useful only to rulers, injurious to the mass of the people, and maintained only by the fear of punishment. 9

So the anarchist view is one of impeded human goodness leading to oppression and the defense of oppression by power and by law. But who administers the laws and who really applies the accumulated power?

> In all times and in all places, whatever be the name that the
> government takes, whatever has been its origin or its organ-
> ization, its essential function is always that of oppressing and
> exploiting the masses, and of defending the exploiters and
> oppressors. Its principle characteristic and indespensible
> instruments are the policeman and the tax collector, the
> soldier and the prison. 10

Tendencies toward sociability are abrogated at least for a span of
history and at least to a certain extent -- the state evolves. It creates,
recreates, accumulates, and defends power, privilege, and wealth, and it
has no other important purpose or capacity.

> Every type of political power presupposes some form of
> human slavery for the maintainence of which it is called into
> being. Just as outwardly -- that is in relation to other states
> --the state has to create certain artificial antagonisms in
> order to justify its existence, so also internally the cleavage
> of society into castes, ranks and classes is an essential
> condition of its continuation. The state is capable only of
> protecting old privileges and creating new ones; in that, its
> whole significance is exhausted. 11

The state and the whole social organization take varying forms and
evolve precisely as the struggle of people's inner natures to assert
themselves affects those forms and moves them ever so gradually toward
political and economic equity. But in the meantime government prevails
and continues by one means or another in its gruesome work. Proudhon's
rather long 'catechism' of the ills of government probably best exemplifies
the anarchist vehemence on the subject if not their clarity of understanding:

> To be governed is to be watched over, inspected, spied
> upon, directed, legislated, regimented, closed in, indoc-
> trinated, preached at, controlled, assessed, evaluated,
> censored, commanded, all by creatures that have neither
> the right nor wisdom nor virtue.... To be governed means
> that at every move, operation, or transaction, one is noted,

registered, entered in a census, taxed, stamped, priced, assessed, patented, licensed, authorized, recommended, admonished, prevented, reformed, set right, corrected. Government means to be subjected to tribute, trained, ransomed, exploited, monopolized, extorted, pressured, mystified, robbed, all in the name of public utility and the general good. Then at the first sign of resistance or word of complaint, one is repressed, despised, vexed, pursued, hustled, beaten up, garroted, imprisoned, shot, machine gunned, judged, sentenced, deported, sacrificed, sold, betrayed, and to cap it all, ridiculed, mocked, outraged, and dishonored. That is government, this is its justice and morality! 12

For the anarchists government is thus the administrative vehicle by which any society's most powerful wealthy groups enforce their wills over everyone else's. Thus, for anarchists, whatever economic socio-cultural form a particular society has, if there is oppression, there is also a state upholding that oppression in the interests of the rich, and to the detriment of everyone else.

In the flow of history one such social economic form that has emerged, that impeded man's natural tendencies and that preserves itself, is capitalism. Anarchists see it as a system of mass robbery wherein those who own steal from those who must sell their labor, while the state justifies and defends the whole process. They feel that under capitalism liberty is a pretense because, although people do have certain freedoms, most are not 'rich' enough, or free enough from their bosses to get any real pleasure from their freedoms. The anarchists, like the Marxists, feel that the whole of society is organized around the maintenance of ruling class wealth to the relative detriment of everyone else's situation and of all people's overall potentials for good.

They feel that capitalism's inequities cause crime and promote false ideas and they feel that the maintenance of capitalism is itself the greatest of all possible crimes because it inevitably leads to pillage, war, persecution, and hardship.

Capitalism is the greatest crime of all; ... it devours more lives in a single day than all the murderers put together. 13

The anarchists perceive that beyond its legal apparatus and its police, capitalism prevails because it sells itself to the people as something worth preserving, fighting, and even dying for. The capitalists are the burglars; the workers are the buglarized, and the state is the vehicle that forces the workers to praise their exploiters. The exploitation is acomplished by means of the laws of the state, its schools, its socialization processes and of course finally by its coercive powers.

> Just now I want to tell you why the worker does not take the burglar by the neck and kick him out; that is, why he begs the capitalist for a little more bread or wages, and why he does not throw him off his back altogether. It is because the worker, like the rest of the world, has been made to believe that everything is all right and must remain as it is; and that if a few things are not quite as they should be, then it is because 'people are bad', and everything will right itself in the end, anyhow. 14

The anarchists see capitalism built on inequity, private accumulation, coercion, the power of the state, and the power of the big lie. They have no faith in the power of reform. They believe that reforming conditions to try to alleviate one problem is most often totally useless, sometimes succeeds in one area to the detriment of some other, and also often incidentally actually works to legitimate the whole system and thus do more harm then good. Malatesta talks at length of the dynamics:

> The fundamental error of the reformists is that of dreaming of solidarity, a sincere collaboration between masters and servants, between proprietors and workers, which even if it might have existed here and there in periods of profound unconsciousness of the masses and of ingenuous faith in religions and rewards, is utterly impossible today.
>
> Those who envision a society of well stuffed pigs which waddle contentedly under the ferule of the small number of swineherd; who do not take into acount the need for freedom and the sentiment of human dignity: who really believe in a god that orders for his abstruse ends, the poor to be submissive and the rich to be good and charitable --

can also imagine and aspire to a technical organization of production which assures abundance to all and is at the same time materially advantageous both to the bosses and to the workers. But in reality social peace based on abundance for all will remain a dream, so long as society is divided into antagonistic classes, that is employers and employees. And there will be neither peace nor abundance. 15

The oppressed either ask for and welcome improvements as a benefit graciously conceded, recognize the legitimacy of the power which is over them, and so do more harm than good by helping to slow down or divert and perhaps even stop the processes of emancipation. Or instead they demand and impose improvements by their action, and welcome them as partial victories over the class enemy, using them as a spur to greater achievements, and thus they are a real help and a preparation to the total overthrow of privilege, that is, for the revolution. 16

Above everything else, then, anarchists are concerned with putting history back on a course aimed toward complete freedom for all. They are revolutionaries and the bulk of their writings and efforts deal with the goals they seek and the methods by which they hope to help all people reach them. Since they see human nature as basically sociable and good, anarchists envision a future society which is completely unleashed from restraint, and in which, as a result, there is the highest possible amount of material and spiritual fulfillment for all. Kropotkin says:

We already forsee a state of society where the liberty of the individual will be limited by no laws, no bonds -- by nothing else but his own social habits, and the necessity which everyone feels, of finding cooperation, support, and sympathy among his neighbors. 17

The anarchists believe such a thing possible precisely because they see that all history shows the only result of coercive institutions is the blocking rather than the fruition of freedom, and this because people tend to sociability naturally and are only hindered by the creation of inequity or the centralization of power. Thus as Emma Goldman says:

> Anarchism is the only philosophy which brings to man the consciousness of himself, which maintains that god, the state, and society, are non-existent, that their promises are null and void, since they can be fulfilled only through man's subordination. Anarchism is therefore the teacher of the unity of life; not merely in nature, but in man. There is no conflict between the individual and the social instincts: the one the receptacle of the precious life essence, the other the repository of the element that keeps that essence pure and strong. The individual is the heart of society, conserving the essence of social life; society is the lungs, which are distributing the element to keep the life essence -- that is, the individual, pure and strong. 18

Anarchists believe societies should serve *each individual's* needs and aspirations as well as those of the *whole collectivity*. They see individual and social needs as harmonious. They thus require elimination of government, private accumulation, and all forms of socially coercive power, precisely because they believe these contribute only oppressions to the societies in which they persist. Anarchists want an end to all obstacles that stand between people and the fulfillment of their needs, and so they want communal ownership, collective participatory decision making, and activity solely through mutual agreements.

> What we want, therefore, is the complete destruction of the domination and exploitation of man by man; we want man united as brothers by a conscious and desired solidarity, all cooperating voluntarily for the well being of all; we want society to be constituted for the purpose of supplying everybody with the means for achieving the maximum well being, the maximum possible moral and spiritual development; we want bread, freedom, love, and science -- for everybody. 19

The anarchists are not content solely with an attack upon the

institutions of old. They believe that during history's passage people have
been mutilated by their conditions and have thereby adopted countless
anti-social counter productive ways of thinking and acting. And these too
have no place in anarchism's future visions.

> It is not only against the abstract trinity of law, religion, and
> authority that we declare war. By becoming anarchists we
> declare war against all this wave of deceit, cunning, exploi-
> tation, depravity, vice -- in a word inequality -- which they
> have poured into all our hearts. We declare war against
> their way of acting, against their way of thinking. The
> governed, the deceived, the exploited, the prostituted,
> wound above all else our sense of equality. It is in the name
> of equality that we are determined to have no more
> prostituted, exploited, deceived, and governed men and
> women. 20

For as Berkman points out :

> Life in freedom, in anarchy, will do more than liberate man
> from his present political and economic bondage. That will
> be only the first step, the preliminary to a truly human
> existence. Far greater and more significant will be the
> results of such liberty, its effects upon man's mind, upon his
> personality. The abolition of the coercive external will, and
> with it the fear of authority, will loosen the bonds of moral
> compulsion no less than of economic and physical. Man's
> spirit will breathe freely, and that mental emancipation will
> be the birth of a new culture, a new humanity. 21

In essence the anarchists are concerned with creating
full communism in people's minds and hearts and in their institutions, but
their methods and priorities are very different from those of the Classical
Marxist Leninists.

The anarchists understand that capitalism exists largely because it is
accepted as just or at least necessary. They realize that "social structure
rests on a basis of ideas, which implies that changing the structures
presupposes changed ideas." 22 They realize that revolution is merely an

excited part of evolution, an excited part of the continual flow of human relations towards conditions of universal mutual aid. And so they realize that "only that revolution can be fundamental which will be the expression of a basic change of ideas and opinions." 23 They know that revolutions break out against bad conditions and in hope of achieving better, and they know that--

> Indispensable for the beginning of any revolution are, first of all, the realization of dissatisfaction with the present, the consciousness of the endlessness of this condition and of its irreparability by customary means, and finally, a readiness for risk in order to change this condition. 24

In the anarchist view *revolution can proceed when there is a mass change of public ideology -- its success or failure depends upon whether the desires of the masses are translated into organic changes or merely misled or redirected into new kinds of oppression,* by the use of bad tactics, by ill preparedness, by ignorances, or by treachery. And so anarchists feel the necessity to determine what should not be done lest they impede revolutionary potentials or subvert the revolution itself, and what should be done to foster revolutionary potentials and to ensure that once revolution breaks out it progresses toward full success.

Anarchist are exceptionally attentive to the possibilities of errors and to the chance of bad means subverting desired ends:

> It all depends, as you see, on what your purpose is, what you want to accomplish. Your aims must determine the means. Means and aims are in reality the same; you cannot separate them. It is the means that shape your ends. The means are the seeds which bud into flower and come to fruition. The fruit will always be of the nature of the seed you planted. You can't grow a rose from a cactus seed. No more can you harvest liberty from compulsion, justice and manhood from dictatorship. 25

> Let us learn this lesson well because the fate of revolution depends upon it. "You shall reap what you sow" is the acme of all human wisdom and experience. 26

The anarchist criticisms of the Bolshevik revolution are virtually merciless and the general lesson they teach is simply that motion alone is not the sole criterion of revolutionary value; rather it is motion to what end, victory with what result. And when anarchists are accosted and told they are too demanding and the pace they would set for the development of revolutionary program is too exacting they reply with no hesitation:

> Maybe you think this too slow a process, a work that will take too long. Yes, I must admit that it is a difficult task. But ask yourself if it is better to build your new house quickly and badly and have it break down over your head, rather than to do it efficiently, even if it requires longer and harder work. 27

Given their overall awarenesses, the anarchists have a few very simple criteria for judging the totality of all their programs:

> ...that is to unite the dissatisfied elements, to promote the acquaintance of separate units or groups with the aspirations and actions of other similar groups, to help the people define more clearly the true causes of dissatisfaction, to help them define more clearly their actual enemies, removing the mask from those enemies who hide behind some decorous disguise, and finally, to contribute to the elucidation of the nearest practical goals and the means of their realization. 28

So in thinking tactically about revolution anarchists oppose the use of any tactics that inhibit revolutionary activities or foster traits which might subvert their ultimate goal. *They oppose the use of centralization because it corrupts leaders and paralyzes followers, they oppose using capitalist methods nad especially a new state formation because such activity would subvert and the rest of their ends, and they oppose sectarianism, arrogance, and the use of repression, and the indiscriminate use of violence because each of these fosters bad attitudes and impedes any intimations of revolutionary possibilities.*

But it is easiest to let them speak for themselves about each of these points in sequence:

Representatively, Rudolf Rocker says of centralism and other capitalist forms:

> For the state, centralism is the appropriate form of organization, since it aims at the greatest possible uniformity in social life for the maintenance of political and social equilibrium. but for a movement whose very existence depends on prompt action at any favorable moment and on the independent thought and action of its supporters, centralism could be but a curse, by weakening its power of decision and systematically repressing all immediate action. 29

> Just as the functions of the bodily organs of plants and animals cannot be arbitrarily altered, so that, for example, one cannot at will hear with his eyes and see with his ears, so one also cannot at pleasure transform an organ of social repression into an instrument for the liberation of the oppressed. The state can only be what it is: the defender of mass exploitation and social privileges, the creator of privileged classes and castes and of new monopolies. 30

And Maletesta argues on the questions of mental attitude, violence, and repression:

> To the 'will to believe', which cannot be other than the desire to invalidate one's own reason, I oppose the 'will to know', which leaves the immense field of research and discovery open to us. As I have already stated, I admit only that which can be proved in a way that satisfies my reason -- and I admit it only provisionally, relatively, always in the expectation of new truths which are more true than those so far discovered. No faith then, in the religious sense of the word. 31

> Violence is justified only when it is necessary to defend

oneself and others from violence. It is where necessity ceases that crime begins.... The slave is always in a state of legitimate defense, and consequently his violence against the boss, against the oppressor, is always morally justifiable and must be controlled only by such considerations as that the best and most economical use is being made of human effort and human sufferings. 32

Terror has always been the instrument of tyranny.... Those who believe in the liberating effects and revolutionary efficiency of repression and savagery have the same kind of backward mentality as the jurists who believe that crimes can be prevented and the world morally improved by the imposition of stiff punishments. 33

Since anarchists believe in the necessity of *creating liberated people as well as a liberated social structure,* and since they believe in the critical importance of education and preparation for administering a new society, their programs generally center around activities aimed at radicalizing workers' initiatives and consciousnesses, and bettering their position to eventually take over society through expropriation and to then administer society in accord with their long accumulated firsthand knowledge. They form organizations that at least try to involve people at all levels and spread skills and information. They do lots of political education, and they prepare workers for the tasks of striking, taking the factories, and then effectively reorganizing society according to new dictates without the imposition of new central authorities.

To these ends they believe in forming industry wide workers' organizations that can strike, and that prepare workers for their eventual 'administrative' roles. They believe in breaking down barriers between town and country and between intellectual and manual workers as early in the organization process as possible. Thus with regard to preparation for new conditions they say:

That reorganization will depend, first and foremost, on the thorough familiarity of labor with the economic situation of the country: on a complete inventory of the supply, on exact knowledge of the sources of raw material, and on the proper

organization of the labor forces for efficient management. 34

And since the anarchists feel that it is necessary for reorganization to be
from the bottom up rather than ordered by a new central authority, they
feel that the revolutionary program must *include means by which workers
gain the personal initiative and knowledge to handle the tasks themselves.*
The strengths of the anarchist perspective reside in the way that it fills
some of the weaknesses of Classical Marxism Leninism: it puts more
emphasis upon people's needs and natures, better grasps the role of
non-material factors in history, understands authority and anti-authoritarianism better, is generally somewhat less sectarian, acknowledges as
more important the roles and dynamics of institutions, work relations, and
especially the state, has a more freeing tone, and puts more emphasis on
the fallibility of its own practitioners and on the need for personal
improvement. In essence it adds to Classical Marxism a *libertarian
emphasis* that overthrows many of Classical Leninism's major precepts,
without eliminating any of its radical content.
      Anarchist weaknesses reside in shortcomings and imbalances.
Anarchism puts more emphasis on individuals than does Classical
Marxism but it still lacks a 'psychological model' that can be a basis for
common collective tactical analyses. It critiques hierarchical authority but
doesn't really offer concrete organizational alternatives. It lacks an overall
theory that can be used not only to support its major general assertions,
but also to help practitioners analyse new situations and further examine
familiar ones. Perhaps most importantly, although it has excellent desires
vis-a-vis political education, increasing popular initiatives, and improving
personalities, it has *little real methodology for accomplishing any such
ends.* It minimizes the importance of impediments and thus fails to even
roughly understand them. Anarchism is a consciousness with important
things to say about revolution but with little power to actually guide one's
activities. It is simply too divorced from the difficulties of mass organiz-
ing/organization and motion. Criticizing centralism and realpolitic to
deserved extremes, its practice and rhetoric both make clear an obvious
gap concerning what should take the place of centralism and realpolitic.
      Though our summary has been very concise, it has nonethless shown
that anarchism is at least as relevant to some areas of our present concern
as Classical Marxism Leninism. Much could be gained by studying

anarchist literature in more detail, in at least as much detail as is given for example, to the works of Classical Marxism Leninism. The one is too 'utopian', the other too 'reactionary', but both can certainly inform us. Further we might resonably guess that whenever a new revolutionary ideology is developed it will not really so much contradict most anarchist perspectives as greatly broaden and enlighten them.

In our next chapter we show how Maoism in fact moves a bit toward synthesizing Classical Marxist Leninist strengths with complementary anarchist ones. We particularly emphasize Maoist efforts to broaden theory, broaden methodology, diminish sectarianism, overcome athoritarianism, overcome economism, and deal better with questions of personality in politics, freedom, centralization, leadership, and strategy in general, all in the context of the specific Chinese socio-political cultural pragmatic situation.

FOOTNOTES

1. Berkman, *What is Communist Anarchism?*, Dover.
2. Bakunin in *Quotations From The Anarchists*, edited by Paul Berman, Praeger Publishers.
3. Malatesta in *Quotations*, op. cit.
4. ibid.
5. Bakunin, *The Knouto- germanic Empire*, quoted in Berman, op. cit.
6. Berkman, op. cit.
7. Bakunin in *Science and the Urgent Revolutionary Task*, quoted in Berman, op. cit.
8. Rudolf Rocker, *Anarcho-Syndicalism*, London.
9. Kropotkin in Kropotkin's Revolutionary Pamphlets, M.I.T. Press.
10. Berkman, op. cit.
11. Rocker, op. cit.
12. Proudhon in *Quotations*, op. cit.
13. Berkman, op. cit.
14. ibid.
15. Malatesta in Vernon Richards, *Malatesta's Life and Ideas*, London.
16. ibid.
17. Kropotkin, op. cit.
18. Emma Goldman in *Anarchism and Other Essays*, Dover, New York.
19. Malatesta, op. cit.
20. Berkman, op. cit.
21. ibid.
22. Kropotkin in *Quotations*, op. cit.
23. ibid.
24. ibid.
25. Berkman, op. cit.
26. ibid.
27. ibid.
28. Kropotkin, op. cit.
29. Rocker, op. cit.
30. ibid.
31. Malatesta, op. cit.
32. ibid.
33. ibid.
34. Berkman, op. cit.

CHAPTER TEN

THE CHINESE EXPERIENCE

Everything reactionary is the same; if you don't hit it, it won't fall. It is like sweeping the floor; as a rule where the broom does not reach, the dust will not vanish of itself .... We must work hard at reworking our world view. 1

Mao-Tse-tung

Comparisons between Classical Marxism Leninism and Maoism generally emphasize bulk differences: peasants versus proletariat; people's war versus class struggle; red bases versus organizing cells; sensitivity to bureaucracy and incentive issues versus espousal of even Taylorism; and so on. But such approaches often bog down by not distinguishing between contrasts due to change of contexts and contrasts due to really significant and general changes of political orientation.

Thus there are major differences between Classical Marxism Leninism and Maoism because of differences between Russia and China but also in some instances because of actual changes in the employed revolutionary paradigm. Our approach is to examine bulk analysis differences with an eye toward distilling the paradigm alterations partly underlying them. We want to show how Maoists and Classical Marxist Leninists not only focus on different aspects of their environments but also even perceive similar things differently, analyze them differently, and then seek to affect them differently, precisely because each sets out with a different guiding paradigm. We want then to consider whether changes from Classical Marxism Leninism to Maoism are helpful, and if so, whether there are any lessons for our own efforts to create paradigm improvements.

In this chapter we will summarily examine Maoist ideology and some of the history of the Chinese revolution. We determine three main things: 1-Maoism goes well beyond Classical Marxism Leninism, 2-Maoism bears out our specific understandings of Classical Marxism Leninism's weaknesses, and 3-Maoism leads us towards a number of new ideas highly applicable to our own situations, though by no means providing a whole new consciousness we can simply adopt in full.

The Chinese say that all their activities are guided by Classical Marxism Leninism coupled with the Thoughts of Chairman Mao. They say Maoist thought is really just strategic and tactical analysis carried on within the framework of China's own concrete problems. 2

We find this misleading and will show that Maoism *alters rather than merely reinterpreting* Classical views. We feel the effort will help explain conflicts between Maoists and Classical Marxist Leninists and between China and Russia, and we also feel it will round out our understanding of past ideologies before we try to draw some lessons concerning what new ones should be like.

THE THEORY OF CONTRADICTIONS

The Maoist theory of contradictions broadens, refines, and extends the applicability of the Classic view. In this section we discuss how, ending with a summary of the change's positive practical effects.

The theory says all things change primarily because of their own inner natures. Thus, "the fundamental cause for the development of a thing is not external but internal; it lies in the contradictoriness within the thing." 3 Nature follows its course due to its own internal tendency for contradictions. Taken as systems, factories change in accord with internal contradictions, and likewise for political parties. Similarly societies evolve because of the natures of their own internal contradictions. But factories, political parties, and societies, are not systems in isolation but in environmental contexts: though their changes are rooted internally, they are cause externally:

> According to materialist dialectics, changes in nature are due chiefly to the development of internal contradictions in nature. Changes in society are due chiefly to the development of the internal contradictions in society, that is, the contradiction between the productive forces and the relations of production, the contradiction between classes, and the contradiction between the old and the new; it is the development of these contradictions that pushes the society forward and gives the impetus for the supersession of the old society by the new. Does materialist dialectics exclude

external causes? Not at all. It holds that external causes are
the conditions of change and internal causes are the basis of
change, and that external causes become operative through
internal causes. 4

As Mao put it, in certain conditions an egg can change into a chicken
but no matter what the environment it will not change into a stone. Its
internal contradictions are the bases for all the change it undergoes. With
an egg there is a potential to be a chicken but none to be a stone. "It is
through internal causes that external causes become operative" for nature
(the egg), and for societies too:

In China in 1927, the defeat of the proletariat by the big
bourgeoisie came about through the opportunism then to
be found within the Chinese proletariat itself (inside the
Chinese Communist Party). When we liquidated the
opportunism, the Chinese revolution resumed its advance.
Later the Chinese revolution again suffered severe setbacks
at the hands of the enemy, because adventurism had arisen
within our Party. When we liquidated this adventurism, our
cause advanced once again. Thus it can be seen that to lead
the revolution to victory, a political party must depend on
the correctness of its own political line and the solidity of its
own organization. 5

All contradictions have two aspects which are in conflict but at the same
time interdependent.
    Again, as Mao put it, with no night there is no day, with no movement
there is no stillness, with no war there is no peace, and with no chicken
there is no egg. Each aspect of a contradiction owes its existence as a
definable thing to the existence of the other aspect. Still at any moment
one aspect or the other holds greater sway and then contributes to the
definition of its encompassing system:

In any contradiction the development of the contradictory
aspects is uneven. Sometimes they seem to be in equili-
brium, which is however only temporary and relative, while
unevenness is basic. Of the two contradictory aspects, one

must be principal and the other secondary. The principal aspect is the one playing the leading role in the contradiction. The nature of a thing is determined mainly by the principal aspect of a contradiction, the aspect which has gained the dominant position. 6

A given system undergoes change only if it embodies a contradiction. And a contradiction exists only if there are two contradictory aspects which are interdependent because they exist in a single thing, because they depend upon one another for their being, and because under the right conditions they can change into one another, as for example war into peace and night into day.

The transformation of one thing into another, through leaps of different forms in accordance with its essence and external conditions -- this is the process of new superseding the old. In each thing there is a contradiction between its new and its old aspects, and this gives rise to a series of struggles with many twists and turns. As a result of these struggles, the new aspect changes from being minor to being major and rises to predominance, while the old aspect changes from being major to being minor and gradually dies out. And the moment the new aspect gains dominance over the old, the old thing changes qualitatively into a new thing. It can thus be seen that the nature of a thing is mainly determined by the principal aspect of the contradiction, the aspect which has gained predominance. When the principal aspect which has gained predominance changes, the nature of a thing changes accordingly. 7

For the Chinese such passages are not abstract philosophical rhetoric but rather a useful outlook that "teaches us primarily how to observe and analyze the movement of opposites in different things, and on the basis of such analysis, to indicate the methods for resolving contradictions," and thus for changing real situations in desirable ways. 8 But since real situations are always highly complex, involving many contradictions, Mao broadens his apparatus accordingly.

Large systems involve many contradictions and undergo many kinds of changes. Maoism says that in all such situations one contradiction is primary even though many may be at work. The primary one affects the others as they ebb and flow, more than vice versa. The primary one's principal aspect is the part of the inner nature of the whole system that predominantly determines the system's overall character and the characters of the changes it can go through.

In societies generally, the primary contradiction is between forces and relations, the old mode and the new mode, the oppressor and oppressed classes. In capitalism in particular, the contradiction is between the social character of production and the private character of ownership, socialism and capitalism, the bourgeoisie and the proletariat. In societies generally and capitalism particularly, other societal conflicts and on-going changes can be best understood in terms of these primary ones rather than vice versa.

For every well defined process there is a primary contradiction and as its two aspects struggle, they exert greater influence on the unfolding of the other contradictions in the process, than the others exert back on them.

> When imperialism launches a war of aggression against such a (semi-colonial) country, all its various classes, except for some traitors, can temporarily unite in a war against imperialism. At such a time, the contradiction between imperialism and the country concerned becomes the principal contradiction, while the contradictions among the various classes within the country (including what was the principal contradiction, between the feudal system and the great masses of the people) are temporarily relegated to a secondary and subordinate position. 9

For Maoists universality is the general fact that all processes have many contradictions, one primary one, two aspects for each contradiction, and one principal aspect for each contradiction. It is the general fact that in all cases the principal aspect of the primary contradiction determines the overall nature of the system embodying that contradiction. It is the fact that when the principal aspect changes from dominating to being dominated by its opposite, there is a new principal aspect and the entire nature of the embodying system changes. And it is above all else the fact that even though contradiction is most evident at points of qualitative alteration, it is always present:

> The universality or absoluteness of contradiction has a twofold meaning. One is that contradiction exists in the process of development of all things, and the other is that in the process of development of each thing a movement of opposites exists from beginning to end. 10

The particularity of contradiction is on the other hand, just the fact that every process has its own unique qualities. It is the fact that for any given concrete system the universal knowledge that there is an internal state of contradiction and so on, is only the first step to full understanding. For what is most crucial are the specific forms each of the universally existent qualities take in each specific case:

> The particular essence of each form of motion is determined by its own particular contradiction. This holds true not only for nature but also for social and ideological phenomena. Every form of society, every form of ideology has its own particular contradiction and particular essence. 11

Mao makes it clear that to understand the particularity of any contradiction it is necessary to understand it in its interconnectedness to other contradictions, as well as to understand each of its aspects. Further, to understand an aspect of a contradiction one had to understand all the forms that aspect takes in its struggle and interdependences with its opposite. According to Mao this is all accomplished by means of "concrete analyses of concrete conditions."

> There are many contradictions in the course of development of any major thing. For instance, in the course of development of China's bourgeois democratic revolution, where the contradictions are exceedingly complex, there exists the contradiction between all oppressed classes in Chinese society and imperialism, the contradiction between the great masses of people and feudalism, the contradiction between the proletariat and the bourgeoisie, the contradic-

tion between the peasantry and the urban petty bourgeois on the one hand and the bourgeoisie on the other, the contradiction between various reactionary ruling groups, and so on. These contradictions cannot be treated in the same ways since each has its own particularity; moreover the two aspects of each contradiction cannot be treated in the same way since each aspect has its own characteristics. We who are engaged in the Chinese revolution should not only understand the particularity of these contradictions in their totality, that is, in their interconnections, but should also study the two aspects of each contradiction as the only means of understanding the totality. When we speak of understanding each aspect of a contradiction, we mean understanding what specific position each aspect occupies, what concrete forms it assumes in its interdependence and in its contradiction with its opposite, and what methods are employed in the struggle with its opposite, when the two are both interdependent and in contradiction, and also after the interdependence breaks down. 12

Thus according to Maoism if we are to use the dialectical method to explain situations or make predictions about them, we must understand *both sides* of each contradiction and aspect in the situation, and also know which contradiction is primary. Dogmatists err by studying only *one or a few of many contradictions*, or only one aspect of each, or by creating formulas and applying them *indiscriminately* without knowing how they emerge or where they actually fit.

Where our dogmatists err on this question is that on the one hand they do not understand that we have to study the particularity of contradiction and know the particular essence of individual things before we can adequately know the universality of contradiction and the common essence of things, and that on the other hand, they do not understand that after knowing the common essence of things, we must go further and study the concrete essence of things that have not been thoroughly studied, or have only just emerged. 13

But what is the actual practical form of contradictions, and most importantly of politico-socio economic ones? Surely it is not something always given but rather something that changes for different systems and in different contexts. Most importantly, Maoists show, in this regard, how resolutions of contradictions which change dominance relations between aspects always cause qualitative changes in system characteristics, but also how these resolutions do not always require violent struggle, or a loss by one or the other combatant.

When, on the one hand, there is a contradiction between forces and relations of production and between classes whose interests lie with one or the other, the clash is antagonistic and resolution only furthers one side's interests. But, on the other hand, when there is a contradiction between two proposed work methods in a factory after a socialist revolution and between adherents of each, resolution favors all strugglers and the process is itself non-antagonistic.

In such cases, though contradictions resolution brings qualitative changes, the old system's characteristics are enhanced rather than undermined. This is the development in Maoism of the theory of *non-antagonistic contradictions*. 14

> Contradiction and struggle are universal and absolute, but the methods of resolving contradictions, that is, the forms of struggle, differ according to the differences in the nature of the contradictions. Some contradictions are characterized by open antagonism, others are not. In accordance with the concrete development of things, some contradictions which were originally non-antagonistic develop into antagonistic ones, while others which were originally antagonreferences forebearers. in contrast there revolutionaries;

Thus in its broadest sense the Maoist theory of contradictions says in summary: The universe is composed of things ranging in complexity from simple 'stones' and 'dollar bills' to highly complex 'classes' and 'governments', and combinations of any and all with each other. There are a multitude of things any one or more of which can be studied as a system amidst many other systems.

Systems go through processes of change in accordance with their internal contradictions. Any system's major characteristics are those of the principal aspect of the primary contradiction of the main process through which the system is going. When systems come into mutual contact (always and inevitably) they affect one another's processes of development, but in no case does an external cause create something that wasn't already potentially existent inside a system's contradictoriness.

Change actually occurs when aspects switch dominance relative to one another. The associated struggle is sometimes non-antagonistic and sometimes antagonistic. In understanding any given process one must fully understand universality and particularity. The Maoist dialectician in accord with the Maoist theory of contradiction continually analyzes systems in terms of the motion of opposites so as to find suitable methods for resolving given contradictions in desirable directions.

Thus Maoism first extends the method of contradiction to all and not just macro-historical systems, and second refines its categories (primary, principal, etc.), and third extends its applicability from changes which only undermine given systems to changes which further them, and form changes brought about only violently to those brought about partly or totally 'persuasively.'

We can expect that these alteration will help Maoists better analyze localized problems; analyze all problems more deeply, methodically, and generally; and also analyze non-antagonistic problems, finally; all of which improvements should contrast mightily with parallel Classical weaknesses.

THEORY OF KNOWLEDGE

The Maoist theory of knowledge, like the Classical Marxist one, centers on reflection but nonetheless also goes somewhat beyond the Classical form. It addresses more carefully how consciousness goes from a blurry image to a fine reflection, and how it then even goes from a fine reflection of surface qualities to a fine reflection of 'essential' ones. In tune with these results it also discusses dogmatism's causes and effects, with an emphasis on methods of prevention. In this section we discuss these results concluding with a summary of their positive practical effects.

According to Mao, knowledge develops from perception to cognition, to practice and back again:

In the process of practice, man at first sees only the phenomenal side, the separate aspects, the external relations of things. For instance, some people from outside come to Yenan on a tour of observation. In the first day or two, they see its topography, streets and houses; they meet many people, attend banquets, evening parties and mass meetings, hear talk of various kinds and read various documents, all these being the phenomena, the separate aspects and the external relations of things. This is called the perceptual stage of cognition, namely the stage of sense perceptions and impressions. That is, these particular things in Yenan act on the sense organs of the members of the observation group, evoke sense perceptions and rise in their brains to make many impressions together with a rough sketch of the external relations among these impressions: this is the first stage of cognition. At this stage, man cannot as yet form concepts, which are deeper, or draw logical conclusions.

As social practice continues, things that give rise to man's sense perceptions and impressions in the course of his practice are repeated many times; then a sudden change (leap) takes place in the brain in the process of cognition and concepts are formed. Concepts are no longer the phenomena, the separate aspects and the external relations of things; they grasp the essence, the totality, and the internal relations of things. Between concepts and sense perceptions there is not only a quantitative but also a qualitative difference. Proceeding further, by means of judgement and inference one is able to draw logical conclusions. The expression in San Kuo Yen Yi, "knit the brows and a strategem comes to mind," or in everyday language, "let me think it over," refers to a man's use of concepts in the brain to form judgements and inferences. 16

Knowledge goes from *shallow to deep*. First it is blurry then clearer; first it is superficial then essential. We know many things loosely from a first perception. We hone that awareness into a finer understanding of essences. We look again guided by the new insights and learn still more.

The process is unbounded.

Knowledge derives from practice, is evaluated by it, guides it, and is in turn guided by it.

> If you want knowledge you must take part in the practice of changing reality. If you want to know the taste of a pear, you must change the pear by eating it yourself. ... If you want to know the theory and methods of revolution you must take part in revolution. ... Hence a man's knowledge consists of only two parts, that which comes from direct experience and that which comes from indirect experience. Moreover what is indirect experience for me is (in the first place) direct experience for other people. Consequently, considered as a whole, knowledge of any kind is inseparable from direct experience. 17

Perceptual knowledge moves beyond obviousness to essence and thus becomes 'theory'. It gives a total picture of how internalities and externalities interact. It allows prediction. It can guide further practice making it more rational. But according to Maoists it never achieves a 'finished form.' For theories must perpetually change, first to correct errors and second to keep pace with the changing realities to which they address themselves.

> ...people engaged in changing reality are usually subject to numerous limitations; they are limited not only by existing scientific and technological conditions but also by the development of the objective process itself and the degree to which this process has become manifest (the aspects and the essence of the objective process have not yet been fully revealed). In such a situation, ideas, theories, plans or programs are usually altered partially and even wholly because of the discovery of unforeseen circumstances in the course of practice. That is to say, it does happen that the original ideas, theories, plans or programs fail to correspond to reality either in whole or in part and are wholly or partially incorrect. 18

And:

> In a revolutionary period the situation changes very rapidly;
> If the knowledge of revolutionaries does not change rapidly
> in accordance with the changed situation, they will be
> unable to lead the revolution to victory. 19

Herein we have the rough idea of a 'growth theory.' To practice effectively Mao says one must have a good theory and also a solid awareness of that theory's inevitable fallibility and need for continual improvement.

Having good theory means specifically understanding things in their generality and essence, in their universality and particularity. It means understanding all contradictions and aspects and most particularly the primary contradiction and its principle aspect, again in universality and particularity. And finally it means understanding that such knowledge is based on practice, good only insofar as it reflects reality well, and deserving alteration insofar as it reflects realtiy poorly and as reality itself changes.

And given this theory of knowledge, Maoism clearly lays out the characteristics of various kinds of dogmatic thinking processes: some dogmatists understand problems only one sidedly, not taking into account particularity, seeing only the smilarities or only the differences between varying compared situations; some don't understand, or at least don't pay any attention to the need for a correspondence between theory and reality, thus not bothering to check and recheck their theories against practical results or always doubting the latter but never the former; and some overlook the fact that realities change over time so that good knowledge yesterday, today, and tomorrow are most often very different from one another, thus becoming tailist or adventurist. And Maoism's entreaties try very hard to offset tendencies in dogmatic directions, and, as we'll see in coming discussions of Maoist practice, very often succeed admirably.

Thus in summary there is a Maoist prescription for gaining knowledge designed to minimize likelihoods of superficiality, onesidedness, over abstractness, dogmatisms, adventurism, tailism, and so on.

> Discover the truth through practice, and again through
> practice verify and develop the truth. Start from perceptual

knowledge; then start from rational knowledge and actively guide revolutionary practice to change both the subjective and the objective world. Practice, knowledge, again practice, and again knowledge. This form repeats itself in endless cycles, and with each cycle the content of practice and knowledge rises to a higher level. Such is the whole of the dialectical materialist theory of knowledge, and such is the dialectical materialist theory of the unity of knowing and doing. 20

Given the improvements in Maoism's understandings of knowledge, we can expect or at least look out to see whether or not the Maoist experience is more aware of the roles of good and especially of bad or dogmatic consciousness than was the Bolshevik experience, and also whether it is more aware of the importance of 'consciousness raising' and more adept at its practice.

CLASSES AND MASSES

Mao has admitted that he was very influenced by populists and anarchists and early in the Chinese experience there were definite divergences from the Russian tenets. In the 1927 Hunan report Mao not only extolled the peasantry and the countryside as the place of immediate motion and battle, but he also attributed to the masses a level of judgement normally reserved to the party. In a populist tradition he said that revolutionary parties and comrades would have to stand before the peasants to be tested and to be accepted or rejected as they decided. His ideas conflicted with those of the strict Marxist Leninists who praised the proletariat, and resolution came only when it became clear that of the two proposed only Mao's way worked.

Although Mao stressed class analysis, as he in some sense had to, to be considered Leninist and revolutionary, he also took a more populist approach as well. He said, "Merge with the Masses," "Learn from the Masses," "Become a Student of the Masses," etc. and he constantly referred to and talked about the whole Chinese People. He understood the importance of class and constantly did class analysis, but he also worked with other approaches and kept a flexible, non-fetishizing attitude.

In general his directives had at least partially the effect of overcoming *the dichotomizing tendencies* of Classical Marxism -- his constant references to the whole organic people is one example, but there are many others that are more obviously consciously aimed:

> In this world things are complicated and decided by many factors. We should look at problems from different aspects and not just one. 21

> We must learn to look at problems all-sidedly, seeing the reverse as well as the obverse sides of things. In given conditions a good thing can lead to bad results and a bad thing can lead to good results. 22

Maoism accepts dialectics, but the theory also works hard to overcome associated tendencies to dogmatism. Much of Mao's thought is designed to help people learn to investigate problems all sidedly and understand their own propensities to exaggeration, subjectivism, and error.

Further, early Maoism had roots in a culture which distrusted large political and economic apparatus; there was an emphasis on regionalism and so there was a kind of populist push towards the people. The earliest Maoist directives constantly reminded cadres that only by merging with the masses practicing first hand, could the cadres learn from them, and thereby efficiently serve and liberate them. There was nothing like this populism in Bolshevism and, given our previous analyses, its addition to Classical Marxism Leninism Chinese style, seems more a matter of a substantial change in body than just a minor refitting to a new country's needs.

Further, all these points concerning anti-dogmatism, populist faith in the masses, and concern about leadership and organization are borne out over and over countless Maoist passages discussing political, social, economic, and organizing questions:

> Within the ranks of the people democracy is correlative with centralism and freedom with discipline. They are the two opposite aspects of a single entity, contradictory as well as united, and we should not one sidedly emphasize one to

the denial of the other. Within the ranks of the people we
cannot do without democracy, nor can we do without
centralism. The unity of democracy and centralism, of
freedom and discipline, constitutes our democratic centralism. Under this system the people enjoy extensive
democracy and freedom but at the same time they have to
keep within the bounds of socialist discipline. 23

There are two methods which we communists must employ
in whatever work we do. One is to combine the general with
the particular; the other is to combine leadership with the
masses. 24

Maoism starts from Classical Marxism Leninism and thus suffers
from many of its weaknesses, but at the same time it attempts to move
further and to rectify as many of those as it can. Mao had to be a Leninist
to be a revolutionary at all -- that he was able to do so and retain an ability
to function at least somewhat outside the ideology and thereby augment it
from his own experiences is likely a tribute to him and to his Chinese
culture. As the above quotations show, Mao accepts the basic dichotomies
of Classical Marxism Leninism, but he then does his best to overcome the
ills that ordinarily follow upon that acceptance.

ECONOMICS AND POLITICS

So, as opposed to Lenin's emphasis on the economic nature of things
and the economic answers to all problems, Maoism emphasizes that
"political work is the lifeblood of economic work" 25 and,where the
traditionalists emphasize the cities, class analysis, and the working class,
Maoists emphasize the country, recognize the importance of non-class
groupings, and emphasize the peasantry. Much of the basis for these
twists and reversals lie in the fact that Maoism has a broader dialectical
method and a different view of people and of the importance of human
interaction, than Classical Marxism does.

One of the crucial problems of any revolution is 'identifying the true
sources of socialist consciousness.' For the Classical Marxist Leninists and
for Lenin in particular, the source was the trained cadre -- indeed the

source was Lenin himself. Maoists find the situation more complex and don't bother hiding their ensuing 'confusion.' Like populists they are non-determinest and feel that actively organizing consciousness alteration is key to ushering in a new socialist era. But at the same time they also feel that peasants are the true repositories of socialist consciousness, and that they alone have the strength, goodness, and awareness, to actually construct socialism. Maoists believe people learn through experiences, and that *those who have never oppressed and have always struggled* are the ones in the best position to teach, even if they must also learn.

> The fighters with the most practical experience are the wisest and most capable. The lowly are the most intelligent; the elite are most ignorant. 26

Maoists have great respect for people's sensitivities and for the long term importance of how people feel about their situations. Maoism understands that human motivation is complex and that inter-human relations can sow either good or bad seeds, and the one or the other can have very critical long term effects. *In China the parallel to politics over economics is the human over the material* -- the result is that tactics are analyzed with reference to their complete effects on all people involved. As just one example, both volunteerism and commandism are ruthlessly criticized precisely because whatever their efficiency might be at one time or another, in the large they inevitably create bad feelings between cadres and masses and thereby undercut crucial goals. Although it's not so written, Maoism does function with a more intimate understanding of human motivation and need than does Classical Marxism Leninism:

> To link oneself with the masses one must act in accordance with the needs and the wishes of the masses. All the work done for the masses must start from their needs and not from the desire of any individual, however well intentioned. It often happens that objectively the masses need a certain change, but subjectively they are not yet conscious of the need, not yet willing and determined to make the change. In such cases we should wait patiently. We should not make the change until, through our work, most of the masses have become conscious of the need to carry it out. Otherwise we

> shall isolate ourselves from the masses. Unless they are conscious and willing, any kind of work that requires their participation will turn out to be a mere formality and fail .... There are two principles here: One is the actual needs of the masses rather than what we fancy they need, and the other is the wishes of the masses, who must make up their own minds rather than our making up their minds for them. 27

The quote couldn't contrast more sharply with Lenin's conceptions of his role and the role of his party to create socialism for the workers even if they should at a moment not want any part of it -- and the Maoist prediction of the results of such aloof authority were also more than adequately borne out by the Russian example. Certainly the Maoists were not perfect but when we consider their practice we will indeed find that psychological overtones do lead to rather important divergences from Classical Marxism Leninism around the questions of communist organization, behavior, thought, values, and goals.

Maoists are historical materialists the same way that they're dialecticians; carefully, so as to take the good and avoid the bad. They believe that the people and the people alone make history, and that *the spirit can be transformed into a material force*. They don't accept the necessity of historical stages and they have a more balanced view of superstructure-base interaction than most Classical Marxist Leninists. They believe that the political often takes precedence over the economic, they believe the superstructure often dominates the base, and don't have any faith that once the base is altered the rest of society must follow. 28 Maoists hold these 'divergent' positions because their experience demands it, and because Mao's thought so alters Classical Marxism Leninism as to make the positions seem not so divergent as they really are. The Maoists are in fact heretics correcting dogma and not just traditionalists reinterpreting it, but at no time in their history was it possible for them to admit this, or in all likelihood even recognize it. The emphasis was necessarily on being a part of a heritage and not on being the creators of something largely new; once a heritage is adopted it becomes especially difficult to move towards renouncing it. It is somewhat easier to merely reinterpret old ideas to suit differing needs. And so in China we come full circle: As time goes along it is in fact Classical Marxism Leninism that is taken in the context of Maoism, rather than vice versa. 29

STRATEGY

Chinese strategy also diverges: the two things we wish most to discuss are the questions of organization and leadership, and the question of the links between revolutionary means and revolutionary ends.

Classical Leninists generally believe in Classical historical materialism. They regard the overthrow of the bourgeoisie as the end of capitalism and the beginning of socialism under the dictatorship of the proletariat. Save the continued presence of counter-revolutionaries, they regard post revolutionary problems as largely economic, and so they stress the need for efficiency, centralism, and discipline in all endeavors.

Applying their broader dialectical methods, Maoists develop a more flexible, rich stand. They believe that classes are defined not only by their abstract relations to the means of production, but also by way of their actual concrete functions, and they also believe that non-class divisions are important. They do see as much significance in the mere change of who controls society as do the Classical Marxists Leninists. For them there are still workers, management, peasants, party and state cadres, men, women, intellectuals, soldiers, family relatives, children, etc. and they see that there are still contradictions among and between these groups (though dominance relations have frequently reversed), and that they must be resolved before there can be any kind of worthwhile socialism. And further as we'll see concretely in later dicussions, and have already seen methodologically, the Maoists also recognize that different ways of addressing these contradictions have differing effects, even to the point where some can do far more harm than good. The Maoists are more attuned to the need for tactical analysis and better equipped to carry it out than were their Bolshevik forebearers.

One of the tactical problems that plagues revolutionary movements and that relates importantly to the question of how to win revolutions and how to also set up better new societies, is, how one compromises between a volunteerist belief in the primacy of the cadre and a non-elitist understanding of the wisdom and centrality of the masses. *How does one balance leadership and participation, centralism and individual initiative, discipline and democracy, how does one avoid authoritarianism and at the same time get things done effectively?*

Marx and Lenin saw little problem: The Party first, and the Central Committee before that, each answering to no one, though perhaps taking some lessons from the people.

The Maoist solution has never really been formalized; it is very flexible and rather populistic. Maoists are in a constant state of enervating tension -- they gravitate from being teachers to being students and back. They don't resolve the organization leadership controversy in one direction or the other, *but instead try to merge the opposites*, to both lead and follow, to trust the masses' spontaneity while teaching and employing discipline as well. The remnants of Classical Marxism Leninism are clearly present but the effort to move foward is also there. In 1933 Mao made clear the thesis "from the masses, to the masses": leadership gathers the ideas of the masses, clarifies and distills them, and then propagates them back so the ideas can be used and refined over and over. Maoists constantly worry about the dynamics of leadership and organizations even if they do accept the Marxist Leninist forms as a starting point. As a result they often move beyond the starting point to realizations well beyond those of any Bolsheviks:

> Apart from the role played by the party, the reason why the
> Red Army has been able to carry on in spite of such poor
> material conditions and such frequent engagements is its
> practice of democracy. The officers do not beat the men; the
> officers and men recieve equal treatment; soldiers are free
> to hold meetings and speak out; trivial formalities have
> been done away with; and the accounts are open for all to
> inspect.... In China the Army needs democracy as much as
> the people do. Democracy in our army is an important
> weapon for undermining the feudal mercenary army. 30

Mao understood that the feelings provoked by organization and leadership were in many ways as important as its efficiency, so his practice always took into account the psychological natures of all situations in question. As an example, the importance of democracy was understood to its fullest depth. There was concern not only with the freedom to participate and the need to participate, but also with creating conditions that actually fostered participation:

> Two principles must be observed: 1-Say all you know and
> say it without reserve; 2-Don't blame the speaker but take

his words as a warning. Unless the principle of "don't blame
the speaker" is observed genuinely and not falsely, the result
will not be "say all you know and say it without reserve." 31

We can only wonder what might have happened if Lenin had followed
Maoist dictates in even his personal relationships with others in his own
party. Perhaps it is not too much to say that the dissident elements on the
issue of factory management might have gotten a better hearing, and
might thereby have strongly affected the evolution of the whole Russian
experience. Certainly that is what Maoists would predict -- that the
incorrect views of the few would be purified by the ideas of the many just as
soon as all were speaking and all were taking heed.

The Maoist movement came in a backward illiterate country where
the need for leadership was obvious. The Maoists recognized this, but also
recognized the need for freedom and dignity. They had faith that the right
mix of leadership and spontaneity would bring out the wisdom of the
masses and thereby lead to good results. Mao makes the point explicit:

Twenty years of experience tell us that the right task, policy,
and style of work invariably conform with the demands of
the masses at a given time and place and invariably
strengthen our ties with the masses, and the wrong task,
policy, and style of work invariably disagree with the
demands of the masses at a given time and place and
invariably alienate us from the masses. The reason why
such evils as dogmatism, tailism, bureaucracy, and an
arrogant attitude in work are definitely harmful and
intolerable, and why anyone suffering from these maladies
must overcome them, is that they alienate us from the
masses. 32

Maoists understand that authoritarianism has a tendency to deaden
spirits and corrupt leaders -- they use exactly the kinds of tactical analysis
that the Classical Marxist Leninists were never able to understand:

Everyone engaged in practical work must investigate
conditions at the lower levels. Such investigation is

especially necessary for those who know theory but do not
know actual conditions, for otherwise they will not be able
to link theory with practice. Although my assertion "no
investigation, no right to speak," has been ridiculed as
narrow empiricism, to this day I do not regret having made
it; far from regretting it, I still insist that without
investigation there cannot possibly be any right to speak.
There are many people who "the moment they alight from
the official carriage," make a hullabaloo, spout opinions,
criticize this and condemn that; but, in fact, ten out of ten of
them will meet with failure. For such views or criticisms
which are not based on thorough investigation, are nothing
but ignorant twaddle. Countless times our Party suffered at
the hands of these "imperial envoys," who rushed here,
there, and everywhere. 33

It is not likely that Mao was referring to a Russian Bolshevik "tribune
of the people" when he described his idea of an imperial envoy but it is not
outrageous to say that he gave a rather good caricature of them anyway.

Another quote will help to show the depth of insight that goes into the
many admonitions against the ills of sectarianism, arrogance, elitism, and
other related 'maladies':

Many things may become baggage, may become encumbrances if we cling to them blindly and uncritically. Let us
take some illustrations. Having made mistakes, you may
feel that come what may, you are saddled with them, and so
become dispirited; if you have not made mistakes you may
feel that you are free from error and so become conceited.
Lack of achievement may even breed pride and arrogance.
A comrade with a short record of struggle may shirk
responsibility on this account, while a veteran may become
opinionated because of his long record of struggle. Worker
and peasant comrades, because of pride in their class origin
may look down upon intellectuals, while intellectuals
because they have a certain amount of knowledge, may look
down upon worker and peasant comrades. Any specialized
skill may be capitalized on and so may lead to arrogance or

contempt of others. Even one's age may become grounds for conceit. The young, because they are bright and capable, may look down upon the old; and the old, because they are rich in experience, may look down upon the young. All such things become encumbrances or baggage if there is no critical awareness. 34

The Maoists have a *humanist* insight. In a subtle way they try to synthesize opposites. They view extreme positions clearly so that they might find middle paths. *They try to resolve the tensions of admiring human potentials and simultaneously warning of possible character related pitfalls.* Mao's thoughts thus have their basis more in an understanding of people coupled with an economic awareness than vice versa.

Means and ends problems are critical to all complex tasks. Will a certain approach to solving an immediate difficulty pay off over the long run as well, or will long run deficits overcome short run gains? Will employing force today to defeat an enemy now so compromise us that it hinders future potentials or will it have a long run value too? Lenin understood such questions were critically important. One of his greatest contributions was an analysis of imperialism and nationalism in light of their overall effects upon long and short run strategic options. But as we have already shown, he had only nominal ability to deal with more intricate problems of this type -- in fact he was usually unaware of their existence. He knew the means-end question was important, but he was poorly equipped to do much about it. He believed in Classical historical materialism. He gave little credence to psychology. He felt that one simply had to overcome each hurdle as it arose and that the end would be reached in due time. The movement was incorruptible and unstoppable; means-ends problems existed, but they weren't likely to be too important or to have too much overall effect. Given an end a means must be chosen. The fact that the means might counter the end or have other adverse effects for psycho-social rather than politico-economic reasons was hardly ever considered.

Mao is different. He follows more in the populist and anarchist traditions; in a sense he is simply more comprehensive. He has a deeper awareness of human interaction, a different methodology, and a skepticism about inevitability, all contributing to his extreme concern with means-ends problems. So, for example, his thoughts about leadership are different than Lenin's. "From the masses, to the masses," represents an attempt to insure that leadership problems are handled so as to lead toward a socialist future rather than so as to put up insurmountable impediments to such a future. Another directive gives a very explicit warning concerning means-ends problems and all tactical questions. It tries to teach people how to think about strategy and how to form programs that might succeed:

> They (the communists) must grasp the principle of subordinating the needs of the part to the needs of the whole. If a proposal appears feasible for a partial situation but not for the situation as a whole, then the part must give way to the whole. Conversely, if the proposal is not feasible for the part but is feasible in the light of the situation as a whole, again the part must give way to the whole. This is what is meant by considering the situation as a whole. 35

The difference between Mao and Lenin lies not only in the emphasis on understanding and coordinating all the implications of a given policy and on ability to do this, but also on exactly what the *whole* really is. For Mao it is communism and the road thereto, while for Lenin it is the next step or the next few steps on the clearly outlined and always to be followed path. The latter approach is dogmatic about whatever is going on, and the former, while dogmatic about the final ends, is largely flexible with regard to the rest. Lenin worries about productive techniques in light of immediate conditions; Mao takes immediate conditions into account in the context of the whole revolutionary process by which socialism is to be achieved.

Maoist criticism/self-criticism is designed to help cadres overcome their weaknesses and especially the ill-effects of power, and at the same time help everyone scrutinize policies so that they might always improve. Tactically, due to his theory of antagonism, non-antagonism, Mao discusses contradictions among the people and contradictions between the people and the enemy in two different ways. He understands the absolute need for *unity* among the vast majority; he understands the negative effects the use of force, coercion, and indoctrination can have on people's feelings and spirits.

Our comrades must understand that ideological remould-
ing involves long term, patient, and painstaking work, and
they must not attempt to change people's ideologies which
have been shaped over decades of life, by giving a few
lectures or by holding a few meetings. Persuasion not
compulsion is the only way to convince them. To try to
convince them by force simply won't work. This kind of
method is impermissible in dealing with comrades or
friends. 36

The kind of problem Classical Marxist Leninists usually ignore or
leave to the forces of economics and history, *the remolding of people's
characters,* the Maoists consider central, and deserving of careful,
complete, tactical analysis. Maoism has a patient but determined view. It
is concerned that the true socialist nature of each individual emerge; it
recognizes that many individuals add up to the whole. Mao's thoughts
constantly analyze situations so that this whole process might well occur.

All our cadres, whatever their rank, are servants of the
people, and whatever we do is to serve the people. How then
can we be reluctant to discard any of our bad traits. 37

It is almost as if, since everyone knows that all people have adopted
some bad traits, the premium is on admitting it and dealing with it rather
than hiding it. Lenin, on the other hand, had no particular worries about
bad traits. He had none and simply discarded anyone else who in his eyes
did.
The effects of Maoism's 'humanism' and its long term biases come
through most clearly in policies aimed at people with wrong or bad ideas.
The traditional way for dealing with such questions is of course well
known, (whether practiced moderately by liberal capitalists or by
Leninists, or whether practiced extremely by fascists or Stalinists), but
Mao's way is not, perhaps because it is so different. He besieges people over
and over:

With regard to people who have made mistakes, stress must
be laid on doing careful and patient ideological work and
truly acting on the principle, "of learning from past mistakes

to avoid future ones," and "curing the sickness to save the patient," in order to achieve the twofold objective of clarity in ideology and unity among comrades. 38

Our very brief analysis of Maoist strategic thought has borne out our expectations reasonably well: in contrast to Leninism, there seems to be less dichotomization, more understanding of the political and human sides of things, more distrust of the large, impersonal, and bureaucratic, and less concern with workers alone and with blind discipline. Maoism tries to teach its people to work and think profitably, it tries to overcome the bad tendencies of centralism, and of all other tactics that involve force, authority, or coercion, and at the same time there is a conscious concern for changing people's beliefs by patient work in the psychological rather than in the economic sphere. We should expect that the Chinese revolution itself will reflect the baggage of Classical Marxist Leninist approaches at the same time that it predicts some of the good new thoughts intrinsic to Maoism.

CHINESE PRACTICE

In the early years of the Chinese Communist Party there were two factions. The first favored a traditional view of the ascendency of the proletariat and the second emphasized the countryside and the peasantry. The majority thought the peasant based approach sacrilegious, the Comintern was the international communist boss and Mao was a kind of sacreligious maverick.

As time went on, despite what the gospel said, the units in the cities atrophied while those in the countryside grew strong. Mao organized a fledgling Red Army, his ideas gained some small legitimacy, and his stature in the movement grew.

Still the Party bureaucracy couldn't bring itself to give in. They issued a call for Mao to take his germinal groups together and start attacking larger cities. Mao thought such an approach backward:

> He felt that the most fertile ground for political work and therefore for military work as well, was far from the cities, where there was little or no civil authority. 39

The Central Committee was effectively adventurist in its designs on the cities, and subjectivist in its views of the working class and in its sectarianism. Mao, on the other hand, was objectively reading the conditions of his environment and correctly assessing the potentials for action. He was putting the long range struggle into an effective political perspective.

In 1930 Mao and his comrade Chu Teh defied Party orders to lay siege to a large city and instead ordered a general retreat to attack again later elsewhere. Their troops followed unhesitatingly, thus making it perfectly clear that their allegiance was to Mao and not to the city Party. The Central Committee was left with no real choice: it censured its own leaders and gave Mao full support. Mao had the only significant support among the people and a split with him would have been fatal to the Party's future.

From then on the Red Army's primary task was gaining footholds in the countryside. Political cadres within and without the army were to radicalize the masses until they fully supported the cause. Mao's whole theory of a *people's war* depended upon the success of the political effort.

The main method of political education was land reform and the redistribution of wealth and power at the local level, but a subsidiary method was the very nature and style of work of the army and its cadres -- they taught and gathered respect due to example, but they also sought to learn and give respect as well. The land reform and all other activities were carefully carried out in ways designed not to create insurmountable private peasant interests, and in ways well suited to the development of political awareness.

A detailed study of Mao's wartime strategy is beyond us here but some of its results might well be mentioned. They show Mao's great ability to think within the context of a total awareness of the whole rather than in only the immediate part. It shows Maoism's patience and maturity in the field, and it shows again how Maoist directives seek to unite traditionally contrary ways of acting into powerful workable combinations. The whole Maoist military program is marked by an ability to synthesize, the patience to apply long term rather than extremist tactics, and the dominance of a 'humanist' perspective. A quotation lends credence to these assertions until such time as the reader can personally check them out:

The Chinese Red Army is an armed body for carrying out
the political tasks of the revolution. Especially at present
(1929) the Red Army should certainly not confine itself to
fighting; besides fighting to destroy the enemy's military
strength, it should shoulder such important tasks as doing
propaganda among the masses, arming them, helping them
to establish revolutionary political power, and setting up
Party organizations. The Red Army fights not merely for
the sake of fighting but in order to conduct propaganda
among the masses, organize them, arm them, and help
them to extablish revolutionary political power. Without
these objectives fighting loses its meaning, and the Red
Army loses its reason for existence. 40

The earliest political military work of this type occurred
in southeast China but it was relatively short lived. In 1934, the Nationalists,
under Chaing Kai Chek, launched a series of massive attacks, and forced
Mao to uproot the Southeastern base area and retreat. The Long March
then went nearly 5000 miles through virtually impassable terrain to the
northwest. During the nomadic journey the communists had to fight
Nationalist troops, warlord troops, and the natural elements. Those that
finally made it were steeled to hardship, they were forged into a kind of
cooperative which later proved totally unbeatable.

The Chinese war with Japan was essentially nationalist, and Mao's
and Chiang's forces both fought the Japanese. But the communists distinguished themselves and won many recruits away from their temporary
allies -- guerilla tactics were highly successful and the Red Army was most
courageous and the people were aware of it. The communist reputation for
fairness and land redistribution survived wherever the troops went. Their
understanding of the importance of how people felt about the left paid off
over and over.

The Long March was followed by a long stay in the northwestern base
area known as Yenan. There many early Maoist tendencies developed
great strength and richness: there was a massive study practice school for
revolutionaries; farming and small industry were successfully adopted,
and the political policies of *democracy, participation, and criticism/self-
criticism were extended.* Yenan thrived -- it was a *red base*, a model for the

Chinese people to see and thereby to understand the potential of a communist state. The Maoists were the first leaders in Chinese history who clearly shared in the fate of the masses while working at their side with mutual respect. As each year passed, support grew; new recruits went constantly to Yenan or organized party units where they lived.

At the end of the Japanese struggle Chiang thought he was China's sole rightful ruler. He refused Mao's offer to form a coalition government and ordered him to disarm the Red Army. The truce formed for fighting the Japanese was quickly annulled and new fighting broke out. Despite massive American aid, Chiang's armies were helpless in the face of Maoist know how and determination. The Red Army used guerilla, unconventional, and conventional tactics; discipline and democracy; had a reputation for honesty, virtue, and land reform; experience and solidarity; and the support of the great masses of the Chinese peasantry. The struggle lasted three years. Chiang wound up on Formosa, Mao was in Peking, and Maoism was in the countryside.

But this was far from the end of the struggle:

> After the enemies with guns have been wiped out, there will
> be enemies without guns; they are bound to still struggle
> desperately against us, and we must never regard these
> enemies lightly. If we do not now raise and understand the
> problem in this way we shall commit the gravest mistakes. 41

When Mao made this statement in 1949, he was in a position of power but China was in a complete shambles. There was no effective transport system, feudal agricultural conditions remained, and the only industry was in the cities, and minimal at that. According to McFarlane and Wheelwright's analysis of the Maoist perspective on these conditions:

> The immediate strategic objective had to be the rehabilita-
> tion of the national economy; in a way that would lay the
> groundwork for the future socialist transformation of the
> economy and the society. 42

This was done by a relatively gradual approach which emphasized the assimilation of old elements rather than their expropriation or eradication. As K.S. Karol put it:

> ...in 1949 China was hardly more developed than Russia in
> 1917...yet this does not seem to have "forced" him (Mao) to
> resort continually to violence. The basis of his system is an
> extensive indoctrination, but the ideological coercion one
> sees being exercised in moments of sharp political conflict
> never develop into bloody persecution. 43

Although we don't have time for details here, one can get a feeling for
how Maoism influenced early development by reading the 1949 essay,
"Methods of Work of Party Committees." It is essentially a set of practical
day-to-day work guidelines, but it is couched in terms of an overall
understanding of China's early situation, its people's potentials, and all
the possible effects of their various possible courses of action.

By 1953 the Maoists felt secure enough to embark upon their first *five
year plan*. They were already building a strong Classical state, there was
much discipline and a huge emphasis on Classical order and effectiveness.
But there was also the Maoist divergence from these tendencies in addition
to the specific qualities of the Chinese situation itself. So there were the
beginnings of a Leninist problem, the early growth of Maoist alternatives,
and the everpresent influence of the whole of China's own specific
heritages.

The slogan adopted was "Learn from the Soviet Union," and the goal
was to build an industrial framework for the support of all future
development. The method was to be one of central planning based on the
Russian model, but despite the desire, the Maoists couldn't really
transplant the 'soviet' approaches. Chinese conditions were different. A
long history of local autonomy pushed successfully towards decentralization. Consumer goods development and distribution, and light industry
development were all handled at the provincial level. The Chinese met and
surpassed their ecpnomic targets but additionally and perhaps more
importantly, their new forms of administration fostered extensive health
and education campaigns which were very successful.

Further, in this first period the agricultural plan aimed at the
introduction of collectivism gradually, in ways conducive to future
consolidation and progress. Cadres joined the peasants in the fields.
Through dialogue and example they established mutual aid teams to deal

with immediate difficulties requiring group labor. They increased membership by convincing through example, instead of using force or economic coercion. And by the end of 1957 a remarkable 88% of China's families had fallen sway to the mixture of moral and material incentive and joined the cooperatives.

Then in 1958 there began the *great leap forward* which we can now recognize as the precursor to the *great proletarian cultural revolution*. The new motion followed Mao's trip to Russia and it seems reasonable that it was the visit that finally convinced him more stringent measures were needed if politics was to really command, and if moral incentives were to dominate material ones. The Russian approaches had to be consciously augmented and even overcome. In 1957 Mao clarified the new position:

> In China, although the main socialist transformation has been completed with respect to the system of ownership, and although the large scale and turbulent class struggles of the masses characteristic of the previous revolutionary periods have in the main come to an end, there are still remnants of the overthrown landlord and comprador classes, there is still a bourgeoisie, and the remolding of the petty bourgeoisie has only just started. The class struggle is by no means over. The class struggle between the proletariat and the bourgeoisie, the class struggle between the different political forces, and the class struggle in the ideological field between the proletariat and the bourgeoisie will continue to be long and tortuous and at times will even become very acute. The proletariat seeks to transform the world according to its own world outlook, and so does the bourgeoisie. In this respect the question of which will win out, Socialism or Capitalism, is still not really settled. 44

The increasing productivity of the Great Leap Forward was not actually Mao's primary goal but rather a welcome side achievement of his other aims. The country's communes developed further, most especially as governmental and productive consumption units. They took over the administration of health, education, defense, and small industry. During the period small and even medium industry developed symbiotically with agriculture, each providing the means for the other and each growing in accordance with the political demands of the people's needs. Almost all efforts were dominated by discussions of *motivation* and the ways one might replace the previous harmful means, notably the use of material incentives. There were certainly many excesses but the gist of the movement was to place human values on a footing above but not totally displacing economic ones. As Mao himself outlined it:

> ...the Chinese people are carrying out a vigorous rectif-
> ication movement in order to bring about the rapid
> development of Socialism in China on a firmer basis. It is a
> movement for carrying out a nationwide debate which is
> both guided and free, a debate in the city and the
> countryside on such questions as the socialist road versus
> the capitalist road, the basic system of the state and its
> major policies, the working system of party and government
> functionaries, and the question of the welfare of the people,
> a debate which is conducted by setting forth facts and
> reasoning things out, so as correctly to resolve those actual
> contradictions among the people which demand immediate
> solutions. This is a socialist movement for the self-educa-
> tion and self-remolding of the people. 45

The movement was successful in that it laid a groundwork for future developments at a later date, but unsuccessful in that it was itself shallow, many of its advances being later temporarily reversed because they had no really strong roots in the minds and ways of the people or the government.

But the Great Leap Forward, because of its great daring, was also quite untraditional and it caused significant concern in the Western communist countries. The Russians withdrew technicians and aid and at the same time China had a number of major natural disasters. The years 1959-61 were thus extremely severe. Agriculture fell off considerably and industry lagged many years behind what could have been justifiably expected.

> As the economic crisis of China deepened with the crop
> failures of '59-'61, the New Economic Policy emerged. It
> aimed to strengthen the authority of management and of

the ministries, while giving more scope for the generation of free market forces in agriculture and industry, at the expense of the authority of decentralized political cadres. 46

During the Great Leap Forward 78 percent of industry went over to local control but much of this motion was reversed during the New Economic Policy period from 1961 to 1964. The NEP fostered private plots, private incentives, and both free-and black-market dynamics. The NEP tactics were capitalist and/or Russian and the accompanying political and philosophical debate set back much of the Great Leap Forward rectification. Profits took command, consciousness suffered, control went to managers and experts instead of union groups, and material incentives replaced moral ones. On one level humanistic Maoist rhetoric flourished but on the others capitalist values emerged anew and the economy began to look somewhat Yugoslavian.

During the period there was a great debate about incentives: the 'real' Maoists insisted that the period was only a temporary crisis reaction while the other 'fake' Maoists argued for its permanence and worth. The 'others' had a concrete advantage in the debate -- With each passing day more and more technocrats and experts got positions of political and economic power and ever widening differences in income and privilege ensued. More and more people gained interests in continuing the NEP. On one side the debate continued, the interest building process continued, and various 'Leninist groups' began consolidating their programs and powers. On the other side Mao began making plans for a new rectification program to restore the ideas of the Great Leap Forward.

Mao never swerved from his desire to have politics in command. He wanted planning to dominate the economy; he wanted humanist values to be the driving forces behind planning; and he wanted moral incentives to be the primary mechanisms for motivating and implementing planning goals. He began assembling 'loyal' forces in '60-'64. He tested the strength of his views in cultural and incentive debate. In 1964 he began decrying revisionism in the Party, and he reorganized the People's Liberation Army according to his policies, with people loyal to his views in leadership.

Whereas Lenin's Classical Marxist goal had been industrialism by any means, and whereas other Chinese groups had adopted that conception and were attempting to carry it out, Mao was still committed to an *all-sided development* by means conducive to political growth and individual remolding. The Russians went 'stage by stage' using modified Taylor methods and whatever else suited and 'coincidently' enhanced the power and wealth and centrality of the leaders; some of the Maoists went that way too and all were certainly partly infected with the involved tendencies. Nonetheless, Maoism asked how a stage could be skipped and carefully considered what to do economically and what to do politically. Mao and Lin Piao began the dynamics of the Great Proletarian Cultural Revolution in the context of the restoration years '61-'64.

The Cultural Revolution was one of the most misunderstood but immensely effective events of modern times. The Chinese people were aroused and carried on a deep political struggle involving criticism of people at every level of the Chinese Communist apparatus. Outsiders projected, and thought it meant Civil War. The movement was virtually unprecedented in international political history: never had so many people been so involved in so huge an undertaking without major warfare ensuing. A political parallel in the United States would perhaps barely exist if all of a sudden a presidential administration gave free wheel to Blacks, welfare recipients, and youths, to correct what they felt were the weaknesses of local and then national conditions by direct, sustained, and largely unsupervised activity. In the United States such a sudden cultural revolution would likely lead to an immense bloodbath and the temporary dissolution of all past order with unpredictable final results.

The Cultural Revolution began actively in the universities. Students started questioning the bourgeois nature of their educations and of their schools' admissions policies. They did it by means of open political debate, mass gatherings, and the unbelievably widespread use of what were called 'big character' posters. The Party bureaucracy tried to redirect student anger from important to lesser targets by a variety of means, but nonetheless the condemnations grew and spread. Soon students began asking and discovering which local party people were implicated in the crimes of the schools.

Mao then wrote his own big character poster called "Bombard the Headquarters," and it called upon youth to carry through their criticism all the way up the party hierarchy so as to weed out those whom Mao called "capitalist roaders in authority." The student movement thus gained immediate confidence, legitimacy, and scope.

Students went all through the country on simulated Long Marches.

They held demonstrations and sit-ins around whatever they didn't like including newspapers and even local party headquarters. Workers and all other people were then more directly affected and thus became more and more involved. People in every city were trying to displace old officials and replace them with others; sometimes it was politically well motivated and sometimes it had more to do with pursuit of wealth or power; in all cases countless factions grew up all over. In essence there were factions around legitimate Maoists, around pretender Maoists who actually had diverging views, and around outright self-interest seekers. In all cases rhetoric masked realities for all but the most initiated, and so for a long time there was considerable confusion. The conflicts were often fierce and violence (almost infinitesimal on a United States scale) frequently broke out. Millions turned out for demonstrations and in the end virtually no one went unaffected. The country resembled a giant university in which every kind of person was involved in very tense conflicts, discovering his or her own allegiances and then acting upon them.

The Cultural Revolution was simply the most recent in a long line of rectification campaigns aimed at undermining bourgeois ideas, actions, and attitudes. The nature of the involved contradictions, and the magnitude of efforts employed to solve them, made the campaign more complex than any that had gone before. Early on Mao realized that since the struggle was between 'him' and another sect of the party, he would have to engage as many non-party forces in the struggle as possible. His first move was to put Lin Piao in charge of the army where he then began a series of political campaigns around the publication of the *Thoughts of Chairman Mao* in the *Little Red Book*.

At the last plenum before the Cultural Revolution visibly began, the Maoist faction and the opposition faction led by Liu Shao Chi apparently both agreed that a wide sweeping rectification program was needed. Both groups felt that the period of the NEP had gone too far and that correctives were needed so as to put China back onto an acceptable course. Both groups were opposed to the consumerist market approaches of the new class of bureaucrats who rose out of the NEP. But each had a very different vision of the right way to go, a different conception of the obstructions to be dealt with, and very different ideas about how they might be overcome.

Mao felt it was necessary to have a *bottom up* campaign of criticism and popular democracy, while Liu's party faction felt it was necessary to have a campaign *led by the party* and aimed at *increasing rather than diminishing party control.* The Maoist approach won out to at least a respectable extent and, as the revolution unfolded, among other occurrences, Liu's men at the highest levels including Liu himself were made the focus of attention and finally removed from office.

To get a firmer grasp on the reasons behind the Cultural Revolution and the differences between Mao and the group he called the capitalist roaders, we will have to speak a little more generally about the nature of revolution and especially revolution in industrially backward countries, though first it might be useful to round out our initial perceptions with some quotations from Lin Piao's speech to the Ninth National Congress of the Chinese Communist Party held in 1969. First he quotes Mao:

> In the past we waged struggles in rural areas, in factories, in the cultural field, and we carried out the socialist education movement. But all this failed to solve the problem because we didn't find a form, a method, to arouse the broad masses to express our dark aspect openly, in an all around way, and from below. 47

And then discussing Mao's slogan "Grasp revolution; promote production," Lin says,

> ...this principle is absolutely correct. It correctly explains the relationship between revolution and production, between the superstructure and the economic base, and between the relations of production and the productive forces. Chairman Mao always teaches us: "Political work is the life blood of all economic work".... Politics is the concentrated expression of economics. If we fail to make a revolution in the superstructure, fail to arouse the broad masses of the peasants and the workers, fail to criticize the revisionist line, fail to expose the handful of renegades, enemy agents, capitalist roaders in power, and counter-revolutionaries, and fail to consolidate the leadership of the proletariat, how can we further consolidate the socialist economic base and further develop the socialist productive forces? 48

This is a kind of Maoist version of a Marxist theoretical analysis. Lin continues by discussing the revolution's resolution by quoting Mao on the process then unfolding in the factories:

> Struggle criticism transformation in a factory, on the whole, goes through the following stages: Establishing a three in one revolutionary committee; carrying out mass criticism and repudiation; purifying the class ranks; consolidating the party organization; and simplifying the administrative structure, changing irrational rules and regulations and sending office workers to the workshops. 49

Finally, after urging everyone to carry out a similar process everywhere, Lin adds a last observation:

> This wide dissemination of Mao Tse Tung Thought in a big country of 700 million is the most significant achievment of the Great Proletarian Cultural Revolution. 50

But what about the political theory of the affair? William Hinton's analysis is a useful place to start. 51 According to him, under socialism the class struggle continues, although now in a highly altered post-revolutionary form:

> The class struggle under Socialism amounts to the bourgeoisie trying to remold the world to suit themselves while the working class tries to remold the world to suit working people. 52

In this remolding 'contest' Hinton says the working class has the benefit of power over the forces of production but the potential new bourgeois ruling classes have advantages in cultural, technical, scientific, and administrative spheres and in the fact that many attitudes from the pre-revolutionary period tend to hang on in people's behaviors even well after the revolution itself.

> In order to consolidate socialism the working class must not only transform the economic base of society but also the

whole superstructure. The ideology, culture, customs, habits of the people must be transformed along with the institutions that reflect and perpetuate them such as schools,religious organizations, trade unions, peasant associations, theatre companies, orchestras, publishing houses, and scientific bodies. New music, art, literature, and drama must be created that is working class in content. Furthermore each individual must conduct an internal struggle to replace bourgeois individualism with proletarian collectivism as his or her motivating thought. Unless all this is carried through the socialist economic base cannot be consolidated. 53

The essence is that revolution creates a society still fraught with contradiction in which, unless old ways and attitudes, are fought they can again gain ascendency: Thus the need for repeated revolution from below and for policies that appeal to people's progressive sensibilities rather than their greed, and that promote collectivity rather than competition. In the beginning of revolutionary development there must be inequities and bad attitudes due to residues from past history. These together foster counter-productive dynamics which if unchecked and especially if exploited by counter-revolutionaries, can lead to restoration of one or another kind. This is Hinton's interpretation of the Maoist theory of struggle between opposing tendencies during the period of socialist construction.

Without a conscious and protracted effort to combat these (negative residue) tendencies they can grow into an important social force. They can and do create new bourgeois individuals who gather as a new privileged elite and ultimately as a new exploiting class. Thus socialism can be peacefully transformed back into capitalism. 54

Hinton points out that all policy debates under socialism, be they about incentives, hierarchy, cadre behavior, education, culture, political organization, or personal study, are really debates around capitalist and socialist roads as the two possible paths to follow, the first pandering either institutionally or ideologically to new or old forms of capitalistic oppression and the latter to new forms of socialistic liberation.

Further in Hinton's view the key aspect of the Maoist understanding of two line struggle is the awareness that frequently it is at the ideological superstructural level that critical phenomena occur:

> Mao, on the other hand, understood that the connection between productive forces, productive relations, and superstructure is dialectical and in constant interaction. Sometimes one aspect is decisive and at other times another. While the forces of production play a major role in determining the contours of human society, there are times when new productive relations are needed to release and develop new productive forces, when changes must be made in the superstructure to bring about changes in the base, times when consciousness determines being, rather than being determining consciousness. At such times massive political transformation is a prerequisite for further productive development. 55

And finally Hinton informs us that though two line struggle is crucially between the proletariat (which we can effectively take to mean the true revolutionaries) and the "people in authority taking the capitalist road" as in the attack on Liu Shao Chi, it is also between people and themselves, between their revolutionary and their residual reactionary aspects, as in the slogan "Fight self; oppose revisionism."

Hinton thus sees the Cultural Revolution as a great rectification program to keep China on the socialist road 1-by exposing and replacing people in authority taking the capitalist road, 2-by reasserting proletarian (revolutionary) politics and culture, and 3-by establishing the principles of continued contradictions and continued struggle even under socialism.

While we accept the bulk of Hinton's analysis as the Maoist position there are still many questions to be answered. What exactly is a capitalist roader, what were the differences between Mao and his 'opponents', and what were the other conflicts and reasons for the Cultural Revolution?

Franz Schurmann says that "as one reads the accusations one sees that the accusation 'capitalistic' meant more than wanting profits or private ownership; it meant authoritarianism, a love of power."56 Technical scientists weren't attacked and their high income status went untouched. In fact only those who were consolidating gains into power or those who were supporting that process from positions of power were attacked.

In 1956 Mao made explicit his thesis that class struggle extends beyond the confiscation of property, and that the key question becomes whether there will be a dictatorship of the proletariat or a dictatorship of the bourgeoisie. Huberman and Sweezy take off from this point in their analysis of the Cultural Revolution. They see the revolution as an attempt to deal with an enormously important historical problem,

> ...the growth in the socialist countries of an increasingly privileged and powerful social stratum in command of society's political and economic apparatus. Along with this growth and intricately connected with it, certain trends in the spiritual and moral spheres develop... The Chinese believe that these trends, if unchecked, must sooner or later culminate in the restoration of capitalism. If we understand them correctly, they do not mean by this that one fine day the state will sell the factories to a new class of wealthy capitalists, but rather that those in command will go on strengthening their positions and gradually transform them into transferable and inheritable property rights. 57

We might add that those in command will go on strengthening their positions not because they are evil, but because they are used to doing it, because it serves their interests, because it corresponds to their talents and personalities, because it corresponds to their training, and because they have a rationalization for it: they believe that it is the best way for them to serve the revolution and the people. In some commanders this 'altruistic' belief really is the primary motive force while in others self-interest is, but all of them have each motive force working and fostering one another to at least some extent. Huberman and Sweezy go on and seek answers to further important questions: what are the reasons for reactionary trends and what are the potential forces that might be organized to forestall them?

Huberman and Sweezy maintain that in a backward country those who have expertise must get enough material support to produce effectively, and further maintain that this is invariably more than what most people can get. As a result, in such circumstances, there is inevitable economic inequity brought on by uncontrollably divergent human needs and economic pressures. As the economy begins expanding, the privileges of certain groups increase in kind until finally that privilege begins creating vested interests which benefitted groups try to defend. Here there is a correlation with Hinton's analysis stressing the on-going influences of old ideas and old behavior patterns: actually it is the dual presence of selfish and elitist attitudes and of privilege which allows each to grow until there are revisionist interest groups. And we add to the analysis *only the realization that privilege need not take only a material form.* The acquisition of influence, rights and powers by party cadres as they employ their expertise in planning (in an non-self-management type socialism) is a very real acquisition of privilege and is at least as important and as inevitable as the development of economic inequities. Certainly Mao's constant warnings against such trends show his awareness of this aspect of the whole problem.

Huberman and Sweezy point out that in third world countries it makes no sense to talk about completely preventing the growth of a privileged stratum which has the potential to become a new ruling class since that is part of the necessary price of economic development (and of the 'necessary' initiation of central planning and inculcation of discipline). But in their view it does make sense to talk about limiting the power of this stratum, keeping its privileges to a necessary minimum, and preventing it from solidifying its position and transforming its interests into trans-ferable property (or political) rights. Who has an interest in doing this? The non-privileged; but their interest, according to Huberman and Sweezy, is usually unfelt because of their old fashioned willingness to submit to authority or expertise. The only people with an immediately conscious interest are thus those who made the revolution and remain uncorrupted. Given the analysis, if these people are unsuccessful in stemming the 'new ruling class' trend, then according to Huberman and Sweezy, their country will take one or another version of what the Chinese have called the capitalist road.

The Maoist solution is not a purge to wipe out newly developing classes or corrupted party elements (the new Stalin would be worse than the old Liu), but the building of *mass-based counter movements* to keep new classes in check, and to create new cadres to replace those who become corrupted. Mao was intent upon dealing with all emerging problems in ways which wouldn't create new problems simultaneously in other areas -- his wish constantly led him to the masses as the chief vehicle of political rectification. The purpose was to stem bad trends, the means was mass-based movements, and the target was those who were misusing political or economic privilege and those in power who were supporting or ignoring such misuses. The 'offenders' were fought not with terror or force, but politically with mass mobilization and with educational campaigns conducted especially among youth and cadres. The goal was not only to right immediate wrongs but also to impede their reemergence by teaching long lasting political lessons to all concerned. The movement's 'targets' weren't evil people so much as good people who gave in to the evil dynamics of underdeveloped growth and Classical Leninist organization: a dynamic Mao seems to have at least in reasonable part escaped because of his deeply ingrained humanist and populist tendencies, and perhaps also because he was always in a good position to be quite objective -- nothing in China could seriously threaten his personal identity, interests, or leadership. He didn't have to worry about protecting himself or defending his own actions even sub-consciously, and he never seems to have internalized much of the kind of elitist, out-of-touch behavior that usually arises from, or leads to such kinds of subjectivity.

The goals of the Cultural Revolution were multiple but integrated. For Liu the problem developing in the sixties was the weakening of local party organs due to excessive restoration of capitalist techniques occurring in the countryside and even in the cities. His solution was to reassert party authority in ways that would continue to augment the powers of the newly emergent class of "red and expert" planning bureaucrats, managers, and party leaders. His faction had control of almost all the local and even city wide communist party committees.

But Mao saw the same rough situation in a completely different way. He had his long time populist tendencies, his trust in the masses, his ultimately libertarian goals, and the example of the degeneration of the Russian revolution guiding his thinking. He felt that restoration tendencies were out of hand and that politics had to be put back in command, but he was interested in accomplishing that end in ways that would further rather than undermine his ultimate goals. He chose the 'socialist road' of attacking the local and even national party structure by unleashing the fury of the students, workers, and peasants, at the 'bourgeois' headquarters. He felt that the revolution had to 'eliminate' those in power supporting the development of a new ruling class, but that it also had to create conditions that would make it increasingly more difficult for the same problems to arise again. He knew that the revolution should eliminate or at least begin to eliminate the vestiges of old thought that stubbornly hung on at every level of Chinese society. He saw the coming events as a great revolution that could touch people to their very souls and aim at solving the problems of their world outlook.

> One cannot have a stable socialist society operating with the motivations of a capitalist society: if the motivations are not changed sooner or later there will be a reversion to a form of capitalism, for the old values of the old society will reassert themselves, helped by influences from outside of both the elite and dissident groups. 58

And a crucial article that appeared in a Chinese newspaper during the revolution made the same points another way:

> Man's social being determines his thinking. But thinking in turn plays a great role, or under certain circumstances a decisive role, in the development of the politics of the economy of a given society... In what does the old ideology of the exploiting classes lie? It lies essentially in self interest -- the natural soil for the growth of capitalism. This explains why it is necessary to start a great political and ideological revolution. It is a revolution to remold people to their very souls, to revolutionize their thinking. That is why in the course of this revolution we must "fight self". 59

And still another passage from Williams and MacFarlane elaborates further:

> A fundamental axiom of Maoist thought is that public ownership is only a technical condition for solving the problems of Chinese society. In a deeper sense the goal of Chinese socialism involves vast changes in human nature, in the way people relate to one another, to their work, and to society. The struggle to change material conditions, even in

the most immediate sense, requires the struggle to change people, just as the struggle to change people depends on the ability to change the conditions under which men live and work. Mao differs from the Russians and from Liu Shao Chi's group, in believing that these changes are simultaneous not sequential. Concrete goals and human goals are separate only on paper -- in practice they are the same. Once the basic essentials of food, shelter, and clothing for all have been achieved, it is not necessary to wait for higher productive levels to be reached before attempting socialist ways of life. 60

Chou En Lai gives essentially the same explanation in a very abbreviated, subtle form:

The goals of our cultural revolution are to workerize our intellectuals and intellectualize our workers. 61

The Chinese have always seen the human aspect of affairs as critical. Solidarity, not economic or physical coercion, is their ultimate 'weapon.' At the center of everything and seemingly symbiotically dominating everything is a desire to create socialist men and women now rather than later.

The Chinese would for example certainly subscribe to Che's formulation of the fundamentally critical moral aspect of revolutionary development, even if he does perhaps give Marxism too much credit for fulfilling them:

Economic socialism without communist morality does not interest me. We are fighting against poverty, yes, but also against alienation. One of the fundamental aims of Marxism is to bring about the disappearence of material interest, the "what's in it for me" factor, and profit from men's psychological motivation. Marx was concerned equally with economic facts and with their translations into men's minds. He called that a "fact of consciousness." If communism fails to pay attention to the facts of consciousness it may be a method of distribution, but it is no longer a revolutionary morality. 62

At another though related level Mao has pointed out that a critical need in the maintenance of revolutionary advance is the on-going rapid development of new revolutionaries. Mao seemed to feel this need for a new mechanism to educate the young very strongly -- in his eyes the only viable means was participation in severe political struggle. A young American in school in China during the Cultural Revolution said:

> The main issue, the real issue was the right to rebel -- to rebel against the bureaucrats and their flunkies the young communists.... The main issue was that youth should directly experiment with the revolution. 63

And here was perhaps the real daring of the Maoist approach and the reason why it had never been attempted before. The Great Proletarian Cultural Revolution put *rebellion on the people's agenda*. It legitimated in general at the same time that it used a specific revolt to foster the spread of a specific *class line*. It takes a great deal of faith in oneself and the masses to risk fostering rebelious attitudes while one is oneself in power; an amount that in fact goes beyond anything ever previously held by people in positions of authority in large societies.

Most of our questions are finally answered. The Cultural Revolution was a large scale tactic aimed at overcoming developmental problems, economic problems, ideological problems, and party authoritarianism problems so as to insure the continuing development rather than the backsliding of the revolution. As Huberman and Sweezy point out:

> There is no guarantee that the cultural revolution will attain its objective, the difficulty of preventing a reversion to class rule in an underdeveloped socialist society is much greater than most Marxists have yet recognized. It is not only that the growth of a privileged stratum is unavoidable but also that old ideas and habits of thought, old world attitudes, ingrained moral and religious values, are enormously persistent and difficult to eradicate; and their very existence creates a soil which is receptive to the seeds of privilege and exploitation. At this stage we can only say that

the Chinese have seen more clearly than anyone else both
sides of this vast problem and are making the only kinds of
efforts to solve it which seem to have any chance of success.
One thing is certain, terror will not solve it. What the
Chinese are now calling "extensive democracy" may. 64

In our brief survey we have emphasized those parts of the Chinese
experience that exemplify the ways it moves beyond the weaknesses of
Classical Marxism Leninism. We've not done any kind of complete job but
enough, it is to be hoped, to make the following assertions: Maoism
as opposed to Leninism "distrusts impositions from above", 65 and the
use of bureaucratic and capitalistic tactics, even though it very clearly
recognizes the need for strong leadership in China. A great deal of Maoist
thought goes into analyzing the means for combining leadership and
spontaneity while fostering chances for reaching communism and
diminishing the chances for falling off into 'capitalist roads'. And perhaps
the most important point is the "Maoist willingness to sacrifice economic
development to preserve what are seen to be essential social and ideological
prequisites for socialism -- and even to abandon the party itself as the
indispensable means to Marxist ends." 66 As Meisner points out in his
article on Maoism and populism:

> Whether Mao is consciously aware of the bureaucratic lim-
> itations of Leninist organizational principles is problem-
> atic; even if he has arrived at such a conclusion, it would be
> impossible for him to acknowledge it without renouncing
> the entire Leninist heritage to which he lays claim, and
> within which he claims to have made creative innovations.
> But Mao has adopted new means and methods which
> implicitly reject the institutionalized, bureaucratic pattern
> of post revolutionary development that so logically flows
> from Leninism, and Mao is sufficiently non-Leninist to
> question the revolutionary legitimacy of the Leninist party
> itself. 67

Still, in any final assessment it must be admitted that Classical
Marxism Leninism remains at the *official* core of Chinese thinking. The
rhetoric about party and authority and discipline still exists, as does one-

partyism, an absence of real decentralist *participatory management*, and significant regimentation in almost all areas of life. The on-going tension between Maoism's libertarian side and its Classical Marxist Leninist side continues, and still confuses Chinese politics. While the Cultural Revolution has at least temporarily overcome certain old aspects, unleashed new forces and new levels of awareness, and ridiculed many old ideas, *it has done little to really institutionalize libertarian gains*. In each city and factory what were called three-in-one committees were established, but experiments in direct popular democracy on the model of the Paris Commune were all unsuccessful and delayed for at least the moment. What will happen in the immediate future is still very unclear. Perhaps the capitalistic and Leninist forces will reassert themselves and slowly recorrupt social dynamics -- and if this occurs, and if Maoist ideology still has the strength, there will be a new cultural revolution of even greater scope and power than the last; but if it occurs, and Maoism is weakened, then China will likely enter onto the road of big power, centrist, bureaucratic, class, authoritarian, capitalistic, Leninistic, politics. And yet there is also the possibility that it will not occur, that the progression will be directly to the left instead, and that the already awakened consciousness of the masses will push steadily for greater and greater democracy until China has new institutions of direct popular control modeled more on the Paris Commune, than on say, General Motors.

Thus the Chinese experience bears out our earlier criticisms of Classical Marxism Leninism while pointing in essentially the same directions as did our own corrective intuitions. Mao had to call himself a Classical Marxist Leninist and even a Stalinist though in fact his political awareness was much richer than their Classical ones. It improved the Classical approaches in many ways (though admittedly also only moderately altering or even exactly recreating certain other failings). It in some senses synthesized certain positive Classical Marxist Leninist and Anarchist views. Before concluding our discussion of Maoism we must here briefly round it out by summarizing how Maoist theory and strategy 1-go beyond Classical formulations, 2-aid us in moving towards a new political consciousness, and 3-still fall short of so aiding us.

THE MAOIST THEORY OF CONTRADICTIONS

The correctness or incorrectness of the Maoist theory of contradictions is not really an issue, for it is *methodology* and thus conceptually definitional. What is important is its power in guiding analysis and in then organizing the results of analysis, manipulating those results, and drawing conclusions from them. This section's main orientation is thus to look at the concrete *use value* of the theory rather than at its abstract and actually tautological rightness-wrongness.

Moreover we are interested in the theory's use value in the United States and not in China. That is, we consider how well it could guide North American analysis, given the specific character traits common amongst the North Americans who would use it. Though we're not prepared to forcefully argue the point, there is an implicit assertion that the analysis is also applicable to China, but to only a lesser degree because Chinese culture and conditions are such that 'Chinese using the theory' can do better than 'North Americans using the theory'.

Thus to begin with we feel that the Maoist emphasis on primary contradictions is misleading and generally quite impossible to effectively apply.

How does one determine the primary contradiction of an unfolding historical process -- surely such determinations are contingent affairs. Take the case where feudal society is rupturing due to an imminent bourgeois revolution. Is the ensuing chaos a manifestation of a primary contradiction or is it merely the resolution of a minor one while the primary one, between perhaps the class nature of society and the humanness of people, is still to unfold? There is no real single right answer to the question. It depends upon how we define process and what time periods we consider.

The primary contradiction in the unfolding of all history is still unknown. The primary contradiction in the disruption of feudalism is supposedly known. Which was more important at any particular moment seems like a meaningless question. Until tomorrow we don't really know for sure what today's primary contradiction was, and even then we probably won't. Were the contradictions in pre-Nazi Germany that created the Third Reich primary, or were they merely secondary and less important than the slowly emerging contradictions between the proletariat and the bourgeoisie? There seems to be no *objective* criteria for any of these determinations except after the fact.

(Further even, though as a bit of an aside, there is also a problem in figuring how one should even define what is the system within which one is looking for a primary contradiction. How did Mao know when to define his system as China and look within, and when to define it as China plus the imperialists, thus looking within/without? Of course one can answer he used common sense, but that is not really a built-in part of the methodology, and in any case not quite as common in most people as it seems to have been in Mao. The United States parallel is, if one is to use the primary contradiction approach, how does one know whether to look for *it* within United States borders or within the entire United States imperialist system, or within the entire world system?)

North American Maoists claim that when the chosen primary contradiction of a process is seen to be less important than expected, an error is at fault -- an error by practitioners and not by the original theoriticians. In the abstract this is of course quite correct, but it solves nothing.

The real crux of the situation is that if this inflexible approach is used, errors are almost inevitable, and that once they are made they tend to be *exaggerated rather than uncovered and reversed*. Most especially in the United States, the extremism of the methodology couples powerfully and destructively with the extremism of the users. Here there is already a strong culturally enforced tendency to polarize and dichotomize, and it is enhanced rather than corrected by the theory, despite Mao's continual warnings of that very possibility.

A North American Maoist picks a primary contradiction even though the choice is historically problematic; he then views all surroundings in terms of that contradiction. Naturally it begins looking more and more central -- the Maoist becomes inexorably but unjustifiably more sure of the validity of his original guess. The Maoist dialectical method pushes the practitioner toward final determinations and away from patient flexibility; it fixates him, and its methods substantiate themselves independently of their real validity. As we'll see, the Maoist theory of knowledge provides only minimal insight for offsetting the process. Mao's warnings provide more, but they are not well heard or heeded in day-to-day North American political struggles. Further perhaps, Chinese culture also provides significant obstacles to the development of these problems, but again these are not operative here, and indeed their North American counterpart cultural forces likely act in opposite directions. Thus we have an argument for the low *use value* of the Maoist theory of contradictions, or at least of the Maoist theory of contradictions unaltered to fit the United

States consciousness context or unaided by complementary methodologies. It has a certain unity of theory and practice, but at least in the
North American setting, very likely it is an *uncorrective* one.

Aside from the ways such fixations invade the body of general Maoist
analysis inside the United States, the best examples of the 'primariness
fixation' problem arise from the practice of Leninist sects trying to
understand and change America. The Labor Committee, as just the limited
paradigm case, felt for a long time that a particular strike in New Jersey was
central to all United States occurrences and more important than any. They
totally fixated on the one strike (later on others, on CIA plots, etc.) and
reorganized the rest of their perceptions to comply. At anti-war meetings
their action proposals inevitably centered in one or another abstruse way
on the need to relate to their primary contradiction strike or whatever.
And though this is a ridiculously extreme example it is only a hair more so
than dozens of others that could be picked from the practice of other sects.
With regard to understanding campus activities, local community
activities, strike potentials, etc., Classical Marxist Leninists continually
focus on one aspect or another to the virtual exclusion of a total
understanding. Further, they do it tenaciously, quite as if their entire
welfare or identity depended upon doing it. Maoism's particular
dialectical entreaties partially cause this fetishism and in the United States
they certainly do nothing effective to prevent it.

In reality all observations are tentative. Almost all conditions are
alterable by history's course and almost all perceptions are subject to
error. It seems resonable to conclude that it is foolhardy and even arrogant
to try to distinguish particular contradictions, forces, ideas, or whatever as
permanently dominant. In a complex society with many spheres
interacting and many contradictions, rather than saying that one
contradiction manifests itself in all spheres and in the resolution of all other
contradictions dominantly, it seems likely it would be *more fruitful* to start
from the perspective that almost all contradictions manifest themselves in
all spheres and in all other contradictions. That way there is some
possibility that the already large 'natural' tendencies to dichotomize and
be inflexible will be offset to some degree. There is more probability of a
balanced rather than a fixated description and thus there is a higher
likelihood of good prediction, and perhaps also a lesser tendency to rush to
conclusions and cling to them despite mounting counter evidences.

Thus it might be wise to stress the idea that 'every' contradiction contains the 'conditions' of every other, and that they all generally develop as an interacting totality where dominance is not so much the important factor, as mutuality and intersection of causes and effects. But for now it suffices to say that the Maoist theory of the primary contradiction is difficult if not impossible to use undogmatically, and further that it tends to push people toward viewing things as being more isolated from one another than they really are.

Any social class has internal contradictions -- as one example, its members' consciousnesses can be either trade unionist or revolutionary about a certain issue -- and if the process of resolution is under way, how does one determine which aspect is dominant and what the extent of its dominance is? In reality their are obviously gradations: various numbers of people can have one or another consciousness, and various individuals (undergoing a personal process parallel to the larger group one) might well be torn between the two forms of consciousness, partially accepting each. The Maoist often tends to miss the complexity of this situation in the effort to make it correspond to simplistic expectations. And it simply doesn't do to say this is the practitioner's fault. There is little or nothing in the theory that opts against such error and in any case one doesn't judge a theory solely by its abstract value but also by its value as it's used by real struggling people.

These criticisms don't seem too different than ones we made previously of the Classical Marxist Leninists. We might deduce, and could show with some effort, that that is precisely because they are holdover weaknesses, offset a bit by a newer better formulation, warned against very strongly by Mao, perhaps less operative and therefore less important in a Chinese context, but still present nonetheless and certainly of significant consequence in any evaluation of Maoist theory for use in guiding United States practice.

To continue, and for a while in the same general vein, the Maoist definition of the principal aspect of a contradiction and of the ways its nature defines the nature of the system of which it is a part, is also highly ambiguous.

A more reasonable formulation of the principal aspect proposition might say that at any given time a system gets its overall nature from all the characteristics of all the various aspects of all its contradictions. In any case it is reasonably safe to assert that one's knowledge of any system is likely valid insofar as it evolves from a *totalistic balanced evaluation*, and likely problematic insofar as it stems from inflexible perceptions about which contradictions and aspects are central and which are not.

Although this type of critique is still at a level far removed from concrete practical situations, we see that it does again imply the kinds of problems Leninist and United States Maoist practice almost always evidences: harping on one contradiction, harping on one aspect of a person's or a group's attributes, working totally from "line" to "line," missing the whole for the part etc. etc.

Perhaps the theory of dialectics has often been formulated in regimented form because it increases its appeal by making it seem more precise and more scientific, and perhaps because the weaknesses of its practitioners simply push them inexorably toward using it that way. In any case the result is a reality that leads to errors of analysis not only in the original efforts of people employing the dialectical method, but also in the whole body of Maoist theory as developed in the United States context.

The lessons of the earlier presentation of Mao's theory of contradictions, of the effects of that theory on Chinese practice, and of the above criticisms seem relatively straightfoward: the extension of methodology to non-macro situations is a great gain. The recognition of and warnings about tendencies to dichotomize and fixate and so on, are enlightening but insufficient to the North American situation. Either adaptation of the methodology or one or more additional augmenting ones is needed. The extension of the concept of contradiction to non-antagonistic situations is a major advance allowing broader, and more pertinent to day-to-day affairs, analyses. Our understanding of these evaluations which springs from our discussion of the whole Chinese experience should be somewhat elaborated in the next three brief concluding sections.

THE MAOIST THEORY OF KNOWLEDGE

Many of our earlier criticisms of the Classical Marxist formulation apply to the Maoist one too. The major gains are the new emphasis on understanding and guarding against dogmatism, the new clarity, and the new applicability to actually guiding one's thought processes. The main problems are the continued belief that practice-theory-practice leads inexorably foward (if only one is careful enough), and the associated and still critical absence of a theory explaining the relation of personality, needs, habits, and whatever else from the psychological realm, to the problems of consciousness and motivation, and thus to the problems of political activism. The lessons are that a new theory should continue moving foward in guaranteeing its own growth tendencies, define its understandings well and clearly enough so that it has high day-to-day use value, and introduce enough of a psychological understanding to answer the many critically psychologically related and quite pressing questions -- not by way of some leaders 'great genius,' which in the United States is highly unlikely to exist and if it did exist likely to be counter-productive anyway -- but by way of a generalized commonally held political awareness.

GENERAL THEORETIC RESULTS

Maoism's broader understanding of social groups, better understanding of revolutionaries, better humanistic-materialistic balance, and greater emphasis on the importance of human character, all suggest directions of possible continued improvment in a 'new United States revolutionary consciousness'. The gains over Classical Marxism are considerable. The view of history and of the roles of groups within it is far more flexible, the understanding of the importance of politics versus the importance of economics is enlightening, and the broader understanding of revolution and of socialism is certainly also a significant advance. The major remaining weaknesses are a still too shallow understanding of human nature and personality and the derivative absence of a significant understanding of racism, sexism, and perhaps authoritarianism. The lesson is that in addition to broadening or repairing methodology, we must obviously also fill in these gaps in any new theory proposed for present United States use.

GENERAL STRATEGIC RESULTS

Obviously Maoism grows off a Leninist strategic root but vastly alters it. It seems to us that it is the direction of alteration that contains the easiest and most important lesson to learn. Mechanicalness, hierarchy, authoritarianism, unconsciousness of means as opposed to ends, unconsciousness of the importance of personality, etc. all diminish in Maoism. The Chinese strategic experience teaches abstract principles of conflict, the extreme importance of political consciousness, the extreme importance of tactics based not only on class analysis but on other social group and even individual person analysis as well, the need for understanding and overcoming problems of central leadership and of lacks of coordination, the need for approaches that bring together all potential allies, the need for overcoming bureaucracy, the importance of cultural and other superstructural issues, and so on, but to try to draw more specific conclusions is laden with difficulty because of the differences between United States and Chinese contexts -- two examples should suffice to prove the point.

In China the setting up of Red Bases, and the partitioning of land to improve material conditions of life played very critical roles in Maoist success. One North American Maoist might well suggest that the lesson for the United States is that developing independent institutions and increasing their power base while simultaneously winning reform demands, aimed at material well being, is central to winning. Another, and we think wiser, North American Maoist might argue instead that developing power within institutions and struggling for ideological and 'governmental' hegemony right there is parallel to Mao's creating Red Bases. A completely different style of life, filling a variety of needs, most especially the need for self-management in a context of sought and won material gains is analogous to Maoism's land redistributions.

In any case it's clear that the problem of deciding strategies for the United States can be aided by studying Chinese approaches, but can only be finally resolved by evaluation through indigenous theory and practice.

Consider as the second example the Chinese method of resolving contradictions within the revolutionary movement or between it and peoples it encounters: criticism self-criticism. All accounts suggest that it was and remains a very effective part of Chinese revolutionary practice. Should we import it? The answer can obviously only revolve around the method's applicability here and not there. In fact new left practice suggested it was not so useful as advance notices portended. Analysis explained that in our society, where competition is one of the pervasive weaknesses, a system of correction based upon finding and announcing weaknesses in one another tended toward back-biting counter produc- tivity, or toward sterile ineffectiveness brought on by defensively avoiding most important or most vulnerable issues. The lesson might well be that the method altered or that the method augmented by another might be effective, while the method in its original form is not.

In any case these specific strategic problems must really await the task of finally drawing lessons from our whole analysis and of then moving on toward new approaches of our own.

For now we must finish out the discussion of the Chinese experience by considering its contributions to revolutionary understandings of societal transitions.

Thus the key strategic lessons of Maoism are not the specifics but the trends toward alteration of Classical Leninism which must be brought even further here in the United States. Maoism hasn't developed alternatives to Leninism but has only reformed and continually struggled to prevent or rectify Leninism's worst effects. As a result it substantiates our critical perceptions of Classical Leninism and shows us directions to pursue but Maoism does not, by any means, supply a model we can slavishly or even flexibly copy. Indeed, only history will show whether Maoist 'reforms' of Classical Leninism were ideal or finally successful in the Chinese context.

GENERAL GOAL RESULTS

Maoist lessons concerning revolutionary goals evolve directly from Maoist theoretical gains. The Maoists tell us that while revolution immediately creates vast changes it does not eliminate all old institutions, old consciousness, old motivations, or old personality types. They tell us that the vestiges of the old society within the recently revolutionized one have the capacity to corrupt its functioning and cause reactionary or even oppressively restorative dynamics. They show us how revolutionary goals must address the full panoply of human needs rather than just the material ones; how they must address efficiency, yes, but also human well being and continued political growth. The Maoists thus make fundamentally clear that revolutionary societies still contain important contradictions and that successful revolutionary programs can't assume continual progress, but must rather create it by addressing reactionary and potentially revolutionary forces at both the institutional and the politico-cultural levels. Whether or not Maoist practice proves itself to have understood these lessons and thereby succeeds, or whether it shows itself instead bound by hierarchically and ideologically induced weaknesses and falls into oppressive days remains to be seen. In either case the validity of the awarenesses and their applicability to all other revolutionary efforts is in no doubt and must be incorporated into future United States ideology and practice.

FOOTNOTES

1. Mao in *Selected Works* and *Little Red Book*, Foreign Languagues Press, Peking, China.
2. See Karol's discussion of the relevant quotations in the *Little Red Book*.
3. Mao, "On Contradiction", *Selected Works, Volume One,* Foreign Languagues Press, Peking, China.
4. ibid.   314
5. ibid.   315
6. ibid.   333
7. ibid.   333
8. ibid.   315
9. ibid.   331
10. ibid.   316
11. ibid.   320
12. ibid.   322
13. ibid.   321
14. ibid.   343-344
15. ibid.   344
16. ibid.   Mao, "On Practice", op. cit. 293-298
17. Ibid.   300
18. ibid.   306
19. ibid.   306
20. ibid.   308
21. ibid.
22. Mao, "On the Correct Handling of Contradictions Among the People", *Selected Works,* op. cit.
23. Mao, *Selected Works,* op. cit.
24. Mao, "The Socialist Upsurge in China's Countryside", Foreign Languagues Press, Peking, China.   287

25. See McFarlane and Wheeiwright, *The Chinese Road to Socialism,* Monthly Review Press, New York.
26. Mao, "The United Front in Cultural Work," in *Selected Works,* op. cit.
27. For all this see especially McFarlane and Wheelwright, *The Chinese Road to Socialism,* op. cit.
28. And yet it is of course true that at any time the Leninist aspects could move to dominance and corrupt the other better ideas and ways.
29. Mao, "The Struggle in Chinkiang Mountain," in *Selected Works,* op. cit.
30. Mao, "The Tasks of 1945," in *Selected Works* op. cit.
31. Mao, "On Coalition Government", *Selected Works,* op. cit.
32. Mao, Preface to "Rural Surveys," *Selected Works* op. cit.
33. Mao, "Our Study and the Current Situation," *Selected Works* op. cit.
34. Mao, "The Role of the Chinese Communist Party in the Nationalist War," *Selected Works* op. cit.
35. Mao in Karol, op. cit.
36. Mao, the "Tasks of 1945," op. cit.
37. Mao, "The Report to the Ninth National Congress of the Communist Party of China," Foreign Languages Press, Peking, China.
38. Karol, op. cit.
39. See Mao, "Strategy in China's Revolutionary War", op. cit.
40. Mao, "Report to the Second Plenary Session of the Seventh Central Committee of the Communist Party of China," *Selected Works* op. cit.
41. Mao, *Selected Works,* op. cit.
42. Wheelwright and McFarlane , *The Chinese Road to Socialism,* Monthly Review Press, New York, N.Y. 32-33
43. Karol, op. cit.
44. Mao, "On Handling of Contradictions Among the People," op. cit.
45. Mao in Wheelwright and McFarlane , op. cit.
46. Wheelwright and McFarlane , op. cit. 67
47. Lin Piao, "Report to the Ninth Congress of the Communist Party of China," Foreign Languages Press, Peking, China.
48. ibid.
49. ibid.
50. ibid.
51. Hinton, *Turning Point in China,* Monthly Review Press, New York, N.Y.

52. ibid. 25
53. ibid. 19
54. ibid. 21
55. ibid. 43-44
56. Schurmann, *Ideology and Organization in Communist China,* University of California Press, Berkeley, California.
57. Paul Sweezy, *The Cultural Revolution,* New England Free Press Pamphlet, Boston, Ma.
58. Wheelwright and MacFarlane, op. cit. 155
59. quoted in Wheelwright and MacFarlane, op. cit. 157
60. Wheelwright and MacFarlane, op. cit.
61. Chou En Lai, "Important Documents of the Great Proletarian Cultural Revolution," Foreign Languages Press, Peking, China.
62. Che quoted in Long, *The Marxism of Che Guevara,* Monthly Review Press, New York, N.Y. 65-66
63. Chris Milton in a New England Free Press Interview Pamphlet.
64. Sweezy, op. cit.
65. Meisner in the China Quarterly, Jan-March 1971. 29
66. ibid. 30
67. ibid. 31

CHAPTER ELEVEN

HUMANIST AND NEO-MARXISM

Marxism, after drawing us to it as the moon draws the tides, after transforming all out ideas, after liquidating the categories of our bourgeois thought, abruptly left us stranded... it no longer had anything new to teach us, because it had come to a stop. Marxism stopped.... Marxism possesses theoretical bases, it embraces all human activities; but it no longer *knows* anything. 1

Jean Paul Sartre

We have thus far critically discussed Classical Marxism Leninism, Anarchism, and Maoism. We've developed awarenesses of a number of general requirements for a workable powerful new ideology; it must 1-incorporate a strong *psychological awareness* for use in both theoretical and also strategic and tactical analysis, 2-broaden and enhance *methodology* for better day-to-day applicability, 3-understand *race, sex, and authority* in accord with their importance to modern revolutionary struggle, 4-understand general institutional relations and specifically *revolutionary and factory institutional relations* well enough to guide related practice, 5-posit understandable, relatively comprehensive *goals*, and 6-generate *workable strategies and programs* suitable to actual, concrete day-to-day conditions and accurately aimed toward desired ends. We've also noted that Marx's own work can valuably aid us in meeting these requirements since it's often vastly superior to the nevertheless more dominant Cassical adaptations we've critiqued.

But even further, since Marx's day, and in parallel to the Classical interpreters, there have been other activists who have come considerably closer than the Classicists to fulfilling Marx's works' own original potentials. Frequently these humanist- and neo-Marxists clearly opposed their Classical contemporaries. They often criticized Classical views due to lessons learned from Second International vulgar determinism, Stalinist

barbarism, fascist reaction, and modern capitalist powers of self-alter-
ation. They were thus motivated by their historical settings and experiences much as we in the new left were pushed to critical views by the
international student upsurge, the Vietnam revolution, the Cuban
revolution, and the Chinese Cultural Revolution.

This chapter thus considers the contributions of Antonio Gramsci,
Anton Pannekoek, Wilhelm Reich, Adam Schaff, Mihailo Markovic,
Svetozar Stojanovic, Paul Sweezy, Charles Bettleheim, Andre Gorz,
Jeremy Brecher, and Stanley Aronowitz. It shows how each responded (or
is responding) to various historical trends by improving old ideology to
meet partially one or more of our above listed six ideological requirements.
The chapter can't approach a total or even fully representative view of
each of these writers, but by foregoing discussion of their actual practice
and of the various historical forces affecting them, it is possible to
emphasize their theoretical contributions, especially insofar as those are
relevant to present-day concerns. This succinct presentation of considerable information will give readers a feeling for each activist's overall
orientation, and 'contemporize' *What Is To Be Undone's* arguments for a
new ideology.

We thus show both how each activist we discuss contributes to
present-day ideological efforts and also how each falls considerably short
of actually succeeding in creating a finished new ideology.

ANTONIO GRAMSCI AND TOTAL REVOLUTION

Antonio Gramsci was an Italian Communist, born on the isle of
Sardinia, but primarily active in Turin, eventually as head of the Italian
Communist Party. His life practice represents a magnificent synthesis of
theoretical and practical work. In this chapter, however, we abstract from
his historical setting and consider his major ideas only in regard to their
modern relevance: we consider Gramsci's belief in the necessity for
broadness of revolution, in the importance of *workers' councils*, and in the
centrality of the ideological contest that Gramsci called the *"struggle for
hegemony."*

Gramsci reacted against the Second International's "wait for the
inevitable revolution" policies by trying to understand capitalism's active
abilities to preserve itself, and by trying to uncover the ways revolutionary
activism could overcome such defenses. He became aware that revolution-

ary activity primarily had to bring the masses from passive acceptance of capitalism to a *revolutionary consciousness* of its injustices and of the need for rebellion. Revolutionary activity would thus have to be premised in understandings of the roots of acquiescent consciousness, of how the state, production, and culture enforce such passive consciousness, and of how alternative views could best be spread. Gramsci understood that waiting for inevitable economically forced revolution was hopeless. Activists must prepare revolutionary potentials *both outside and inside the masses, both organizationally and in consciousness.* A precondition of total social revolution was a prior or at least simultaneous subjective revolution in the ways people think and live, how they perceive their worlds and act upon their needs.

Thus for Gramsci revolution required development of revolutionary consciousness among the masses of workers. Revolutionaries could aid such development by spreading their awarenesses and skills, but it was crucial that such acts actually foster real worker initiative. Gramsci knew the critical importance of *mass communication* of ideas and of non-elitist organizing methods:

> To create a new culture does not only mean to make *original* discoveries on an individual basis. It also and especially means to critically popularize already discovered truths, make them, so to speak, *social*, therefore give them the consistency of basis for vital actions, make them coordinating elements of intellectual and social relevance. That masses of men be led to evaluate in a coordinated way the present reality is, philosophically speaking, a much more important and original fact than the isolated philosophical genius's discovery of a certain truth, which is then left in heritage to small intellectual groups. 2

Gramsci also realized the necessity for creating a new type of intellectual who could really communicate well with workers by sinking roots among them:

> The mode of existence of the new intellectual can no longer consist of eloquence, the external and momentary arousing of sentiments and passions, but must consist of being

actively involved in practical life, as a builder, an organizer,
"permanently persuasive" because he is not purely an
orator -- and nevertheless superior to the abstract math-
ematical spirit; from labor-technique he reaches technique-
science and the humanist historical conception, without
which he remains a "specialist" and does not become a
"leader" ... 3

Gramsci felt education critically important because he saw that
revolution had to be *total* -- political, economical, social, and cultural -- or
it would not succeed at all. Weaknesses due to ignored concerns could
subvert all other effective efforts. For Gramsci, therefore, "communists
must ensure the development of spiritual premises of a new order." 4

Further Gramsci saw that the process of developing a full worker's
revolutionary awareness was one that could only occur in context of
worker self-organization, self-activity, and revolutionary activism:

The real process of the proletarian revolution cannot be
identified with the development and action of revolutionary
organizations of a voluntary and contractual type such as
the political party and the trade unions. These organizations are born on the terrain of bourgeois democracy and
political liberty, as developments of political freedom.
These organizations, insofar as they implement a doctrine
that interprets and predicts the revolutionary process, are
the direct and responsible agents of the successive acts of
liberation that the entire working class will launch in the
course of the revolutionary process. And yet they *are not*
this process, they do not go beyond the bourgeois State, they
do not and cannot encompass all of the revolutionary forces
that capitalism provokes in its implacable path as a
machine of exploitation and oppression. During the economic and political predominance of the bourgeois class, the
real unfolding of the revolutionary process happens under-
ground, in the darkness of the factory, in the obscurity of
the consciousness of the countless multitudes that capitalism subjugates to its laws. This will be done in the future
when the elements that constitute it (sentiments, habits,

seeds of initiative and mores) will be developed and purified by the evolution of society and of the new place that the working class will occupy in the field of production. 5

Gramsci recognized that workers would become revolutionaries by developing revolutionary consciousness through analysis of their own activities in context of advice afforded by the more advanced new type of intellectual activists. He saw that the real organizations of revolution were the workers' own *self-constituted councils,* where the workers not only gathered the strength necessary to taking over the means of production, but also gained the skills and solidarity to then administer them.

He saw the councils as organic centers of factory life that were simultaneously *weapons* of revolutionary struggle and *prefigurations* of the coming revolutionized society. The council structure could above all else, make the working-class see itself as an *active subject of history.* Gramsci saw that councils could give workers a direct productive responsibility, improve their work, create voluntary self-conscious discipline, create a psychology of the producer and of the "creator of history," and thus that they could prepare workers to win, create, and live in a new type of *self-managed society.* Gramsci saw that rather than abstract ownership rights, the really central issue was *day-to-day management of production and surplus,* and the beliefs that such various types of local management could "engender." 6

Thus where the Bolsheviks, for example, destroyed indigenous workers' councils, Gramsci always struggled to defend and support them. They could initiate revolution *in the workplace itself,* where it was most critical. Where the Bolsheviks saw the councils as a contrary power which had to be eliminated lest it interfere with the state's implacable will, Gramsci saw the councils as themselves the correct vehicles of decision-making, the correct vehicles of workers' control of production:

The factory council is the model of the proletariat state. All the problems inherent in the organization of the proletarian state are inherent in the organization of the council. In the one and in the other, the concept of the citizen declines and is replaced by the concept of the comrade; collaboration to produce wealth... multiplies the bonds of affection and brotherhood. Everyone is indispensable; everyone is at his

post; and everyone has a function and a post. Even the most
ignorant and backward of the workers, even the most vain
and 'civil' of engineers eventually convinces himself of this
truth in the experience of factory organization. Everyone
eventually acquires a communist viewpoint through understanding the great step forward that the communist economy represents over the capitalist economy. The council is
. the most fitting organ of reciprocal education and development of the new social spirit that the proletariat has
succeeded in creating.... Working-class solidarity... in the
council is positive, permanent, and present in even the most
negligible moment of industrial production. It is contained
in the joyous awareness of being an organic whole, a
homogenous and compact system that, by useful labor and
disinterested production of social wealth, asserts its sover-
eignty, and recognizes its power and its freedom as a creator
of history. 7

Finally Gramsci also formulated the concept of *hegemony* and
hegemonic struggle: every society has an order "in which a certain way of
life and thought is dominant, in which one concept of reality is diffused
throughout society in all its institutional and private manifestations,
informing with its spirit all taste, morality, customs, religious and political
principles, and all social relations, particularly in their intellectual and
moral connotations."8 The hegemonic struggle thus itself determines
which "concept of reality" will infuse all social relations and thoughts. *It is
a cultural, ideological, and institutional struggle to establish the dominance of a new revolutionary world view over and above the previous
dominance of the old bourgeois world view.* It is a struggle which Gramsci
considers crucial because holding hegemony over a society's world view
implies holding support of the masses and is thus essential to revolutionary success. Further, Gramsci recognizes how shared ideology is a
prerequisite to collective action for both the bourgeoisie and the proletariat. In this context, Gramsci's workers' council is a vehicle for the
proletariat to understand its own views, needs, and visions, one by which
they can propel that awareness to the central position of "infusing all
social relations and thoughts," so that revolution can gain mass allegiance
and thus the ideological and material power to collectively win full victory.

Gramsci's thought is a powerful *counter* to both Second International economist determinism and Leninist over-concerns with state power. It offers insights into cultural and workplace dynamics insofar as they affect human consciousness and it recognizes the central importance of creating and spreading revolutionary ideology. It puts *consciousness* in a central position and it emphasizes total revolution, the struggle for hegemony, and the power of workers' councils. To learn more from Gramscian thought a modern activist would extend its dimensions in both the workers'-council and the psychological-awareness directions. Thus these are precisely the types of contributions made by the next two activists whose works we consider.

ANTON PANNEKOEK AND COUNCIL COMMUNISM

Anton Pannekoek was perhaps the most famous of the European Council Communists and was the principle target of Lenin's derogatory polemic, *Left Wing Communism: An Infantile Disorder.* Pannekoek was one of many libertarian Marxists who shared Gramsci's general concerns, but where the others (Lukacs, Bloch, etc.) put most of their time into studying culture, Pannekoek emphasized issues of state power, workers' management, and workers' councils. His work thus continued the Gramscian corrective to old ideology by specifically furthering the understanding of authority, hierarchy, and workers' institutions.

Pannekoek's vision of a revolutionary society thus rested first and foremost on desires for *workers' self-management* without any accompanying party coercive apparatuses. He felt that workers' powers could only reach maturity in context of a parallel decline in traditional state power.

Governments were necessary, during the entire period of civilization up to now, as instruments of the ruling class to keep down the exploited masses. They also assumed administrative functions in increasing measure; but their chief character as power structures was determined by the necessity of upholding class domination. Now that that necessity has vanished, the instrument, too, has disappeared. What remains is administration, one of the many kinds of work, the task of special kinds of workers; what comes in its stead, the life spirit of organization, is the constant deliberation of the workers, in common thinking attending to their common cause. What enforces the accomplishment of the decisions of the councils is their moral authority. But moral authority in such a society has a more stringent power than any command or constraint from a government. 9

Thus Pannekoek's goal is an active working-class administering its own collective life through *self-organized councils.* Collaboration is to replace command, solidarity is to replace fear:

Thus council organization weaves a variegated net of collaborating bodies through society, regulating its life and progress according to their own free initiative. And all that in the councils is discussed and decided draws its actual power from the understanding, the will, the action of working mankind itself. 10

Obviously this is in sharp contrast with Bolshevik desires for discipline and the subordination of workers to managers and the state. For the Bolsheviks the economy must be set right by imposition of authority. For Pannekoek the economy can only thrive if *workers take the initiative,* thereby contributing incomparably to the powers of production. For Pannekoek the Bolshevik mistake was in subjugating workers rather than propelling them, and in destroying their organs of power rather than fostering them, not only for reasons of freedom and prevention of bureaucracy, as important as those are, but also for reasons of *economic efficiency.*

State socialism is a design for constructing society on the basis of a working class such as the middle class sees it and knows it under capitalism. In what is called a socialistic system of production the basic fabric of capitalism is preserved, the workers running the machines at the command of the leaders; but it is provided with a new improved upper story, a ruling class of humane reformers instead of profit-hungry capitalists. 11

History has of course demonstrated the plight of these well-motivated new ruling reformers under the pressures of maintaining their own powers and self-conceptions.

Pannekoek understood revolution as a process wherein workers continually develop ever-widening revolutionary awarenesses. Struggle after struggle would perpetually enhance awareness of capitalist injustices and revolutionary alternatives until such time as the councils could command power themselves. He felt that the key to revolutionary victory was to avoid taking reactionary roads within capitalist-based institutions:

> The old forms of organization, the trade unions and political party, and the new forms of councils (soviets) belong to different phases in the development of society and have different functions. The first was to secure the position of the working class among other classes within capitalism and belongs to the period of expanding capitalism. The latter has to conquer complete dominance for the workers, to destroy capitalism and its class divisions, and belongs the period of declining capitalism. 12

The sin of hierarchical parties should be avoided: "The belief in parties is the main reason for the impotence of the working class.... we avoid forming a new party not because we are too few, but because a party is an organization that aims to lead and control the working class..."13 The education of the masses should take place in context with their continual ever growing spontaneous rebelliousness, and in ways that depend upon and foster *self-activity*: "The insight needed cannot be obtained as instruction of an arrogant mass by learned teachers, possessors of science.... It can only be acquired by self-education, strenuous self-activity. [There should not be] the one sided teaching of doctrines that can only serve to breed obedient followers." 14

Pannekoek believed *mass action* carried on through workers' councils was the best way for workers to develop their own awarenesses. He felt that during unstable times self-preservation instincts dictate worker acquiesence to societal rules and lead to general worker passivity, but that in troubled, disrupted times, especially when well-posed alternatives seem better than old ways, the reverse phenomenon becomes true and preservation instincts push workers toward rebellion. Thus the miracle of the revolutionary energy of aroused masses, and thus also the importance of capitalist "breakdown" to Pannekoek's view.

Finally, like Gramsci and in opposition to determinist views, Pannekoek saw that the key to a full victory over all capitalist institutions was a *prior conquest of capitalist ideology.* Like Gramsci's hegemonic perspective, Pannekoek felt that workers must defeat old ideas and hold new ones if they are to have the initiative, morale, knowledge, and solidarity to practice effectively. Workers must overcome capitalism's spiritual sway over their minds before they can gain the insight and spirit necessary to also throw off its institutional yoke. Thus "capitalism must be beaten theoretically before it can be beaten materially." 15

> But the fight will be long and difficult. For the power of the capitalist class is enormous....firmly entrenched in the fabric of state and government. It disposes of all the treasures of the earth, and can spend unlimited amounts of money...to carry away public opinion. Its ideas and opinions pervade the entire society...and dominate the minds of even the workers.... Against it the working class, certainly, has its numbers.... It has its momentous economic function, its direct hold over the machines, its power to run or stop them.... Number and economic importance alone are as the powers of a sleeping giant; they must first be awakened and activated by practical fight. Knowledge and unity must make them active power. Through the fight for existence... through the fight for mastery over the means of production, the workers must acquire the consciousness of their position, the independence of thought, the knowledge of society, the solidarity and devotion to their community, the strong unity of class that will enable them to defeat capitalist power. 16

Council Communism is important for its emphasis on revolutionary institutions, for its awareness of the negative effects of capitalist and of all hierarchical institutions, for its insights into the importance of mass revolutionary consciousness, and for beginning the necessary effort of describing socialism and particularly the day-to-day nature of its alternative working relationships. On the negative side, however, Council Communism loses track of Gramscian cultural-consciousness lessons: it overemphasizes the likelihood of capitalist collapse, and underemphasizes the need to understand how capitalism's psycho-social dynamics and social divisions impede possibilities for worker activism. Council Communism relies too much on spontaneous revolution. It doesn't pay sufficient attention to what forms impediments to revolution take, and to discussing tactical means for overcoming those impediments. To extend Council Communist awarenesses it's necessary to add a strong psychological aspect to its already well-developed political one. Perhaps the finest work in such directions comes from the revolutionary psychologists themselves, and most principally from Wilhelm Reich.

WILHELM REICH: THE PSYCHO-SOCIAL FACTOR

Despite the unbalanced nature of some of his later work, Wilhelm Reich was in the main one of the most creative of all "modern" Marxist activists. His books are finally receiving attention in the United States and the results are likely to be both far-reaching and positive. Reich's main contribution was to extend revolutionary awarenesses into recognition of the vital importance of interaction between and among authoritarian character structure, revolutionary and reactionary consciousness, sexual needs, and sexual repression. His weakness was his fixation on sexual needs alone (while largely not understanding sexism itself) and his inability to gain a fair hearing from his contemporary revolutionaries, a fair hearing which could have led finally to a dialectical growth and improvment of his ideas.

Reich understood that history is at least as much determined by *what's in people's heads* as by "more material" matters. In their daily lives from birth onward people develop character structures or personalities which then mediate between their actual needs and their social contexts. Therefore to understand how economic and political events manifest themselves in real people's behaviors and consciousnesses, one has first to understand the nature of psychic character structure and the ways its mechanisms can react to societal occurrences.

Further for Reich one of the key problems in making a revolution is

overcoming *ruling-class ideology*. Thus it is necessary for activists to
understand not only how ruling-class ideology is pushed upon the
oppressed, but also why they frequently tend to hold onto it despite its
reactionary affects.

> ...every social order creates those character forms which it
> needs for its preservation. In class society, the ruling class
> secures its position with the aid of education and the
> institution of the family, by making its ideology the ruling
> ideology of all members of society. But it is not merely a
> matter of imposing ideologies, attitudes, and concepts on
> the members of society. Rather it is a matter of a
> deep-reaching process in each new generation, of the
> formation of a psychic structure that corresponds to the
> existing social order in all strata of the population. 17

Reich wants knowledge that can help revolutionaries create day-to-
day programs. He wants to understand how people develop character
traits which generally respect private property, respect established
authorities, and often fail even to recognize or admit the injustice of many
quite obvious oppressions. *He wants to know how acquiescent personalities are rooted in the forces of daily life and thus how they might be
positively affected by revolutionary activity centered around explaining or
altering daily life.* He wants to know at the need/consciousness level why
people generally support the status-quo instead of actively rebelling
against it or at least hoping for opportunities to do so. He believes that only
this type of knowledge can help revolutionaries orient programs toward
affecting the real obstacles to mass revolutionary activism. Reich finds
most of his answers at the micro- and psychological rather than macro-
and sociological or economic levels of social life:

> The revolutionary movement also failed to appreciate the
> importance of the seemingly irrelevant everyday habits,
> indeed, very often turned them to bad account. The
> lower-middle-class bedroom suite, which the "rabble" buys
> as soon as he has the means, even if he is otherwise
> revolutionary minded; the consequent supression of the
> wife, even if he is a communist; the "decent" suit of clothes

for Sunday; "proper" dance steps and a thousand other "banalities," have an incomparably greater reactionary influence when repeated day after day than thousands of revolutionary rallies and leaflets can ever hope to counterbalance. Narrow conservative life exercises a continuous influence, penetrates every facet of everyday life; whereas factory work and revolutionary leaflets have only a brief effect. Thus it was a grave mistake to cater to the conservative tendencies of workers by giving banquets as a means of getting to the masses. 18

Here Reich recognizes the importance of analyzing tactics to determine how they affect worker consciousnesses in light of an understanding of worker character types, and also points out the importance of confronting not just in-the-factory abuses but also *the totality of everyday life under capitalism.* Reich continues by finding that the key element in inculcating false ideas and reactionary lifestyles into the bulk of any oppressed citizenry *is sexual repression.* Sexual repression is seen as contributing to the development of authoritarian domineering and passive personalities, and as enforcing continuation of such personalities once they take root.

For Reich class-consciousness means having: 1-the knowledge of one's fundamental needs, 2-the knowledge of the possible ways of satisfying those needs, and 3-an understanding of how capitalism and capitalistic ways of thinking and acting are the chief obstacles to satisfying those needs while worker solidarity is the chief prerequisite of all means of satisfying them. Reich sees that class-consciousness is impeded among other ways by all authoritarian and sex-repressive interrelations. 19

Thus for Reich the revolutionary problem becomes how to choose tactics and organization so as to *overcome passive and authoritarian tendencies,* while simultaneously fostering real revolutionary working class consciousness. Like the Council Communists Reich believed in the crucial role of direct worker activity, self-education, and self-organization, but he was also aware of the many psychological impediments to effective worker activism. He thus favored a *totalist organizing focus aimed at all facets of daily life, including work, but also including sex life, home life, culture, sports, and so on, through the whole gamut of activities that make up the bulk of any individual's daily concerns.* For example, he severely criticized the pre-Nazi German left for its unwillingness to address the question of revolution in human relations until after a revolution in power relations. Further, with regard to the issues of sex life he developed a Sex Pol program, stressing youth centers, health clinics, and the distribution of sex information, to try to counter Classical party inadequacies. His extensive studies of the psychologies of youth, women, workers, and other strata attempt to provide a bedrock of useful information for strategic and tactical thinking. For example, using his psychological insights in tactical evaluation, he suggests setting up sex hygene clinics, youth centers, and radical theatres, not overemphasizing ruling class strength in ways feeding working class insecurities, and acting carefully toward the police so that they might be won over or at least neutralized rather than thoroughly polarized. 20

Although Reich's contributions centered too exclusively on sexual need, they do offer many lessons about how to add a psychological dimension to revolutionary political and economic awarenesses. Readers who are convinced of the importance of such a task should read Reich and also a number of more recent authors who, while not quite sharing his perspectives, do share his overall psychological concern and do offer up a number of interesting psychological perspectives on modern problems. The bibliography in this book (see pp. 322-332) provides a considerable number of annotated references both to Reich's own work and to the work of some other more recent radically-oriented psychologists.

EAST EUROPEAN MARXIST HUMANISM

The East European Marxist Humanists address their efforts primarily to overcoming Stalinist residues in their own countries by charting humane alternatives to state, bureaucratic, or in some cases, mixed market socialism. Their advances centrally focus on issues of human nature, human consciousness, and human psychology, both in the abstract and as they affect and are affected by actual social institutions, particularly bureaucracy.

More concretely, in arguing the need for more emphasis on people and their natures, Mihailo Markovic says that "the idea of making a world more humane presupposes a well-developed idea of the nature of man, and what it means to exist in an authentic way as a true human person"21 and "that there is no Marxist economy, there is no revolutionary theory without a theory of man and human nature."22 And Markovic adds that the Classicists haven't nearly accomplished these ends and explains why East European efforts to do so are not more prevalent:

> Apart from some very general phrases about the greatness of man, alienation in capitalism, freedom as knowledge of necessity, and practice as a "criterion" of truth, philosophers of dialectical materialism have not developed any conception of human nature based upon an in-depth understanding of praxis, involving true, human needs and basic capacities, positive freedom, alienation, and human emancipation. Yet all of these are major themes in Marx's philosophical works. "Dialectical materialism" became a rigid ideological system in a time when some of the most important Marxist philosophical works were not yet known. But there is also method in this neglect: it involves deliberate rejection of these problems for obvious ideological reasons. Only in the light of Marx's humanism can one have an overall critical view of the whole history of socialist society, and only comparing the present-day reality with Marx's humanist project can one fully grasp how much the former is still far from the latter and how little resemblance there is between present-day bureaucratism and Marx's idea of self-government. Knowing what *alienated labor* and *political alienation* are, it should not be difficult to find them in a society which claims to have built socialism a quarter of a century ago. That is why Marx's early philosophical writings had to be classified as Hegelian and not Marxist. 23

Similarly Adam Schaff says that "it is common knowledge that psychology is the Achilles' heel of Marxist research into social problems." And goes on to say that

> One reason for this is surely to be sought in the simplified approach to the base superstructure relationship that seemed to eliminate the operation of the psychological factor. The Marxist lexicon includes, it is true, such categories as "national character," "national mentality,"

"cultural tradition," etc., but these can hardly be said to
have been seriously considered in analyzing questions
concerning the ideological superstructure of society. 24

Schaff notes that obviously in different social environments "similar
changes in the base cause different transformations in the consciousness
of a given society." He asks how this could be and recognizes that the
answers have a psycho-social core and "are not purely academic. They also
concern such issues as the reason why similar changes in bases of socialist
societies lead, in some of them to a relatively smooth and rapid collectivi-
zation, while in others they fail to transform the obstinacy of social
consciousness." 25

Schaff knows that people create their environs, both base and superstructure, and therefore realizes that a fuller understanding of base and
superstructure and indeed of any social dynamic *depends upon a fuller
understanding of human activity and thus of human motivation, consciousness, and psychology.* In his formulation people are the "go-
between " "mediators" who translate base-superstructure influences
back and forth. Schaff thus says:

Whether we speak of the psychology of a given society, or of
the historically formed character of men -- in fact whatever
we call this issue -- we shall still remain within a sphere of
rather vague definitions each of which requires further
clarification. What matters in all these cases is certainly the
entire range of mental attitudes, the emotional dispositions
of men, their readiness to accept certain systems of values,
and even the irrational component of the human mind
which may be rationally explicable from the viewpoint of its
genesis. If all this, and perhaps something else as well,
makes up what we call the human "character," it is
something that varies in the course of history and has been
shaped by society. It consists of two factors: the psycho-
somatic, which is a social product in phylogenesis, and the
effects of social stimuli in the life of the individual, which
are the product of ontogenesis. Their sum total constitutes
the filters that sift and direct the stimuli of the base.
Knowledge of these filters is essential for our ability to

predict the influence of the stimuli and thus for conscious planning of our behavior. It is also important as far as changes of the "filters" themselves are concerned, since, however reluctantly and slowly, they too are susceptible to such changes. 26

In this passage Schaff gives a substantial part of the argument for expansion of radical awareness in psychological directions and thus makes a very significant contribution. Markovic even goes so far as trying to posit human nature as a series of *innate capacities* upon which, social interaction constructs *personalities*. He says that all people have capacities for unlimited sensory development, reason, imagination communication, creative activity, harmonization of interests in groups, discrimination among alternative possibilities, and development of clear self-consciousness. Regrettably, however, Markovic does not explain anything significant about how people form beliefs and personalities and choose their actions based on their capacities, and so he in fact gives us no reason to believe that his choice of a model of human nature is a particularly powerful or valid one; but he does at least admit the need for such knowledge in order to solve many critical problems, not the least of which is that of "irrational" behavior:

If we want to understand why many ordinary Russians admired and many adored Stalin in spite of all his monstrous crimes, if we want to understand how it is possible that even persons who suffered unjustly in concentration camps for years were later again ready to die with Stalin's name on their lips, a behaviorist will not help much. As has sometimes been said, "We must understand the Russian Soul." 27

Marxist Humanism is concerned to put people and their capacities in priority at the concrete political revolutionary level. The entire East European Marxist Humanists orientation thus centers on the need to *free human beings to be themselves* by freeing them from alienation, ignorance, and institutional oppressions. As Schaff says, Marxist Humanists are interested in understanding how to "transform this inhuman world, in which things rule men, into a human world, a world of free human beings who are architects of their destiny and for whom man is the supreme good. A humanism of this kind is a theory of happiness. The prime objective is to make people happy, *to make them capable of happiness.*" 28

And as Markovic says:

> The essential characteristic of revolution is a radical tran-
> scendence of the essential internal limit of a certain social
> formation. Consequently the basic theoretical question of
> revolution is the establishment of this essential internal
> limit. Only when we establish which basic social institutions
> make a society nonrational and inhuman, only when we
> establish the historical possibility and the paths for abolish-
> ing these institutions and replacing them by others which
> ensure more rational and more humane social relations,
> can our idea of revolution become sufficiently clear and
> concrete.... 29

Thus for the Marxist Humanists:

> The task of a critical scientific analysis is then, a) to show
> what institutions and structures make social relationships
> irrational and inhumane, b) to show what real historical
> forces could possibly abolish them, and c) to clarify how
> these forces could be strengthened by appropriate practical
> collective engagement. This is the only way to make it clear
> under what historical conditions, with what concrete objec-
> tives and by what actions a radical change is possible, and
> what course must be taken from the initial transformations
> towards the realizations of the ultimate goal. 30

But East European Marxist Humanism does not tell us what the central "critical scientific theory" that will aid us in accomplishing these tasks on a day-to-day, institution-to-institution, struggle-to-struggle level looks like. It does, however, recognize the crucial import of self-management and in Stojanovic's words posits that

> A political movement which does not strive to create
> real possibilities for the introduction of workers' self-

management is not a workers' movement in the full sense of the term. The criterion for this should be the extent to which the movement takes advantage of all opportunities to achieve this goal, not only after it has come to power, but while in opposition as well. 31

Schaff, because of both his opposition to Stalinism and his awareness of the keen, critical importance of people, recognizes further that *ideologies and institutions can also gain lives of their own* which extend beyond the economic factors and influence social reality well beyond Classical expectations:

But once an ideology has been created, it begins to have a life of its own, and to acquire a relative autonomy, as shown by its repercussion on the base of a society. Ideology may shape human behavior, the further evolution of ideology itself through a filiation of ideas, and by a conservative perseverance that enables it to resist transformations of the base. 32

In their social life, men enter various relationships which arrange themselves in permanent structures, most often in the form of institutions: the state and its bureaucratic apparatus, political parties, nations, social classes, professional groups, family, and so on. I have deliberately listed different types of human relations, with their different structures and institutions. All of them, however, have something in common. Once they are constituted as an institution (state, party, family, etc.) or as a permanent form of social organization (people, class, professional group, etc.) they begin to live an autonomous life independent of the will and choice of the individuals who are born into these institutions and forms of social organization and absorbed by them.... In some cases, particularly when the state is involved, the [resulting] estrangment of the human product is exceptionally harsh, painful, or even destructive of the individual. 33

And Stojanovic adds a further awareness concerning the characteristics of "life-taking" bureaucratic parties:

> In those communist parties in which the monolithic
> conception prevails it is characteristic that the ideological-
> theoretical monopoly of the leadership is constantly being
> renewed. This ideological centralism, a consequence of
> political, organizational, and staff centralism, has devasta-
> ting consequences in the realm of ideas. All the most
> important theoretical initiatives are awaited from the party
> summit, so that it remains for the lower levels to merely
> accept them and work them out. Thus the theorists are
> divided into "party" and "non-party" elements, even
> within the party. 34

But at this point the growing incisiveness of the Marxist Humanists
begins faltering. They, for example, urge workers' control but in the fight
against bureaucracy only seem to offer minimal *correctives*, rather than
real alternative ways of organizing a revolutionary society's institutions:

> A developed society which already possesses the possibility
> of creating all these institutions of self-management should
> make resolute efforts to prevent all those processes which
> lead to bureaucratization such as: a) fusion of the victorious
> party and state; b) professionalization of the leading
> political functionaries; c) privileges for performing political
> functions; d) monopoly of the mass media of communica-
> tion; e) public property being used for the private benefit of
> permanent leaders; f) allowing the cult of certain personal-
> ities. Analogously to the norms of ancient democracy it
> should be a matter of revolutionary ethics to remove
> potential charismatic leaders from the positions of power
> and influence and to transfer to them other important
> social functions. 35

> In an early phase of the struggle against bureaucracy, while
> the critical social self-consciousness is still in *statu*

nascendi, the most important means are *truth,* bold *demystification* of existing social relationships, *dethronement* of deified persons and institutions, and above all a *great moral strength.* It should be borne in mind that bureaucracy sometimes survives long after it has lost any historical justification because it succeeds in breaking psychologically the most active progressive elements in society. 36

In conclusion, Marxist Humanists see the need for psychology, recognize the imbalance of Classical base-superstructure ideas, and partially understand the dynamics of ideologies, institutions, and especially parties gaining extreme powers and "lives" of their own, but do not go deeply enough in any of these directions, do not provide sufficiently useable understandings of how people's consciousnesses form and are formed by revolutionary practice, do not adequately consider issues of class and other social groups, and do not even really venture to discuss alternative institutional relationships. Their whole East European thrust seems quite positive as a philosophical counter to Stalinist anti-humanism and bureaucracy, but their usefulness here in the United States is primarily in the questions they generate, rather than in any specific answers they finally give. Stojanovic is not merely rhetorical when he asks:

Can dictatorship lead to democracy? Coercion and violence -- to freedom? Class struggle to classless society? Can uniformity yield diversity? Should we expect absolute state power to usher in a society without a state, a self-governing community? How can socialist revolution, itself a part of prehistory, lead to the beginning of mankind's true history? Can the revolutionary, himself belonging to the old world, create a new life and educate the new man? Who is to educate the educators? 37

And for attempts to furnish answers we must turn our attentions to some more western theorists.

PAUL SWEEZY AND CHARLES BETTLEHEIM:
REVOLUTIONARY TRANSITION

Paul Sweezy and Charles Bettleheim are the deans of modern revolutionary economics. Their recent *Monthly Review* debate about "socialist transition" is a very interesting Western response to essentially the same issues and events which created Eastern European Neo-Marxist Humanism.

The debate centers around the problem of how a society can be transformed from capitalist to socialist dynamics once a successful transfer of power from the bourgeoisie to the proletariat and its representative party has occurred. The key agreement is that after this power transfer and before the actual success of the revolution there's a transition period during which old and new factors (market and plan; material and moral incentives; competitive and cooperative ideology; etc.) exist simultaneously. The problem then is determining which transitional features will foster socialism, which will impede it, and what programs might combat the latter while propelling the former?

Sweezy begins the debate by asserting: 1-enterprises run by small groups for profit embody the essential social relations of capitalism, so 2-control of an enterprise residing internally plus market distribution plus material incentives creates capitalist divisions and mentality and thus pushes toward capitalist restoration, no matter what property and governmental control regulations prevail, so that 3-market socialism is a contradiction in terms because during transition helping rather than fighting market relations equals helping rather than fighting tendencies toward return to capitalist dynamics.

Bettleheim replies by urging that the factors Sweezy emphasizes (market, incentives, and profit-seeking local management) are really only economic reflections of more fundamental political phenomena: principally the succession of a revolutionary bourgeois class to power. Bettleheim asserts that market relations per se don't propel either socialist or capitalist dynamics but rather that market relations only in the context of *who is in power* have such effects. For Bettleheim markets used by truly socialist authorities are socialist; markets used by capitalist authorities are capitalist.

Thus Bettleheim asserts that the key transitional problem is *power*, and that in the event of the successful solution of that problem, temporary economic retreats (like Lenin's use of capitalistic forms) are okay.

Sweezy replies that he doesn't mean that market, incentive, and profit seeking dynamics preclude socialism, but just that, though such features must temporarily exist, they are dangerous and must be carefully controlled.

Sweezy believes markets, individual material incentives, and profit-seeking create competition, advertizing, inequality, mis-directed production and consumption priorities, and general productive-place and consumption-place alienation.

Sweezy outlines his vision of potential negative transitional possibilities: power seizure leads to *bureaucratic control,* which, diminishing mass participation in politics, increases *authoritarianism,* which generates *worker depoliticization,* governmental rigidity, and general alienation, which finally causes *economic problems* due to worker hostility, passivity, and frustration/laziness, all causing worker disobedience and production decline. According to Sweezy the revolutionary party (the supposition of the whole presentation is that revolution is accomplished with a party at the helm and that transition is administered by that same party) then combats the economic problems by choosing either cultural revolution, as in China, to bring the masses back to lively participatory awareness, or capitalist incentive and management organizing techniques, as in Russia, to more directly reinforce productivity. In the former event reaction is hopefully warded off by a reassertion of revolutionary dynamics and values. In the latter case, however, there develops a *managerial elite* who subsequently struggle with and eventually overcome the programless bureaucrats and then institute the essentials of *state capitalist organization.*

Bettleheim responds at length, saying that an advance toward socialism equals a growth of self-control of producers, so that central plans -- the assumed alternative to Sweezy's disliked markets -- can mean an advance toward socialism if their content and implementation increase producers' control over economic life, but can also mean a return to capitalism if their processes of creation, content, and implementation throw up obstacles to producers' control over economic life.

He says that, contrary to Sweezy's implicit urge to focus on plan/market contradictions, analysts should instead look first and foremost to the condition of the *class struggle* for power. Who is in power gives reality and content to the plan-market choice and determines the direction of social evolution, and Bettleheim says that focusing attention on plan-market dynamics can obscure these more critical relations. Bettleheim thus rightly points out that *plans need not equal a force for socialism* and that *markets need not equal a force for capitalism,* and that it's important to examine power relationships as well as technical and tactical ones. He realizes that plans and markets have some aspects that reflect or depend upon "more essential" class power dynamics, but he doesn't realize that they also have *intrinsic features of their own* which *tend to affect people in capitalistic or socialistic ways no matter who is in power.* Thus Bettleheim rightly recognizes that transitional conditions can degenerate due to bourgeois elements taking positions of power, but he fails to recognize that another threat is that those in power (workers or otherwise) can *be made bourgeois* by their very efforts to employ capitalist or authoritarian methods.

In the next round Sweezy accepts Bettleheim's definition of the direction of socialist progress as power to the producers but then asks, what if the proletariat is in power and uses market relations? Won't such practice lead to competition, inequality, and so on, and won't all such trends tend to create reactionary forces and even to promote capitalistic type revisions? How do we know whether any chosen tactic is fostering socialism; what determines if socialism is going foward or backward; how do we know if the proletariat is actually in power; and why will it necessarily be the proletariat and not some other sector or alliance of sectors?

Bettleheim replies first giving his criteria for progress towards socialism, the continued enhancement of proletariat control over production, and then quoting Lenin favorably to the effect that *State power* is absolutely central to all revolutionary activity.

He continues, however, by arguing that for success, the state *must be separated* from the masses, and that policy must *promote workers' control* over their own situations and over the economy rather than state or party control over the workers. For him, the state must seek *without coercion* to push the proletariat to act in its own best interests. During the transition continued class struggle is necessary to eliminate old societal dynamics and must be led by the party and state. Precisely *how* they will accomplish such ends, however, or why *they alone* are suited to accomplish such ends, is never made explicit.

Thus Bettleheim recognizes the need to overcome bourgeois divisions of labor, old ideologies, separations between manual and mental labor, between leadership and performance roles, between theoretical knowledge and practical skills, but regrettably posits no concrete way to accomplish these tasks, save the enlightened application of proletarian policies by a proletarian government.

So the essence of the debate is that Sweezy asks what is the criterion for judging whether transition to socialism is proceeding well and for judging whether any particular tactic is having capitalist or socialist effects. Bettleheim replies that the criterion is the increase of proletarian control, and tactical evaluations, then, are to be based on their effects on proletarian control.

Well enough, but then Sweezy tries to make a fundamental advance: market relations, individual material incentives, and profit-seeking, all used by a proletarian party/state might be differently motivated than when similarly employed by a bourgeois state, but still a number of their capitalistic oppressive characteristics survive, and so a good part of their practical effect is to *induce capitalist ideology, institutional relations, and even class divisions* irrespective of who is in power; i.e., a whip in proletarian hands is perhaps a little gentler than a whip in bourgeois hands but it is a whip nonetheless.

Regrettably Bettleheim 'solves' Sweezy's problem much as Lenin did similar earlier problems, by putting more or less enlightened demands (anti-sectarianism, bring power to the proletariat) on the same old party and state institutions which are so ill-suited to meet these demands instead of describing new institutions more suited to the task of bringing power to all people and then helping them collectively hold that power.

The debate makes some headway over Classical views by emphasizing: 1-issues of producers' control and 2-the potentially capitalistic effects of markets and other traditional methods; but fails to make really significant advances because *it never questions the necessity and worth of hierarchical parties as vehicles to producers' power.*

In a discussion of Soviet and Polish experiences that closes the published debate, Sweezy makes some additional interesting points. In transition, policies should satisfy private needs only to the extent that such satisfactions can be produced in enough abundance to go around. Policies should be aimed at social improvement and social justice and inhibit development of divisions based on inequities of power or wealth. Short of being able to meet individual needs by producing enough for all, policies should aim only at solving problems by affecting collective well-being: thus, for example, public-transit investment rather than automotive investment. Similarly, since solidarity is the key to the development of revolutionary consciousness and behavior, while competition conversely fosters capitalist relations, *all private incentive procedures should be replaced by collectively-oriented ones.* Sweezy shows how in Poland "representatives of the proletariat in power" became essentially bourgeois due to their use of counter-productive techniques in society and in their own party relations. He argues that the transition from capitalism to socialism has potentials for reversion *because residues of capitalist relations at both the human and institutional levels* provide a basis for backward-looking elements to exert authoritarian and capitalistic policies. Thus, according to Sweezy's view, its always necessary to examine transitional methods to insure that they foster socialist rather than capitalist tendencies, and its never sufficient to rely solely on the enlightenment of the party in power.

Nonetheless both Sweezy and Bettleheim are, with reference to the United States, far too narrow in examining the problems of the ideological and institutional effects of racism and sexism, and far too cautious with the problem of creating new day-to-day useable methods for social investigation, new understandings of the relations between revolutionary consciousness and daily revolutionary activities, and new models of revolutionary political organization, leadership, and discipline more suited to the problems of both gaining and then effectively employing power in the United States.

Further, both Sweezy and Bettleheim unquestioningly accept the idea that gaining revolutionary power is a bureaucratic affair inevitably involving party and then government control. Although the thrust of many of their ideas is the *necessity to counter bureaucratic deformations* after power take-over, neither entertains the idea that the methods and institutions of power transfer could in themselves mitigate or solve the problems of bureaucratic control *before and during* rather than only after power transfer. Obviously also neither addresses the likelihood that hierarchical organizations in the United States wouldn't in fact be able to garner enough worker allegiance to manage a takeover in the first place, let alone deal with deformation after a takeover. These weaknesses seem to stem from a Sweezy and Bettleheim misunderstanding, or rather too literal understanding, of Maoist lessons: for Maoism primarily struggles against Classical difficulties in a reformist way without totally overcoming the use of Classical rhetoric, Classical ideas, and especially some forms of Classical organization, both on the road to taking and then also in the process of holding power. How much the Chinese in their particular situation will suffer for this is unclear; that Sweezy and Bettleheim are in error to assume they won't suffer at all, and moreover to assume that a similar understanding is also applicable in the United States is even more problematic. For Sweezy and Bettleheim to really push their debate forward they must recognize that it's necessary to struggle against the old society's "baggage" after reaching the new society, but also that, especially in the United States, it's necessary to do so even while fighting to reach the new society, and further, that this struggle must apply to all methods of investigation, conflict, and pre- as well as post-revolutionary organizational forms. Then Sweezy and Bettleheim would be better able to recognize and address the presently central question of how a United States revolutionary movement could best organize itself to insure its chances of gaining societal self-management and decentralized libertarian socialism without simultaneously creating any significant bureaucratic or authoritarian deformations to be countered, if such countering is really possible, later. Moreover Sweezy and Bettleheim don't seem to yet realize that as our earlier disscussions of Leninism emphasized, a creative approach to revolutionary organizational forms is critical not only to *perfecting* but also even to *generating* United States revolutionary activity --precisely because such activity will inevitably address societal anti-authoritarian and self-management needs, as well as material needs.

The importance of the Sweezy-Bettleheim debate is thus primarily not in any answers it develops but rather in the questions it raises for others to address. Like the East European Marxist Humanists Sweezy and Bettleheim only manage to find possibly fruitful directions of further inquiry, teaching us as much by what they leave out of view as by what they actually do discuss. Some other more strategy-oriented modern activists come still further along the road of demystifying past ideological conceptions and fulfilling the kinds of new revolutionary needs we outlined at the beginning of this chapter.

ANDRE GORZ AND REVOLUTIONARY PROCESS

Andre Gorz is perhaps West Europe's best-known, practically-oriented, neo-Marxist. His works are aimed at concretely suggesting and analyzing programmatic ideas suitable for affecting real world conditions. The core advances of his work are extensions beyond Classical aware-nesses of *intra-class dynamics,* of the importance of *revolutionary goals,* of the nature of *revolutionary organizations,* especially parties, and of the possibility of *"non-reformist reform"* strategies that lead to progressive development of mass revolutionary consciousness. His modern impact is deservedly great, but what is lacking *from a United States orientation* is enough analysis of the impact of racism and sexism, enough day-to-day useable methodology, enough discussion of the concrete ways revolu-tionary programs could affect worker consciousness, and a willingness to advance to the stage of actually describing what revolutionary organizations should look like.

For Gorz capitalism is a total system whose overthrow demands total opposition:

> The dictatorship of capital is exercised not only on the production and distribution of wealth, but with equal force on the manner of producing, on the model of consumption, and on the manner of consuming, the manner of working, thinking, living... over the society's vision of the future, its ideology, its priorities and goals; over the way in which people experience and learn about themselves, their poten-tials, their relations with other people and with the rest of the world. This dictatorship is economic, political, cultural, and psychological at the same time: it is total. That is why it is right to fight it as a whole, on all levels, in the name of an overall alternative.... The cultural battle for a new concep-tion of man, of life, education, work, and civilization, is the precondition for the success of all the other battles for socialism because it establishes their meaning. 38

For any revolutionary movement to succeed against advanced capitalism it must recognize that people are not going to move on the basis of oppression alone, but instead also because envisioned liberated conditions make revolution too desirable to pass up:

What has changed, however, is that in the advanced countries the revolt against society has lost its *natural base.* As long as misery, the lack of basic necessities, was the condition of the majority, the need for a revolution could be regarded as obvious. Destitute proletarians and peasants did not need to have a model of future society in mind in order to rise up against the existing order: the worst was here and now; they had nothing to lose. But conditions have changed since then. Nowadays, in the richer societies, it is not so clear that the status-quo represents the greatest possible evil. 39

Further Gorz therefore knows that for a revolutionary process and strategy to gain adherents it must not only point out present oppressions but *also describe and even prefigure future liberations.*

[The revolutionary project] can only constitute...a total stake justifying a total risk if the action of struggle has already been an experiment for them in self-organization, in initiative and collective decision-making, in short, an experiment in the possibility of their own emancipation. 40

A revolutionary movement always feeds itself on the radical and total rejection of the existing order and all its possible improvements. But it can move forward, assert itself and bite into the existing order only if, in its progess, it evolves the outlines of a new kind of society, the instruments of its future development. 41

Gorz knows that "the working class will not unite politically or man the barricades for the sake of a ten percent wage increase or an extra fifty thousand dwellings. It is unlikely that in the foreseeable future there will be a crisis in capitalism so acute that, in order to protect their vital interests, workers will resort to a revolutionary general strike or armed insurrection."42 Therefore "the main problem confronting socialist strategy is consequently that of *creating the conditions,* both objective and subjective, in which mass revolutionary action becomes possible and in which the bourgeoisie may be engaged and defeated in a trial of strength."43

But Gorz also recognizes the depth of capitalism's abilities to administer itself, deceive and mystify its potential opponents, and even convince those it oppresses that their condition is in fact not so negative: "Domination produces an ideology that justifies domination as natural and necessary and makes non-acceptance of it a crime. The deeper the oppression, the greater the inability of the oppressed to think of themselves as possible subjects and agents of their own liberation and to create a consciousness of their own." 44

Gorz knows that capitalism oppresses, that it creates many needs it cannot meet, but also that such inadequacies are not always easy for the oppressed to identify fully and act upon. He knows that the "theory of immiseration" can only lead to sterile inactivity:

> This theory becomes a crutch: like the theory of the inevitability of catastrophic crises which was current in the Stalinist era, it bases itself on the *growing discontent of the masses* as if that were an absolute impasse toward which capitalism were headed. Convinced that capitalism can only lead from bad to worse, the theory foresees its absolute intolerability. This allows it to dispense with the elaboration of a strategy of progressive conquest of power and of active intervention into capitalist contradictions. 45

For Gorz the revolution is a process during which masses of workers and others become progressively more aware and begin to act both against the ills of present society and for the positive aspects of an envisioned future society. Therefore the problem is how can present revolutionaries best propel such a process -- to insure that it occurs at all, since it's not inevitable, and to cause it to happen as rapidly and with as little social friction as possible. Most importantly, in the context of this same problem, Gorz realizes that capitalism's police and military capacity demands revolutionaries *rely on more than spontaneity;* while capitalism's abilities to coopt or thwart misconceived opposition necessitates that revolutionaries also *not rely on demagogy, hierarchy, and or a blind discipline of the Leninist variety.* Thus "one of the intrinsic difficulties of revolutionary leadership and education is that they can be entrusted to neither an 'enlightened' and self-appointed vanguard, nor the spontaneity of the masses...."46

Further, and in parallel to the awareness that the "education problem" must be sovled in ways prefiguring new societal potentials, Gorz recognizes that the "power problem" also requires a creative libertarian rather than the traditional centrist solution:

> The key issue, therefore, is not getting working class parties into power; it is the building up of a genuine power of popular self-determination and self-government in opposition to centralized state power, which is the supreme instrument of bourgeois domination by which the social division of labor is perpetuated. Indeed, the question of winning power is practically meaningless unless a certain number of things have been done or have happened to liberate repressed needs and aspirations, promote the capacity of popular self-rule and effectively raise the issue of alternative power. 47

Given all his concerns for revolutionary process, and for the importance of practice prefiguring goals, Gorz readily understands the centrality of the problem of revolutionary organization, seeing first that revolutionary organization must have *a real basis in worker activities,* and second that it must take a non-Classical form fulfilling a number of requirements which Lenin wrongly discounted. Thus "the first prerequisite for building a revolutionary movement is not the creation of a new party organization -- however 'pure' and 'genuinely revolutionary' its program and ideology -- but rousing the workers to fight for things that are within their reach and can be realized by their own direct actions: namely, working conditions in the factories. Self-determination of the purposes and methods of struggle; self-management of strikes and/or production through permanent debate in open assemblies; the setting up of strike committees at the factory and shop level, whose elected members are answerable to the general assembly of workers and may be recalled at any time -- all are liberating experiences that reveal to the working class its capacity for self-rule and for mastering and modifying the work process, and prepare it to refuse domination by management and by the state as well as by party and union bureaucracies."48 But once there's a real basis for revolutionary organization it must be remembered that its organizational goals must be to *strengthen but not dominate* the movement, creating the means for workers to take societal powers unto themselves. For Gorz, such a revolutionary organization, which he still calls a party, must grow *up from below* in accord with developing worker conscious- nesses and in tune with their needs for *anti-authoritarian* self-manage- ment and for the development of the skills necessary to effectively *administer society and their own lives.* Thinking in terms of the ills of traditional Leninist parties, Gorz sees the need for a party as a *necessary evil,* and tries to describe criteria for structuring one that would have a minimum of weaknesses:

> Insofar as the party is a central organization it is to be regarded as a necessary evil: necessary because there has to be a center where local experience can be compared and coordinated, where it can achieve a unified outlook and be transformed into a political strategy to confront the bour- geois state. But nevertheless an evil because, facing a centralized power, it reflects the necessity to centralize a revolutionary undertaking of which the final aim is to do away with *all* state centralization. As a central organization, the party must be understood to be a temporary structure necessary for getting rid of the bourgeois state but *which must thereafter get rid of itself.* 49

Regrettably, however, Gorz never moves on to consider if there could be an organization which might serve the positive functions he outlines above, without, on the other hand, having any of the traditional negative aspects of the central parties. Could there be a people's organization which could accomplish coordinating, communicative, and even planning and strategic functions, without at the same time garnering for itself any undue authority or power, without stifling initiative, and without becom- ing an eternal obstacle to the final appearance of a revolutionary and decentralist society? *Could there be a people's organization which prefigures, propels, and then melts into a decentralized decision-making mechanism for a new society?*

Gorz does however set stringent libertarian criteria for his revolu- tionary "party":

It is natural, therefore, that all those political parties that aim at controlling the state apparatus and modern capitalist society but not at changing them, should model their own structure on that of the state as it exists. A revolutionary party, on the other hand, is distinguished by its assault, both theoretical and practical, on the authoritarian centralist nature of the state as an expression of bourgeois monopolist rule; and by an ability to destroy the illusion that this degree of centralization is unavoidable in a modern industrial state, whether capitalist or socialist. The destruction of this myth entails in the first place that the party should not behave as -- and should not be considered as -- a machine for winning power for itself and for its leaders. It must be viewed not as the *holder* of future power but as the *instrument* whereby all the power will be transferred to the people and exercised by themselves. Not the winnng of state power but the destruction of the state as a separate center of power ruling the people, is the revolutionary goal. 50

Gorz knows that with a creative new "party," the revolutionary process has a good chance of success: he sees growing numbers of activists, growing revolutionary consciousness, and a growing scope for revolutionary programs, causing a strategic flow leading to eventual revolutionary victory. Therefore in Gorz's view the working hypothesis on which the revolutionary party must base its activity is no longer a sudden seizure of power, made possible by the breakdown of capitalist mechanisms or a military defeat of the bourgeois state, but that of a patient and conscious strategy aimed at provoking a crisis in the system by the masses' refusal to bend to its logic, and then resolving this crisis in the direction of their demands.

Revolution is to be an on-going flow of conflict during which continually more people become politically consicous and active -- the crisis precipitating an actual trasfer of power comes then, not as a result of internal economic dynamics alone, but rather as a result of revolutionary opposition itself rupturing society's orderly capabilities. The conditions of revolutionary transfer of power from central institutions to people's institutions is accomplished by the long hard work of conscious revolutionary activists.

Further, Gorz feels that though capitalism is a total system, the locus of anti-capitalist activity must begin with the work situation and develop from there:

> It is from the *place of production* that the struggle must necessarily begin. For: 1- it is at the place of production that the workers undergo most directly the despotism of capital, and have the direct experience of their social subordination; 2- it is there that capital, by methods of the division of labor which, often without *technical* necessity, constitute *methods of domination,* puts itself to work producing decomposed, molecularized, humiliated men which it can then dominate in society; 3- finally, and especially, it is only there that the workers exist as a group, as a real collective force capable of a collective action which is direct and daily, and which can just as well modify their condition in its most immediately intolerable aspects as it can force the enemy to confront them as he really is. 51

Gorz also recognizes that within any factory there are not just two opposing classes but *many sectors,* each of which must be treated differently in revolutionary thought, propaganda, and tactics. He sees differences not only between boss and worker, but also between skilled, semi-skilled, and unskilled workers, black and white workers, male and female workers, white- and blue-collar workers, totally oppressed workers and workers who partly carry out orders that oppress others, and so on. Gorz believes people's consciousnesses develop primarily through analysis of personal experience. He feels that for real successes the critical awarenesses that can thusly develop must be combined with positive aspirations as well -- for it is the positive aspirations that create the possibility of revolutionary praxis:

> The politicization of the masses doesn't start from politics, nor action or struggle alone. Political commitment and choice, are in fact, the final position of a development of consciousness...which never starts with politics, i.e., with the problem of the organization of society and social

relations, but from the direct and fragmentary experience of a change *which is necessary because it is possible.* The demand for change, in other words, does not arise from the *impossibility* of accepting what is, but from the *possibility* of no longer accepting what is. 52

Gorz's ultimate solution to the revolutionary problem of creating the *objective and subjective* preconditions of revolution is to work in such ways as to continually augment worker consciousnesses of present injustices and future alternatives, and create *a long march of non-reformist reform struggles.* The workers organize to win concrete demands but when they accomplish those immediate ends, rather than merely recreating stability, their victory instead creates more favorable conditions for the next round of conflict. Thus the reform struggle is a successful part of real revolutionary process when it "sets up objectives beyond the realm of wages, when it carries on despite management concessions of wages, when it provokes a heightening of consciousness, and when it does not end before having raised additional demands, which, being unsatisfied, will resurge and reappear on a higher level in further actions," and when in victory it creates a better balance of forces for the next worker-management conflict.

Thus in clarifying his revolutionary reformist approach Gorz says:

What in practice distinguishes a genuinely socialist policy of reforms from reformism of the neo-capitalist or "social-democratic" type is less each of the reforms and goals than, first, the presence or absence of organic links between the various reforms, second, the tempo and method of their implementation, and third, the resolve, or absence of resolve, to take advantage of the imbalance created by the initial reforms to promote further disruptive action. 53

Therein lies the profound difference between reformism and socialism. It is the difference between conceded reforms which perpetuate the subordinate position of the working class in the factories and in society and reforms dictated, effected, and controlled by the masses themselves, based on their capacity for self-management and their own initiative. 54

Gorz's work is important to the left because he begins to challenge dogmas about *revolutionary goals, revolutionary organization,* and the existence of differing problems for each *different sector* of the working class. But he doesn't progress to the point of positing *clear goals* or describing concretely how *tactics can prefigure new possibilities;* he doesn't go beyond pushing stringent demands on a new revolutionary party to the task of explaining how a *new revolutionary organization* might actually be structured to meet those demands. The problems of revolutionizing different working-class sectors and different social groups with different consciousness and therefore different taking-off points is not adequately developed. Finally though Gorz does recognize the *totalist nature* of capitalist oppression, he focuses too single-mindedly on the workplace as the scene of revolutionary struggle. He doesn't give enough consideration to the possibility for consumer, neighborhood, caste, sex, service-institution, ecological, and state-sector political struggle in themselves and as they interrelate with workplace struggle. He does however recognize the need for separate struggles and movements to be tied together in ways going beyond the limitations of traditional alliances:

> The weakness of the traditional type of alliance is that it consists of separate group interests and sectional grievances that are merely added together and turned into a list of demands that never amount, in their sum total, to a comprehensive critique of the existing order and to a unifying vision of the struggles to be waged for its super-session. 55

But since he doesn't investigate the full variety of such sectional struggles, he gives no real ways for accomplishing this unifying task at either the ideological or the programmatic level. All in all he provides a powerful basis for further progress but does not show the precise ways to accomplish such further gains.

A MODERNIZED COUNCIL COMMUNISM

Stanley Aronowitz and Jeremy Brecher in a sense combine Pannekoek's political awarenesses and Reich's psychological awarenesses into a new and more powerful Council Communist position. Like Pannekoek they emphasize worker self-activity, worker self-organization, and the need to avoid and overcome the negative effects of hierarchical parties and trade unions. But they also go beyond Pannekoek's belief in the ease-of-worker-arousal to a more Reichian awareness of the kinds of socio-cultural forces impeding the realization of revolutionary consciousness.

Thus Brecher's major work, *Strike,* essentially charts a history of mass strikes in the United States, showing that they were mostly rank-and-file, often opposed rather than supported by organized trade unions, and that they sometimes offered up alternative direct factory-council organizational forms that had significant revolutionary potentials.

He shows how *mass strikes generating worker self-organization* are especially important for challenging authority, promoting solidarity, and giving workers new skills for controlling their own lives. The implication is that if workers were also guided by their own revolutionary ideals, goals, and programs, mass strikes could be truly effective revolutionary tactics.

Thus in a summary of his position published in "Radical America," Brecher first describes what he understands to be revolutionary consciousness:

> The "consciousness" necessary for socialist revolution consists in workers' shared understanding that they can collectively initiate and control their own action to meet their own needs. Such an understanding does not flow directly and automatically from the position of workers in production, although that position is what makes workers potentially powerful. Nor does it arise primarily from the speeches, manifestos, and other "consciousness raising" activities of the Left, though they may make some contribution to it. The working class can come to understand its power to act *only by acting.* 56

He then alludes to some adverse factors he finds prevalent in present United States working class consciousness: "On the contrary, it was because it [*Strike*] took the actual activity of the working class as its basis for evaluation that it found individualism, conservatism, racism, sexism, nationalism, and passivity to be real factors shaping working-class practice."57 Brecher draws the rather straightforward conclusion that revolution in the United States will require a developmental process in which *conscious revolutionaries must play significant organizational and educational roles:*

> The working class is potentially revolutionary, and socialism would be the natural result if one tendency of its development were carried to its logical conclusion. But if this were the only tendency in effect, the workers would all be revolutionaries and socialism would have been achieved long ago. To ignore the factors which currently lead workers to adapt to existing society instead of trying to abolish it is to give up the ability to understand "the real, existing American working class with all its limitations." To ignore those limitations is to lose the power to grasp the process that will be necessary to overcome them. 58

> ...it is hardly the function of radicals to say "amen" to whatever the working class may do. Those who accept rather than challenge the institutions and attitudes through which workers' subordinations to capital is mediated are the true "spontaneists".... For those of us who aim for the replacement -- and not merely the "humanizing" -- of capitalism, the least we can learn from the past is how to avoid contributing to the perpetuation of the system we want to abolish. That requires a willingness to criticize the Left of the past, not just for one or another "incorrect line," but for its most basic principles and premises. The purpose of such a critique, however, is by no means to discourage action; it is to see that our own action actually contributes to our liberation, rather than to our firmer enslavement. 59

Because he feels that hierarchy and authoritarianism breed passivity in workers and elitism in revolutionary cadres, in contrast to worker self-activity which leads to worker self-management, Brecher has a straight-forward criterion for judging revolutionary organization: "If socialism means the organized direction of society by the producers themselves, then socialist organization is that by which people develop their ability to initiate and control their common activity to meet their own needs." 60

In this same context Brecher revealingly defends *Strike* and implicitly Council Communism against a particular form of prevelent criticism:

> Why then is *Strike* sometimes interpreted as advocating "spontaneous," as opposed to organized, activity? This criticism grows out of a different conception of organization, one which has been more common in the history of the socialist movement than the one I have proposed. According to this view, the working class is seen as organized to the extent that it is enrolled in formal organizations, particularly trade unions and radical parties. The possibility that such organizations might represent the disorganization of their members -- their inability to initiate and control their actions themselves -- is not apparent from this point of view. And activity not originating with such organizations is by definition "spontaneous." 61

Finally Brecher makes explicit his reasons for believing in the revolutionary viability of workers' councils:

> Workers' councils do not possess any secret quality which makes them, by virtue of their form, revolutionary. They do, however, have several characteristics which make them different from unions. First, they are based on the power of workers who are together every day and exercise continuous power over production. Second, they are already controlled by the workers themselves, who can recall their delegates at any time. Third, they follow the actually existing organization of the working class in production, rather than dividing it along lines that quickly become obsolete, as has happened over and over again in the history of unionism. 62

Brecher's ideas are a fundamental return to Council Communism with an increased awareness of race, sex, authority, and psychology related concerns, and as such represent significant contributions to the task of creating a new United States revolutionary ideology.

Aronowitz has a similar orientation but greater experience and thus an even more effective and broad formulation. His recent book, *False Promises,* includes a general theoretical presentation of his viewpoints in the context of a discussion of modern worker activism, the history of the development of various sectors of the American working class and of American working class struggle, and of the culture of the American working class. The work is a major contribution to an understanding of United States history, of present United States conditions, and of Council Communist ideas adapted to a modern setting.

Aronowitz starts off with a strategic aim: "The fundamental question to be explored in this book is why the working class in America remains a dependent force in society and what the conditions are that may reverse this situation."63 To answer why workers acquiesce to their oppressive conditions, Aronowitz recognizes that he "must examine daily life, for it is in the structures of everyday existence that the social structure is reproduced in the minds of its participants."64 He finds that the confusion of American worker consciousness arises in the first place from the mystifying dynamics of their involvement in production:

> Commodities appear to assume value in exchange rather than in production and the relations between men are perceived as relations between things. The worker values himself as one values all commodities -- by his selling price. Thus all relations appear as object relations. The very existence of the worker is bound up with the sale of his labor power. Individual worth is measured by how much labor can bring in the market place. People become identical with their occupations, consumption styles and social prestige and the self has no autonomy apart from its exchange value. The subordination of the self to the labor process takes on the appearance of blind economic law, so that the domination of man by man no longer appears an injustice but a biological or legal necessity. The power of the employer over the worker has the force of economic necessity and its human substance is entirely suppressed. 65

And in the second, from the effects of society's various socializing institutions:

> The main institutions within and against which the individual confronts society prior to entering the work-world are family, schools, religion, and more recently mass culture These institutions mediate between the social relations of production and individual consciousness by communicating to the individual his place in the social division of labor while providing contrary symbols that hold out the possibility of transcending the fate of previous generations. 66

> The importance of the socializing institutions is that they make unnecessary the open use of force, because workers in their earliest experiences find themselves at the bottom of a pyramidal structure within these institutions and come to expect that all social institutions will asign them the same position. Theories of human nature are constructed that elevate this experience to a level of belief. The superiority and inferiority ratings of human beings based on the criteria of adaptive intelligence justify the hierarchical organization of labor, the domination of political institutions over individual lives, the tracking system in the schools, and the differential treatment accorded members of a person's family by parents. 67

> Indeed, the child learns in school. But the content of the curriculum is far less important than the structure of the school itself. The child learns that the teacher is the authoritative person in the classroom... 68

Aronowitz thus sees socialization as primarily a process of acclimating people to their niches in society, such that they will accept those niches and even feel them deserved, no matter how oppressive and unjust they might actually be. Like Pannekoek, he sees that authority relations play a central role in all such socialization and control, especially in the case of workers. But unlike Pannekoek, Aronowitz has no naive belief in the consciousness-raising effects of immiseration -- he neither expects worsening conditions, nor believes that if adverse changes did somehow occur, workers would thus be radicalized:

What has developed in the twentieth century is the *partial*
utilization of knowledge, sufficient to maintain a level of
economic growth adequate to the criterion of the profitab-
ility of production and to the maintenance of relatively high
living standards...it seems clear that if the proletarian
revolution awaits the economic crisis it may remain little
more than a fantasy. 69

The theory of revolution as the outcome of manifest
economic crisis of capitalism encounters a second difficulty. There is absolutely no evidence that depressions in
themselves lead to a rise of revolutionary activity, much less
revolutionary consciousness among the workers. On the
contrary, workers tend to become profoundly conservative
under conditions of increasing material deprivation. They
organize themselves only to fight against wage cuts or to
force the government to undertake programs that increase
relief payments and job-creating projects such as public
works. The economic crisis of the 1930's resulted in the
strengthening of the capitalist state rather than the development of a large revolutionary workers' movement.... 70

Further Aronowitz discusses Reich's analysis of Germany favorably,
agreeing on the importance of distorted sexual and authority relations to
all that transpired there:

...the question of politics of the working class and its
movement cannot be decided by reference to political and
economic leadership alone. Reich argues that it was the
authoritarian character structure of the German working
class that provides the causal explanation for the revolutionary failure of the 1930's German society, he asserts, as
mediated through the authoritarian family, repressed the
instinctual need for freedom....the working class was
predisposed to seek the solution to the world crisis of
capitalism in authoritarian institutions because it failed to
wage a struggle against authoritarianism within its own
organizations.... Workers were subjected to a consistent

pattern of repressed social relations in the entire compass of
everyday life... 71

Aronowitz thus realizes the complex nature of political motion and
recognizes the absolute requirement that left organization not merely
mimic traditional hierarchical modes. He says of the left's organizations in
Germany, "the left-wing parties and the trade unions reflected the
hierarchical relations of capitalist society no less than the corporations
and the family," and points out that for so long as the left offers no real
structural alternatives vis-a-vis issues of authority, it will be powerless in
competition with even far more authoritarian, tighly knit organized right
wing elements. He realizes thus that "the existence of radical organizations enjoying the support of the masses could constitute a brake on
revolutionary activity if they reinforced the system of domination,
especially sexual repression, already existing within the culture."72 And
he agrees with Reich that the fundamental question is "the transformation of workers' consciousness, not only at the point of production and
within political struggle, but also in their daily lives, in the fulfillment or
denial of their needs -- especially their sexual needs." 73
Further Aronowitz says that, "Daily life provides clues for both the
liberatory and the authoritarian tendencies with the working class as well
as all social groups. It is the critical institutions of family, peer groups,
school, church, and the voluntary associations, and the workplace itself
that structure the way people respond to events as well as create them." He
then spends much time doing fine, relatively detailed analyses of how
those institutions actually operate in the present United States setting. 74
Predictably Aronowitz is opposed to trade unions and all other
hierarchically organized or capitalistically entangled institutions: "The
trade unions have become an appendage of the corporations because they
have taken their place as a vital institution in the corporate capitalist
complex." 75
Further Aronowitz feels that organizing solely around wage problems
is at best a partial and at worst a counter-productive approach. It is the
totality of oppression that must be confronted most particularly by
focusing on issues of management and alienation:

The most important issue to be addressed in defining the
tasks ahead is not the question of inflation, wages, or

general economic conditions. No matter how inequitable
the distribution of income, no matter how deep the crisis,
these conditions will never, by themselves, be the soil for
revolutionary consciousness.
Revolutionary consciousness arises out of the conditions of
alienated labor, which include economic conditions but are
not limited to them. Its starting point is in the production
process. It is at the point of mental and manual production,
where the world of commodities is produced, that the
worker experiences his exploitation. Consumption of waste
production, trade union objectives in the direction of
enlarging wages and social benefits, and the division of
labor into industries and sections are all mediations which
stand between the workers' existential exploitation at the
workplace and their ability to comprehend alienated labor
as class exploitation. 76

For Aronowitz the revolutionary task is for activists and workers
together to understand *both the personal and the political obstacles to
fulfillment* and to then organize struggles designed to raise the type of
revolutionary consciousness that could overcome those obstacles. Thus for
Aronowitz "the first step in the reeducation of workers is to help them
become aware of their own biographies, that is, the ways in which they
have been educated so that their character structure is harmonious with
the structure of domination." For Aronowitz the new left's great success
was to realize the necessity of merging the political and personal, but its
great failure was in not extending the awareness of this need from women
and students to the workers themselves. Activists must not make the
mistake of thinking that workers live only an "economic" existence lest
they become "coconspirators with the corporations in the cultural
impoverishment of the working class. 77
    Culture is central as one aspect of the consciousness-life of all
workers. Aronowitz thus sees that "the struggle of workers' self-
management at the shop level cannot be waged successfully as long as
corporations and the government have cultural hegemony over the
workers,"78 and feels that:

...the central mechanism of this hegemony is the control

over unbounded time and its consequent rationalization analogous to the rationalization of industrial production. Consumerism, mass media, spectator sports, and educational institutions prepare workers to view themselves as objects of manipulation, to view their lives as outside of themselves, to surrender their subjectivity to the spectacle and to destroy their imagination. 79

Aronowitz thus sees that "the central task of a New Left among the working class is to create the conditions for the separation of popular culture from mass culture,"80 because he feels the crucial need for workers to exert *creative initiative over control of their own leisure lives,* both to break down capitalist control and to begin exercising worker alternatives.

Aronowitz understands at least some of the implications of his anti-authoritarianism for questions of revolutionary organization. He sees that the task of a new radical left is to create a self-organized working class actor in history. He feels correlatively that radicals must avoid "vanguard politics" for three reasons:

First, the working class in America does not need such a vanguard because it has the objective possibility of comprehending its own experience and leading itself. Second, the left has no credentials for assuming the role even if it were needed; its contributions to working class struggle, however considerable, have never transcended the level of consciousness of the workers themselves, and have often seriously impeded that consciousness. Third, it is not the job of the left to reproduce authoritarian social relations in the workers' movement. Instead, its first responsibility is to help create a movement that prefigures a non-authoritarian society -- a movement that is aware of the dialectic of domination and subordination within the structure of society as well as the character structure of the workers themselves and tries to transcend these syndromes, even as it simultaneously struggles every day in the workplace against the assault of capital on work conditions. 81

In line with his Council Communist heritage, Aronowitz feels that the ultimate vehicle for accomplishing the necessary revolutionary tasks can only be the workers' own self-organized councils:

> Workers' councils or committees can only become serious expression of working class interests when they challenge authority relations in the enterprise, are based on some understanding that the prevailing division of labor rein- forces these relations, and when they possess the power and the desire to transform the workplace in accordance with a new conception of the relations between work and play and between freedom and authority. Workers' control demands that are instruments of trade union and bureaucratic institutions merely reinforce the powerlessness of workers because they sow the seeds of cynicism concerning the possibility of actually achieving the vision of a self-managed society. 82

In a real sense Aronowitz's politics synthesize the advances of humanist and neo-Marxism. The gain beyond previous sectarian conceptions is certainly obvious enough, but the remaining gaps are also quite pronounced. *Still to be incorporated is a good understanding of the roles of Black and women's struggles, consumer struggles, and the importance of the state sector and of directly anti-state struggles.* There is still no well-delineated discussion of *revolutionary goals*, still no really workable ideas on how revolutionary structures should look, and perhaps most important of all, there is still very little *activist orientation.* For even though Aronowitz does focus strategically on the question, "What are the impediments to revolution?" and even though he tries to give broad answers on how to counter those impediments, he does not develop a *methodology activists can learn and employ in their own efforts.* There is no set of tools that can be used to analyze tactics or programs that can overcome impediments of specific local work institutions, neighborhoods, or schools. Creating such tools is the crucial next step that could rekindle United States left motion. Developing a complete, popularly readable theoretical perspective, including goal orientation, theoretical tools, and an overall strategic awareness is the next major task for the left. Whether it can be accomplished within the rough outlines of Aronowitz's modern

Council Communism, or whether it will require several new theoretical (feminist, racial, psychological?) categories remains an open question. What this book has however hoped to demonstrate is the variety of ways in which a new ideology must transcend Classical Marxism Leninism, Anarchism, and Maoism; and the nature of the "success criteria" it must fulfill in order really to provide viable tools for guiding a new United States revolutionary praxis.

FOOTNOTES

1. Jean Paul Sartre, *Search for a Method,* Alfred A. Knopf, New York. 21, 28.
2. Antonio Gramsci quoted in the article, "Antonio Gramsci: The Subjective Revolution" by Romano Giachetti, in *The Unknown Dimension,* edited by Dick Howard and Karl E. Klare, Basic Books Inc, New York. 151.
3. Ibid. 158.
4. Ibid. 162
5. Ibid. 157-158.
6. This is a crucial point in the sense it goes beyond Classical preoccupation with forces of production to a fairly clear perception that really far more important are the relations of production and of life in general.
7. Antonio Gramsci in *Antonio Gramsci and the Origins of Italian Communism,* John M. Cammett, Stanford University Press. 82.
8. Ibid. 204.
9. Anton Pannekoek, *Workers' Councils,* A Root and Branch Pamphlet, 275 River Street, Cambridge Mass. 52.
10. Ibid. 54.
11. Ibid. 33.
12. Anton Pannekoek quoted in the article "Left-Wing Communism: The Reply to Lenin," in *The Unknown Dimension,* op. cit. 181.
13. Ibid. 182.
14. Ibid. 177.
15. Anton Pannekoek, *Workers' Councils,* op. cit. 29.
16. Ibid. 34.

17. Wilhelm Reich quoted in the article "The Marxism of Wilhelm Reich," by Bertell Ollman, in *The Unknown Dimension,* op. cit. 205.
18. Wilhelm Reich, *The Mass Psychology of Fascism*, Farrar, Straus, & Giroux, New York. 22-23.
19. See the essay "What Is Class Consciousness" in Wilhelm Reich, *Sex-Pol*, Vintage Books.
20. ibid.
21. Mihailo Markovic, *From Affluence to Praxis,* University of Michigan Press. Ann Arbor, Michigan. 139.
22. Ibid. 73.
23. Ibid. 56.
24. Adam Schaff, *Marxism and the Individual,* McGraw Hill Paperbacks, New York. 40.
25. Ibid. 40.
26. Ibid. 41.
27. Markovic, op. cit. 19.
28. Schaff, op. cit. 8.
29. Markovic, op. cit. 191-192.
30. Ibid. 214.
31. Svetozar Stojanovic, *Between Ideals and Reality,* Oxford University Press. New York. 115.
32. Schaff, op. cit. 115.
33. Ibid. 119.
34. Stojanovic, op. cit. 85.
35. Markovic, op. cit. 204.
36. Ibid. 206.
37. Stojanovic, op. cit. 178.
38. Andre Gorz, Karl Klare's introduction to *The Unknown Dimension*, op. cit. 10-11.
39. Gorz, *Strategy for Labor,* Beacon Press, Boston Mass. 3.
40. Gorz in *The Unknown Dimension,* op. cit. 18.
41. Gorz, *Socialism and Revolution,* Doubleday Anchor, New York. 36.
42. Ibid. 136.
43. ibid. 135.
44. Ibid. 15.
45. Gorz, *Strategy for Labor,* op. cit. 23.
46. Gorz, *Socialism and Revolution,* 31.
47. Ibid. 32.

48. Ibid. 33.
49. Gorz, *Socialism and Revolution,* op. cit. 176.
50. Ibid. 63.
51. Gorz in Howard, in *The Unknown Dimension,* op. cit. 406.
52. Ibid 405.
53. Gorz, *Socialism and Revolution,* op. cit. 141.
54. Ibid. 158.
55. Ibid. 57.
56. Jeremy Brecher, *Radical America,* "Who Advocates Spontaneity?" 91-92.
57. Ibid. 93.
58. Ibid. 94.
59. Ibid. 110.
60. Ibid. 98.
61. Ibid. 99.
62. Ibid. 106.
63.Stanley Aronowitz, *False Promises,* McGraw Hill, New York. xi.
64. Ibid. 6.
65. Ibid. 7.
66. Ibid. 10.
67. Ibid. 60.
68. Ibid. 75.
69. Ibid. 53.
70. Ibid. 53-54.
71. Ibid. 54-55.
72. Ibid. 55.
73. Ibid. 55.
74. Ibid. 55.
75. Ibid. 219.
76. Ibid. 255.
77. Ibid. 435.
78. Ibid. 435.
79. Ibid. 436-437.
80. Ibid. 437.
81. Ibid. 441.
82. Ibid. 426-427.

CHAPTER TWELVE

A NEW "NEW LEFT" IN THE SEVENTIES

I am a fanatic lover of liberty, considering it as the unique condition under which intelligence, dignity, and human happiness can develop and grow; not the purely formal liberty conceded, measured out and regulated by the state, an eternal lie which in reality represents nothing more than the privilege of some founded on the slavery of the rest; not the individualistic, shabby, and fictitious liberty extolled by the school of J.J. Rousseau and the other schools of bourgeois liberalism, which considers the would be rights of all men, represented by the state which limits the rights of each -- an idea that leads inevitably to the reduction of the rights of each to zero. No, I mean the only kind of liberty that is worthy of the name, liberty that consists in the full development of all the material, intellectual, and moral powers that are latent in each person; liberty that recognizes no restrictions other than those determined by the laws of our own individual nature, which cannot properly be regarded as restrictions since these laws are not imposed by any outside legislator beside or above us, but are immanent and inherent, forming the very basis of our material, intellectual, and moral being -- they do not limit us but are the real and immediate conditions of our freedom. 1

Mikhail Bakunin

In chapter two we discussed and generally elaborated T.S. Kuhn's method of understanding scientific progress. Since then we've struggled to demonstrate that Classical Marxism Leninism is inadequate to present daily revolutionary needs, and that though Anarchist and Maoist alternatives offer additional insights, they too are inadequate.

The present United States situation is grossly unjust though also obviously pregnant with immense liberatory possibilities. To release these possibilities requires revolution, and revolution presupposes powerful revolutionary ideology.

Past paradigms can't do the now necessary job: we must create a new one that can. That is this book's 'message' and the effort it tries to support.

Over the next few years left praxis must create new ideology and movement. As a contributory step we now distill from our critical understandings of past ideologies an awareness of what a new ideology must be like: what it must explain, what it must enable us to do, how it must be the same and different from past ones, how it must alter over time, and how it might be created through our activities.

The most general summary answer to these questions is that our efforts at creating a new revolutionary paradigm must continue the trend we saw in the developmental transition from Classical Marxism Leninism through Anarchism and into Maoism. Methodology must be further improved, and psychological consciousness awarenesses further enlarged, both at our new ideology's roots, and then derivatively all throughout it.

The coming American revolution will be a collective anti-authoritarian mass-based process. It needs non-elitist theory with methods all people can use, and with growth dynamics that will fight all tendencies toward sectarianism. It cannot be built on the Classical Marxist Leninist or even the Maoist dialectical methodologies alone; those will have to be simplified, and amended as well.

In the United States, dynamics between individuals and between people and the 'roles' they must fulfill are very critical to day-to-day revolutionary affairs. Sexism, racism, and authoritarianism are crucial factors in all people's lives and in all revolutionary calculations. *The psycho-social side of societal relations is equally as causal in social movement dynamics as the material-economic side.* A new theory must perceive that reality, understand it, and create strategies to change it, in ways relevant to our specific contexts. It will need to arm us for answering the crucial questions of revolutionary day-to-day work. Why do people often do things detrimental to their own welfares? What prevents people from fighting the injustices around them? How do varying organizing approaches affect people's attitudes toward the left? What tactics should we use, what programs are important, what tasks must we undertake today? In each specific daily situation, how do people's feelings or habits, or the dynamics of institutional arrangements or of culture, or of personal interaction, affect revolutionary potentials?

Such a theory needs also to arm us to answer the larger questions that affect people's overall values, motives, morale, and style. What is it in history that gives us a right to have faith in reaching a better future? What is it in 'human nature' that can give us the values we require for a new society? What are the needs a new society must fill and what are the things its organization must accomplish? What is oppression? How did it arise in history, why does it persist, and to what extent can we eliminate it? Why are some societies stable and others not? Which are the institutions, productive relations, and ideologies that are fostering change, and which are impeding it? Which groups are capable of revolutionary motion and which will likely oppose it? In essence, what in the national and what in particular local situations in the United States fosters revolution, what hampers it, and how can our various tactics affect each?

Classical Marxism gives us criteria for a new theory, Maoism and Anarchism give us insight into directions it will likely take. We can thus expect that our theory will be very concerned with the roles of ideas, race, sex, and authority, and that it will be aware of the multiplicity of dynamics that actually constitute most historical situations. We can reasonably expect that it will have a powerful perspective that sees in human nature a relatively constant good, or at worst a neutral basis upon which personality develops, due to upbringing, education, culture, work, and all other kinds of 'socialization.' And we can expect that it will study the process of personality development and that it will understand the interrelation of human nature, personality, institutions, cultures, and economies.

But a new ideology won't stop with theory. Our study of Classical Leninism suggests that a new strategy must be concerned *both with society's power relations and with its interpersonal ones.* It needs to provide guidelines for *building* a movement, *contesting* the authorities for power, and *developing* the institutions and values of a new society.

It must give us *criteria for our day-to-day activities.* It needs to take into account our weaknesses and strengths, and needs to work to hamper the former and foster the latter. It needs to understand centralization, bureaucracy, and work styles, decentralization, democracy, and spontaneity. It needs to instruct us as to the nature of good organization, and help us move towards it. It needs to tell us what good leadership is, and help us move towards that too.

Our new strategy must enable us to find *revolutionary potentials* in each of society's sectors and in its various dynamics and institutions, and help us bring those potentials to fruition. It needs to have methods of communication, organization, and struggle that are suited to the abilities of involved groups, applicable to the dictates of present conditions, and carefully aimed towards future goals.

Based on the lessons of Anarchism, we can expect that such a new strategy will include a process through which revolutionaries not only contest power, but through which they also learn how to create and 'administer' a new society. We can expect that within factories, schools, hospitals, and all other institutions, the new strategy will call for the creation of more and more revolutionaries, each of whom is self-confident, and able to function strategically, and thereby able to contribute to the development of a wholly new society.

We know from our understanding of the new left that a new strategy needs to have workable methods for its practitioners *to use in fighting their own weaknesses,* while also making themselves continually more revolutionary in personality. It needs mechanisms that insure wide participation at every level of analysis and planning, as well as very clear well outlined methodologies and values. Everything needs to revolve around the dual problems of *growing in size, commitment and ability, while also effectively dealing with all those supporting the status-quo.*

A new strategy should thus give its practitioners a strong identity without making them sectarian or extremist. It should provide methods for analysis while not hampering people with excessively positive attitudes about themselves or their environments. It should provide a context that fosters desires for growth rather than desires for ego-fulfilling stagnant 'correctness.'

At present America's status-quo forces have material strengths, organizational strengths, and structural and ideological weaknesses. Revolutionaries have material weaknesses, personality weaknesses and strengths, potential ideological strengths, and of course great strengths based on the potential emergence of revolutionary tendencies in all oppressed Americans. As a result, the status-quo task is to use material force to annihilate everything threatening, while also guarding against the weaknesses which could further provoke revolutionary strengths. The revolutionaries' task is to translate the potential inadequacies of the status-quo's relations and the power of their own new ways and new ideas into concrete gains leading to eventual victory -- while at the same time also guarding against their own weaknesses and most especially the tendencies to use self-defeating oppressor-oppressed behavior patterns. A new strategy needs safeguards against internal weaknesses that can couple effectively with methodologies aimed at increasing membership and material strength.

Based on our understandings of Anarchism's emphasis on the need for mass consciousness changes we expect that a new strategy will include very detailed processes for consciousness changing -- processes that provide new visions while at the same time overcoming old ones, without creating 'ego' problems like those that plagued the new left.

We expect that *a new revolutionary process will unfold internally as a mechanism for creating liberated people and externally as a mechanism for confronting the injustices of the United States*. It will be guided by a methodologically and humanistically broadened new theory. It will be rooted in an all-sided understanding of present realities, including an understanding of where people's consciousnesses are at. It will be aimed at creation of a new society that will be at least clearly enough envisioned so we can always successfully communicate about it, and successfully orient our tactics towards actually reaching its goal.

But how will such a strategy and the theory and goal behind it come into being, and then enter people's consciousnesses? Certainly herein we've given only a few criteria for their content. What are the steps which might actually bring them into being, and how might people embark on the involved tasks? Where might they start; how should they proceed?

We should clarify -- the process as the last chapter suggested has already long since begun. We see two main directions of its present development.

First, and as has thus far been primarily the case, people can return to Marx's own writings and essentially begin anew in light of their own criticisms of Classical interpretations and in accord with their own present 'experience lessons.' Such efforts seek to stay within overall Marxist frameworks, making additions and alterations with it as base. Frequently they begin by uncovering Marx's own actually varied understandings of human behavior and consciousness formation (passed over by the Classicists and in some sense even by the pragmatic Marx himself because of their then untranslatability into practical prescriptions) and by moving off those to altered historical and strategic results. For this approach, theories of alienation play growing roles as do understandings of the mediating agencies between production, daily living, and revolutionary practice and consciousness formation. Views of history become altered with economic but non-technical, and also non-economic factors playing ever greater roles. Power and control factors play greater roles in analysis and are seen as more important in real life history. Strategic orientations derivatively become more flexible, reflect greater understandings of human needs, motivations and potentials, and generate anti-hierarchical organizational desires. Growth orientedness becomes a sought after end. In essence, as in the last chapter, the Classical view is subjected to thorough overhaul in light of various Anarchist, Maoist, and New Left lessons, *all within the basic confines of Marx's own conceptual categories.*

Second, people can start anew, working from criteria developed from understandings of old ideologies, but initially, right from the start, developing their own more modern descriptive categories, terminology, methods, and so on. They'd be motivated in a similar way as the neo-Marxists (and also study Marx's own writings in addition to criticizing Classical interpretations) with but one significant addition -- they would feel that the likelihood of creating successful new ideology would hinge at least in part on getting away from habitually misused concepts, though not from the real power of the understandings often lurking behind those concepts. We would thus expect people of this second orientation to create new views translatable to the language of the neo-Marxists, but perhaps better suited to present needs in their own category/terminology, and also perhaps going a bit beyond what the neo-Marxists themselves generate, precisely because of the new approach's complete escape from traditionally habituating formulations.

In any case, which ever approach one takes, an early step in the task will be the development of a usable *'psychological picture' of how people act*, of what they are like, and of what they want, and then the incorporation of that understanding into creation of a generally broader political perspective. As a result we also expect creation of some form of a rather more organic theory of history that puts significant emphasis on race, sex, ideology, authority, and personal relations, and that has a powerful understanding of how consciousness and behavior mesh with, cause, and are caused by material interactions. We expect that, though such a theory would begin taking shape 'on the desks' of people who have been active in the movement, it would take usable form only in the hands of actually practicing revolutionary activists. 2

We might reasonably expect people to move from first discussing Classical ideas toward a wide debate on new theoretical outlines, new strategic orientations, new goals, and especially new understandings of organizational and organizing methodology. Then we expect such views would be used and simultaneously evaluated, and continuously improved upon. We would expect collective agreements to emerge, a rough ideology to evolve, and a movement, essentially already in existence, to adopt it all. Then since the ideology would be growth oriented we expect that with time it would get ever better, especially as more and more people of varying backgrounds contributed their insights and analyses of their own particular situations.

Such a new ideology would aid our manner of revolutionary struggle. It would help us create solidarity and provide a large context within which revolutionaries could all function together. It would provide work guidelines and a common language for communication. It would provide strength and identity but it would also foster an abhorrence for sectarianism and a desire for truth. It would be self-consciously self-critical. It would deal with all forms of oppression and liberation in organically unified ways. *It would give local practitioners the means to create programs, evaluate them, and carry them out.* It would help people become interested members of an on-going process of personal and political growth -- a process that would go from experience to knowledge to change and back to knowledge, over and over, right up through development of a new society and a whole new way of life. Such a new ideology will be 'friendly' and it will also work. The debate between it and Classical Marxism Leninism and Maoism will end precisely as larger and larger numbers of previously apolitical people gravitate toward the new paradigm's movements, much like the way the debate between Mao and the Classical Leninists ended with the growth of the Red Army among the peasants.

Perhaps by way of conclusion we can go somewhat out on a limb and 'fantasize' a contrast between Classical Marxism Leninism and such a new ideology as if it already fully existed.

Both Classical Marxism Leninism and the 'new' ideology employ a materialist perspective. Both use a dialectical method, both use abstraction, and both believe in the primacy of practice as the final arbiter of truth. But the new ideology changes the dialectical method a bit and also adds a number of other new, useful, broadening methodologies. The result is a better basis for all-sided analysis, and a much lesser tendency towards fetishism and sectarianism.

Both ideologies believe that the ways humans interrelate and learn are important. Both believe that history flows not according to plan, but according to the dictates of chance and necessity within a framework of largely understandable contradictions, causes and effects, but each has a somewhat different view about what is most important to the involved processes.

Classical Marxism Leninism puts the base and superstructure of each society in relief with the base getting the most attention; the new ideology puts the base and superstructure together as well as the totality of things in people's heads in relief, with all getting equal attention. Classical Marxism Leninism focuses in on the class struggle while the new ideology adds the dynamics of caste, movement, and group struggle in equal weight to those of class. Classical Marxism Leninism sees the main struggle at the productive level between forces and relations, whereas the new ideology sees main conflicts actually between oppressive and liberating potentials at all of society's levels. Classical Marxism Leninism sees the defining conflict rooted in the dynamics of production, while the new ideology sees it rooted in the dynamics of given human natures and formed human personalities in given historical contexts.

The new ideology has significant psychological insight; Classical Marxism Leninism abstracts it out. As a result the new ideology deals far better with racism, sexism, authoritarianism, classism, and sectarianism.

Classical Marxism Leninism feels that beliefs follow after practice and so doesn't worry so much about their inner consistency. The new ideology realizes that beliefs and practice can each lead or hinder the other's validity and so worries about both.

The Classical Marxist theory of revolution is a theory of class interaction propelled by contradictions at the society's material base; the new theory of revolution is a theory of human interaction propelled by contradictions arising directly from human needs, desires, and potentials, operating at the intellectual, physical, productive, and social levels of society. It is a macro theory but it is also able to analyze micro situations. It corresponds to Classical Marxism wherever Classical Marxism is correctly applicable but goes beyond Classical Marxism wherever a situation's complexity so demands. It is comprehensive but always growing. It is powerfully suited to day-to-day use by real down-to-earth in-the-world people.

Classical Marxism Leninism aims at changing the world in accord with the 'dictates' of the flows of its economic base -- in some sense the value is to reach that which will inevitably be reached. The new ideology aims at changing the world in accord with human nature's present historical potentials, and human fulfillment's present historical demands.

The value is to reach that which can be reached and is most desired. The contrast is between decentralist, self-management goals of the new ideology and various centralized socialisms and communisms of the old.

The Classical Leninist strategy is narrow; it doesn't sufficiently understand motivation, bureaucracy, authority, the ties between life, practice, and consciousness, or the real dynamics of corruption and cooptation. The new strategy is broader and better understands each of these things. It is more balanced; it is better rooted in the present and better aimed at a desirable future. It has better knowledge of real-world people.

The Classical Marxist Leninist's organizational forms rule their revolution; the new ideology's forms melt into the dictates of their revolution's needs. Classical Marxist Leninist top-down discipline stifles creativity, spontaneity, and initiative while also creating a new group of oppressors. The new revolution's self-discipline combines creativity, spontaneity, and initiative, with organization, in a collective assault on all oppressions.

The new revolutionist has a better understanding of tactical alternatives than the Classical Marxist Leninist and so he or she comes up with more varied and better programs, and what's more, in the new movement everyone is in a position to analyze social conditions, form programs, and evaluate results, precisely because all method and information is widely shared, while hierarchies of experience are continually struggled against.

The new revolutionist's identity is tied up in change and constant growth and the new theory helps foster those dynamics. The Classical Marxist Leninist's identity is tied up in the longevity of his or her ideology, and so the theory generally stagnates, while its users 'defend' it against all change.

Obviously a new ideology of the type "intimated" above doesn't yet exist and can't for some time to come. Still the fanciful comparison we've done graphically illustrates the type of qualities a new ideology must have if it's to adequately aid future United States left practice.

In any case it's clear from our critical studies and from the lessons of modern revolutionary thinkers and recent revolutionary experiences that it is time for some ideological and practical creativity. Continued esoteric exhumations of old writings will not turn us around the next revolutionary corner nor even necessarily bring us to its vicinity. Theoretic work must stop looking for miracles from the skies or from the graves of old 'masters.'

It no longer suffices for us to speak precisely but continually say nothing really practically useful. In now creating new theory we must aim first at useability and thus take primary account of what our experiences have taught us, what our present conditions are, and of what our present organizing needs are, in factories, and also in communities, schools, and even households, and in all cases with reference to actual day-to-day activity. Only by struggling to create new ideology that can guide and in turn be enlarged by new practice can we truly confront the American beast and propel the next American revolution.

FOOTNOTES

1. Quoted in Noam Chomsky's essay "Anarchism" which appears in *Essays On Socialist Humanism,* The Bertrand Russell Peace Foundation Limited.
2. As a possible starting point for discovering such a psychological picture, people might especially want to read the works of Wilhelm Reich, Abraham Maslow, and R. D. Laing, as well as the recent book, *Toward A Marxist Psychology,* by Phil Brown, Harper Colophon Books, New York.

SELECTED BIBLIOGRAPHY FOR FURTHER READINGS

ON MARXISM LENINISM AND THE RUSSIAN REVOLUTION

The Selected Works of Marx, Engels, Lenin, and Trotsky; especially *The Communist Manifesto, What Is To Be Done,* and *Left Wing Communism: An Infantile Disorder.*

Karl Marx, edited by T.B. Bottomore, McGraw Hill Paperbacks.
   A good collection of short excerpts on just about everything. A good introduction to Marx's own thoughts.

The Grundrisse, Karl Marx, edited and translated by David McLellan, Harper Torchbooks.
   Very good for understanding Marx's more sociological insights and especially those having to do with alienation.

The Formation of the Economic Thought of Karl Marx, Ernest Mandel, Monthly Review Press.
   A rather scholarly tracing of the flow of Marx's thoughts; useful but difficult.

Human Nature: *The Marxian View,* Vernon Venable, Meridan Books.
   Perhaps the best book for understanding Marxism as a whole theory of history, succinct and not very difficult to read.

Marxism and The Human Individual, Adam Schaff, McGraw Hill.
   A lot of what I think is convoluted apology but also a lot of interesting ideas on people and politics.

Marx's Theory of Alienation, Istvan Meszaros, Harper Torchbooks.
   A very complete and interesting, but also very difficult book. This one is no introduction.

Lenin: A Study on the Unity of His Thought, Georg Lukacs, MIT Press.
   An adoring work that is nonetheless informative and pleasantly quite concise.

A History of Bolshevism, Arthur Rosenberg, Doubleday Anchor.
A very excellent, perhaps the best, short history of the revolution. A critical but sympathetic well written account.

The History of The Russian Revolution, Leon Trotsky, MacMillan.
Revealing even if not totally comprehensive.

The Russian Revolution, Rosa Luxemburg, University of Michigan Press.
All of Rosa Luxemburg's writings are a cut above almost everyone else's best. This one is well worth reading and so are the various collections of her essays; so is Nettl's biography of her.

The Solidarity Pamphlets on Marxism and on the Russian Revolution, and especially *The Bolsheviks and Worker's Control,* Maurice Brinton.
All the pamphlets are nice as Solidarity publications are rather insightful and stimulating. Brinton's booklet is a masterpiece of research and reasoning that is 'must' reading both for its critique of the Bolsheviks and for its own general political insights.

The Anarchists on the Russian Revolution and Marxism, especially *My Disillusionment in Russia,* by Emma Goldman, Apollo, *Memoirs of a Revolutionary,* by Victor Serge, Oxford, and "Listen Marxist" in *Post Scarcity Anarchism,* by Murry Bookchin, and any of Bakunin's, Berkman's, or Rocker's anti-Marxist essays.
Goldman and Serge give very readable personal accounts that are tremondously insightful not only for their politics but also for their emotional involvement. Bookchin's essay is a biting attack on Marxism Leninism that is pithy and usually right even if not well argued at its roots. And the anarchists on Marxism are all fine, showing their insight, creating good criticism, and also creating good new political ideas. All this material is worth reading, pleasurable and easy.

The Russian Anarchists, Paul Avrich, Princeton University Press.
Rather scholarly but interesting including a section on Makhno, on whom there is not much anywhere.

"The Worker's Opposition," Alexandra Kollontai, Chicago.
A fine firsthand document important for the light it sheds on

opposition to the Bolsheviks and also for its own political worth.

Obsolete Communism: The Left-Wing Alternative, Gabriel and Daniel Cohn-Bendit, McGraw-Hill.
    The section on Bolshevism is brief but very fine. Excellent on the Makhnovites, and on Kronstadt.

History of the Makhnovist Movement, Peter Arshinov, Black and Red, Detroit.
    An excellent moving description of the Ukrainian Anarcho- peasant movement. Particularly useful in undermining the thesis that the Civil War made "progressivism" impossible, and in describing Anarchist modes of non-authoritarian organization and the Bolshevik ways of destroying those same modes.

The Unknown Revolution, Voline, Free Life Editions, New York.
    I 'discovered' this book after compositing *What Is To Be Undone*. It is a masterpiece: readable, comprehensive and well reasoned. It deals especially with the period before the Revolution (1825-1905), the period of the 1905 revolt, the general Anarchist influence in the Revolution, and the Bolshevik dynamics, as well as the Kronstadt and Makhnovist experiences. Although the book is not good on the fate of worker's management and the soviets, it is very good on Bolshevik and Anarchist politics and the flow of the whole revolution. The book is similar though not as fully elaborated as ours and goes beyond it in explaining the positive aspect of the Anarchist programs and the fierceness of the Bolshevik repression.

ON MAOISM AND THE CHINESE REVOLUTION

The Collected Works of Chairman Mao, Mao Tse-Tung , People's Publishing House.

The Little Red Book, Mao Tse-Tung edited by Lin Piao, People's Publishing House.
    A lot of wisdom in a little space. If you can't read him in the large, it's worth reading him in the small.

The Chinese Road to Socialism, Wheelwright and McFarlane, Monthly

Review Press.
> A very good book despite it's being repetitive. The documentation, analysis, and politics are all very good. It is about the best book for developing a fairly quick understanding of the whole of the Chinese revolutionary experience.

Red Star Over China, Edgar Snow, Grove Press.
> A 'classic' on the early years of the revolution with interesting conversations interspersed.

The Yenan Way in Revolutionary China, Mark Selden, Harv. Univ. Press.
> A detailed work on the nature of the Red Base areas in North China.

Fanshen, William Hinton, Monthly Review Press.
> A mammoth book of mammoth value. A chronicle of the revolution in a rural village. An excellent look at what the old society was like and at what the revolution meant in human terms. If you read one book on China this should be it - but no one should read just one.

Ideology and Organization in Communist China, Franz Schurmann, University of California Press.
> I think this may be the longest book I've ever bought. It is hard reading and literally immense. But if you're interested in detail and can read a little at a time for a long time, then this book is worthwhile.

Important documents on the Great Proletarian Cultural Revolution in China, Foreign Languages Press.

Report to the Ninth National Congress of the Communist Party of China, Lin Piao, Foreign Languages Press.
> Very interesting for its content and also because it is an actual party document.

The Cultural Revolution in China, Joan Robinson, Penguin Books.
> The first book on the topic and still one of the best. Very clear with a good introduction.

Shanghai Journal, Neale Hunter, Beacon Press.
> A fascinating account of how the cultural revolution actually went on

in China's biggest city. It explains a lot, not only about what happened but also about where the Chinese people are now. It gives a very balanced and honest view.

Turning Point in China, William Hinton, Monthly Review Press.
The Maoist line of the Cultural Revolution. Very readable, very informative, and rather good politics. The best available analytic material on the topic.

"Interview on the Cultural Revolution" with Chris Milton, New England Free Press.
A very nice, simple commentary showing what it felt like from a young boy's perspective.

"Leninism and Maoism: Some Populist Perspectives on Marxism Leninism," Maurice Meisner appearing in the China Quarterly, Jan.-March, 1971. #45.
A well argued essay that largely follows the line taken in this book.

ON ANARCHISM:

Anarchism, Daniel Guerin, Monthly Review Press.
A very good summary analysis of the various trends in anarchist thought. Well worth reading despite a little too much emphasis on Max Stirner.

Anarchism and Other Essays, Emma Goldman, Kennikat Press.
Very clear, very concise, and very good.

The Political Philosophy of Bakunin: Scientific Anarchism, edited by G. P. Maximov, Glenco, Illinois.
This is a collection of excerpts. It's very fine but more difficult than reading full essays, though more comprehensive.

Bakunin on Anarchy, edited by Sam Dolgoff, Vintage Books.
A little easier to read because of the layout but otherwise similar to Maximov's work though less comprehensive.

Anarchy, Errico Malatesta, London.
A biography and a collection of excerpts. Excellent because

Malatesta, of all the anarchists, is the clearest and most relevant to our modern situation.

Anarcho-Syndicalism, Rudolf Rocker, London.
A relatively unknown classic. The best on its topic.

Collected Writings of P.J. Proudhon, edited by Stuart Edwards, Anchor Books.
Primarily good for the scholar interested in the roots of anarchism or in Proudhon himself.

What is Communist Anarchism? Alexander Berkman, Dover Publications.
A very comprehensive easy to read introduction to all aspects of anarchist thought with sections on analysis of capitalism, anarchist goals, anarchist methods, and the Russian Revolution.

Mutual Aid, Peter Kropotkin, Porter Sargent Publisher.
A theoretic argument about the goodness of humanity based on evolutionary analysis. Like all Kropotkin's works, it is very readable, warm, and intelligent.

Kropotkin's Revolutionary Pamphlets(two volumes), MIT Press.
Excellent material on just about everything from analysis to goals to strategy. Beautifully written. Each essay is self-contained so it is a great book for people who like to read a little at a time but like that little to be complete unto itself.

The Anarchists, edited by Irving Horowitz, Dell Publishing.
A fine collection of relatively short essays from a large number of anarchist sources. A good overview.

Anarchism, George Woodcock, Meridian Books.
A good history with very nice biographical analytic sketches of many major anarchists.

The Anarchists, James Joll, Universal Library.
Same as Woodcock's but a little deeper and I think a little better.

Lessons of the Spanish Revolution, Vernon Richards, Freedom Press.
  Excellent for developing an understanding of the events, and even
  more important for its anarchist views, and its critique of the way the
  Spanish anarchists fell short of their own ideological perspectives.

ON THE NEW LEFT

The New Student Left, edited by Mitchell Cohen and Dennis Hale, Beacon
Press.
  A very fine collection of early new left writing, well worth reading for
  its on-going value and also for an understanding of the new left.
  Especially good are the excerpts from the Port Huron Statement, an
  essay by Stokely Carmichael, and a speech by Carl Oglesby -- all of
  which are new left classics.

Up Against the Ivy Wall, Jerry Avorn, Atheneum Books.
  Good as a chronicle of the Columbia struggle, for understanding the
  student movement, and for understanding something about Mark
  Rudd and the roots of the Weathermen.

Student Power, edited by Alexander Cockburn and Robin Blackburn,
Penguin Books.
  Difficult but informative campus oriented articles.

Soul On Ice, Eldridge Cleaver, Delta Books.
  A must for understanding racism and the Panthers. Beautifully
  written, it is one of the new left's major works.

Eldridge Cleaver, edited by Robert Scheer, Ramparts Books.
  A well written collection of Cleaver's essays and speeches showing the
  politics of the time and also the progression of Cleaver's own politics
  and personality.

Conversations With Eldridge Cleaver, Lee Lockwood, Delta.
  A very warm little book that has the politics of its time and reflects
  Cleaver at his best.

Blood in My Eye, George Jackson, Random House.

A too "violent" book that nonetheless shows where many of the Panthers politically wound up. Reading this after reading George's brillant first book of prison letters teaches a great deal.

"The Myth of the Vaginal Orgasm," Anne Koedt; "Politics of Housework," Pat Naimandi; "Families," Linda Gordon; "Women: The Longest Revolution," Juliet Mitchell; and "Liberation of Women: Sexual Repression and the Family," Laurel Limpus. All New England Free Press Pamphlets.
A fine collection of women's new left writings that shows the basis of their movement; these writings have value also for their contributions to leftist thought.

Sisterhood is Powerful, edited by Robin Morgan, Vintage Books.
The best available collection on the women's movement and on sexism.

The New Radicals, Paul Jacobs and Saul Landau, Vintage Books.
A good history with an interesting section on SNCC.

The New Left Reader, edited by Carl Oglesby, Grove Press.
An intellectual collection good for understanding the politics of the new left and good also for understanding some politics that go beyond what the new left practices. Especially nice are the essays by Oglesby, Kolakowski, Castro, and Deutschke.

The New Revolutionaries, edited by Tariq Ali, William Morrow Books.
A fairly heavy collection with overall good insights.

Prelude to Revolution, Daniel Singer, Hill and Wang.
A fine analysis of the 1968 French uprising relevant to understanding the new left and to critiquing it. Readable and worthwhile.

AND A FEW 'CONTEMPORARY' WORKS
USEFUL FOR FORMING A NEW IDEOLOGY

Mass Psychology of Fascism, Wilhelm Reich, Noonday Press.
Useful for the general problem of creating psychological insights with

applicability; particularly useful for the task of understanding the place of sexual repression and authoritarian personality traits in the dynamics of Fascism. A very important book, well worth reading.

Sex-Pol, Wilhelm Reich, edited by Lee Baxandall, Vintage Books.
Very good, especially the essay "What is Class Consciousness" which should be must reading for the left.

Character Analysis and *The Sexual Revolution,* Wilhelm Reich, Noonday Press.
Useful for developing a better understanding of the dynamics of human nature and human personality, especially concerning the role of sex needs in each.

Toward a Psychology of Being and *Motivation and Personality,* Abraham Maslow, Van Nostrand.
Very good for forming a psychological picture that is easily usable by political activists, also clear and readable.

On Becoming a Person, Carl Rogers, Houghton Mifflin Company.
Good for general understandings of personality change and also for insights it gives into possible methodologies of internal movement growth efforts. Also very readable and clear though a bit repetitious.

Post Scarcity Anarchism, Murray Bookchin, Ramparts Books.
A lot of creative thinking about goals and methods with emphasis on ecology.

Workers' Councils, Anton Pannekoek, Root and Branch.
An important short exposition of the ideas of Council Communism. Easy to read, clear, and a fine example of Marxist thought that goes beyond Classical weaknesses, especially those of the Leninist 'Party worshipers.'

Transition to Socialism, Paul Sweezy and Charles Bettelheim, Monthly Review Press.
An important, but in many places muddled, contribution to the problems or creating a successful revolutionary transition in an

advanced Capitalist society.

Monopoly Capital, Baran and Sweezy, Monthly Review Press.
A good first work effort at understanding the dynamics of the United
States. Very much worth reading.

The Sick Society, Michael Tanzer, Holt Rinehart and Winston.
A fine study of the United States with chapters on the economy,
political power, overseas involvement, racism, alienation, crises, and
prospects for America. I think this will soon be a left text.

Counter Revolution and Revolt, Herbert Marcuse, Beacon Press.
A lot of interesting thoughts on strategy and overall perspective.

An Essay on Liberation, Herbert Marcuse, Beacon Press.
A difficult but fine work essentially on human nature and
revolutionary goals.

Pedagogy of the Oppressed, Paulo Freire, Herder and Herder.
Enlightening on consciousness and methods of education but very
difficult to read -- a peculiar combination of insight about
communication, and poor style for communicating.

False Promises, Stanley Aronowitz, McGraw-Hill Book Company.
A modern Council Communist perspective with improvements due to
better cultural and psychological insights.   One of the finest recent
United States contributions to revolutionary analysis.

Strike, Jeremy Brecher, Rolling Stone Press.
A good history of United States working-class struggle with emphasis
on the roles spontaneity and worker self-organization have played.

Strategy for Labor, Andre Gorz, Beacon Press
A modern discussion of revolutionary possibilities and of the role of
reform struggles within a revolutionary process.

Socialism and Revolution, Andre Gorz, Anchor Books
Wide ranging essays on the problems of revolutionary strategy and
socialist practice. Excellent throughout.

The Fiscal Crisis of the State, James O'Connor, St. Martin's Press.
A very detailed and well researched description of the modern

American political economy and some of its major internal contradictions. Hard to read.

There are a number of books by neo- Marxists coming out of East Europe. They generally deal with problems of human nature, alienation, bureaucracy, and the need for a humanization of Marxist practice. Two that I've liked are Svetozar Stojanovic's *Between Ideas and Reality,* Oxford University Press; and Gajo Petrovic's *Marx in the Mid Twentieth Century,* Doubleday Anchor Books. Also important, however, and discussed in *What Is To Be Undone,* is Mihailo Markovic's *From Affluence to Praxis,* University of Michigan Press.

Antonio Gramsci and the Origins of Italian Communism, John M. Cammett, Stanford University Press.

This is the classic biography of Gramsci and admirably includes his ideas, integrated into the historical situations he confronted.

INDEX

Anarchism, 189-204
  and history, 189-193
  and oppression, 190-193
  and government, 193-194
  and capitalism, 194-195
  and revolution, 196-203

Shlomo Avineri
  on Marx, 82,83

Stanley Aronowitz, 304-309

Mikhail Bakunin, 146.
  on political power, 102
  on history, 190
  on property, 191
  on power and wealth, 191
  on freedom, 314

Daniel Cohn-Bendit
  on Makhnovites, 118
  on Kronstadt, 125
  on Bolshevism, 127

Alexander Berkman
  on Anarchism, 189
  on authority, 191
  on government repression, 193
  on capitalism, 194-195
  on goals, 198
  on methods, 199
  on revolutionary process, 200, 202-203

Charles Bettelheim, 284-289

Black Panthers, 33-36

Murray Bookchin
  on parties, 184.

Bolsheviks, see Russian Revolution

Jeremy Brecher, 298-304

Maurice Brinton
  on workers' control, 106
  on authority, 109
  on Leninism, 142, 143-144, 185

Paul Cardan
  on Russian Revolution, 102
  on Trotsky, 112
  on Bolsheviks, 128.
  on ideas, 134
  on consciousness, 161-162

E. H. Carr
  on workers' councils, 106
  on early trends, 109

Fidel Castro, 52, 176

Che Guevara, 248

China
  revolutionary practice, 230-251
  early years, 230-235
  Great Leap Forward, 235-237
  New Economic Policy, 237-238
  Cultural Revolution, 238-250

Noam Chomsky, 6

Eldridge Cleaver, 35

Frederick Engels
  on metaphysics, 55
  on superstructure, 63
  on forces of production, 63
  on history, 75
  on contributions of Marx, 76
  on party, 82

Emma Goldman
  on soviets, 104-105
  on Russian Revolution, 107, 128
  on goals, 197

Antonio Gramsci, 264-269

Andre Gorz, 289-298

William Hinton
  on Cultural Revolution, 241-243

Samuel Hurvitz
  on Marxism, 54

Idealism defined, 55

J. M. Keynes
  on avarice, 80

Kommunist on workers' management, 112

Peter Kropotkin
  Letter to Lenin, 127
  on soviets, 133
  on law, 192
  on revolutionary goals, 196
  on revolution, 199
  on revolutionary process, 200

T. S. Kuhn
  quoted, 42, 43, 44
  criticized, 53

Kuhn's Theory of Science
  paradigm, 42
  normal science, 43, 45
  crisis science, 43, 45
  revolutionary paradigm, 44

Chou En-Lai,
  on Cultural Revolution, 248

Lenin, 134, 80
  on strategy, 81
  on tactics, 81
  on "leftists," 86
  on political parties, 87
  on workers' consciousness, 89
  and imperialism, 90
  on authority, 94
  on state capitalism, 95, 97
  on workers' management, 96
  on factory relations, 98
  on early years, 105
  on factory authority, 111
  on workers' management, 114-115

on compromise, 140
on capitalist organizational forms, 142
on human nature, 143

Leninist Strategy, 80-99

Criticisms of Leninism, 133-145, 181-187
  of party and revolutionary organizational
  views, 134-140

Georg Lukacs
  on Lenin, 84, 88

Rosa Luxemburg
  on Leninism, 89, 90, 136, 138, 141
  on Russian Revolution, 105

Wheelwright and McFarlane
  on early practice, 233
  on NEP, 236-237
  on Cultural Revolution, 247

Errico Malatesta
  on Bolsheviks, 127, 129.
  on social ills, 190
  on reforms, 195
  on goals, 197
  on consciousness, 201
  on violence, 201-202
  on terror tactics, 202

Mao Tse-tung
  on reaction, 206
  on contradiction, 207-212
  on knowledge, 214-218
  on democracy and centralism, 219
  on investigation, 219
  on leadership, 220
  on politics and economics, 220
  on peasants, 221, 225
  on revolutionary process, 221
  on revolutinary strategy, 224-230
  on bad traits, 229
  on correcting past errors, 229
  on practice, 230
  on the Red Army, 232
  on socialism, 235
  on the Great Leap Forward, 236
  on the Cultural Revolution, 247

Maoism
  Theory of Contradictions, 207-212, criticized, 251-256
  Theory of Knowledge, 214-218, criticized, 256-257
  Classes and Masses, 218-220
  Economics and politics, 220-222
  Strategy, 223-230, criticized, 257-259
  Means and Ends, 227-228, criticized, 259-260
  criticism/self-criticism, 228-229
  compared to Leninism, 222-223, 224, 227, 228, 230, 237-238, 250

Herbert Marcuse
  on Marxist theory, 179

Mihailo Markovic, 276-283

Karl Marx
  on dialectics, 56
  on human nature, 57-58
  on knowledge, 59
  on stages of economic organization, 61
  on role of labor, 62
  on tools, 62
  on social relations, 62
  on production relations, 64
  on revolution, 65
  on class, 67, 68
  on socialist revolution, 69
  on modern industry, 71
  on the proletariat, 72
  on Marxism, 76
  on party, 82

Classical Marxism, 54-77
  Historical Context, 55-56
  Theory of Dialectics, 56-57
  Theory of Knowledge, 58-60
  Historical Materialism, 60-66
  superstructure and base, 60-64
  mode of production, 62
  classes, 61, 66-69
  ruling class, 68
  View of Capitalism, 70-73
  and revolution, 73-77
  and dictatorship of the proletariat, 74

Critique of Classical Marxism, 146-179
  weaknesses listed, 146-149
  Theory of Dialectics, 153-154
  Human Nature, 154-158
  Theory of Consciousness, 158-163
  Historical Materialism and Class, 163-173
  Historical Materialism in use, 173-176
  alternative views, 168-170
  Views of Capitalism, 176-179

Classical Marxism Leninism
  defined, 4.
  criticized, 180-187

Mayday, 18.

McNamara, 11

National Liberation Front (NLF), 21

New Left, 5-40.
  lessons of, 7-10
  analyzed, 10-13
  internal weaknesses, 11
  student movement, 13-20
  student strategies, 16-17
  anti-war movement, 20-26, 7-10
  anti-war strategy 23-24
  Weatherman, 26-29
  Yippies, 29-33
  Black Panthers, 33-36, 7-10
  Women's movement, 36-38, 7-10

Carl Oglesby, 10

Anton Pannekoek, 269-273

Black Panthers, 33-36, 7-10
  Program, 34

Peguy, 133

People's Coalition for Peace and Justice, 24.

Gajo Petrovic
  on approach to Marxism, 2
  on human nature, 155

Lin Piao
  on Cultural Revolution, 240, 241.

Maurice Merleau-Ponty, 180

Paul Potter
  on New Left, 15

Progressive Labor Party, 14.

Proudhon
  on government, 193-194.

Wilhelm Reich, 273-276
  on human nature, 156-157

Rudolf Rocker
  on dictatorship, 126
  on power, 138-139, 192
  on state, 193, 201
  on centralism, 201

Arthur Rosenberg
  on early years, 105
  on Russian Revolution, 93, 94, 95,

Russian Revolution, 102-132
  Brest-Litovsk, 108
  Workers' Management, 111-116
  Makhnovites, 116-120
  Kronstadt, 120-125
  Kronstadt statements, 124

Seattle Liberation Front, 17.

Student Non-Violent Coordinating Committee, 33

Jean Paul Sartre
  and organization, 135
  on Marxism, 263

Adam Schaff, 276-283

Michael Schneider
  on Marxist Leninist sectarianism, 176

Franz Schurmann
  on Cultural Revolution, 243-244

Svetozar Stojanovic, 276-283
  on Marxist Sectarianism, 186

Huberman and Sweezy
  on Cultural Revolution, 244-246, 249

Paul Sweezy,   284-289

Leon Trotsky
  on revolutionary upheaval, 103, 104
  on workers, 110, 96
  on Civil War, 111
  on workers' management, 114, 115
  on Kronstadt, 126

Tomsky, 97

Voline
  on elitism, 102
  on Russian Revolution, 108

Kurt Vonnegut, 187

Woodrow Wilson
  on imperialism, 71

Weatherman, 26-29

Yippies, 29-33

DATE DUE